METAPHORIC NARRATION

Luz Aurora Pimentel

METAPHORIC NARRATION
Paranarrative Dimensions in *A la recherche du temps perdu*

UNIVERSITY OF TORONTO PRESS

Toronto Buffalo London

© University of Toronto Press 1990
Toronto Buffalo London
Printed in Canada
Reprinted in 2018
ISBN 0-8020-2735-0
ISBN 978-1-4875-8077-3 (paper)

Printed on acid-free paper

University of Toronto Romance Series 61

Canadian Cataloguing in Publication Data

Pimentel, Luz Aurora, 1946–
　Metaphoric narration

　(University of Toronto romance series ; 61)
　Includes bibliographical references.
　ISBN 0-8020-2735-0

　1. Proust, Marcel, 1871–1922. A la recherche du temps perdu.
　2. Proust, Marcel, 1871–1922 – Technique.
　3. Narration (Rhetoric). 4. Metaphor.
　I. Title. II. Series.

　PQ2631.R63A894 1990　　843'.912　　C90-094367-X

This book has been published with the help of a grant from the Canadian Federation for the Humanities, using funds provided by the Social Sciences and Humanities Research Council of Canada.

Contents

Preface / vii

Introduction / 3

PART ONE: METAPHORIC NARRATION / 9

1 **Metaphor within the boundaries of the sentence: the phrastic or lexematic level** / 11

  1 The semantic operation of addition and suppression / 14
  2 Conjunctive and disjunctive relations / 17
  3 Poetic metaphor: an illustration / 21

2 **Metaphor as a discursive phenomenon: the transphrastic level** / 27

3 **The narrative dimension of metaphor** / 34

  1 Metaphoric narration: the level of the manifestation in language / 38
  2 Metaphoric narration: the level of the organization of a narrative text / 40
    2.1 Metaphoric articulation of narrative sequences / 40
      2.1.1 The actual mode of articulation / 40
      2.1.2 The virtual mode of articulation / 43
      2.1.3 A mixed mode of articulation / 47

2.1.4 Different forms of narrative isotopy in metaphoric articulation / 50
2.2 *Metaphoric construction or configuration of narrative sequences* / 55
2.2.1 Lexicalized metaphor as an implicit narrative program / 55
2.2.2 The process of metaphorization as the constructive principle in certain narrative sequences / 56
2.2.3 The metaphoric configuration of a narrative sequence on the pattern of another / 59

4 **Metaphor and metaphoric narration: an illustration** / 68

PART TWO: METAPHORIC NARRATION AND NARRATIVE STRUCTURE / 79

5 **Metaphoric narration and the temporal structures of narrative** / 83
1 Order / 84
  1.1 Metaphoric narration as prolepsis and analepsis / 86
  1.2 The analeptic sequence as a constituent of metaphoric narration / 91
2 Narrative tempo (duration) / 96
  2.1 The role of metaphoric narration in narrative tempo / 99
3 Frequency / 106
  3.1 Metaphoric narration and iterative narrative / 106
  3.2 Metaphoric narration and repetitive narrative / 108

6 **Narrative modulations** / 114
1 Distance / 114
  1.1 Metaphor in descriptions of diegetic space / 116
2 Perspective: metaphoric narration and focalization / 120
  2.1 Metaphoric narration and ambiguity in focalization / 130

7 **Narrative voice** / 136
1 Metaphoric narration and narrative level / 139
2 Metaphoric narration and vocal ambiguity / 145

Conclusion / 153

Appendix: The operational concepts / 159
Notes / 165
Bibliography / 199
Glossary / 203
Index of authors cited / 215

Preface

In its earliest phase, this book was conceived as a comparative study of Marcel Proust's *A la recherche du temps perdu* and José Lezama Lima's *Paradiso*. Despite the temporal and cultural distance between the two, it seemed to me that both the French writer and the Cuban offered profound and original meditations on the role of metaphor in their work. In fact, both have elevated metaphor to an aesthetic principle, to a veritable expression of their *Weltanschauung*.

In Proust, the whole world is read through the powerful lens of metaphor; everything, from politics, war, snobbery, friendship, or love to the very notion of time and mortality is consistently interpreted and explained, analogically, by means of the stylistic device of metaphor. For, according to Proust, metaphor is the essence of literature, which in turn is the only form of authentic living: 'La vraie vie, la vie enfin découverte et éclaircie, la seule vie par conséquent réellement vécue, c'est la littérature' (*Le temps retrouvé*). As for Lezama Lima, metaphor is such a vital concern that he claims it is akin to breathing, that it is at the source of human identity and creativity. Only the poet, he says, is capable of encompassing the totality through metaphor: 'sólo el poeta, dueño del acto operando en el germen, que no obstante sigue siendo creación, llega a ser causal, a reducir, por la metáfora, a materia comparativa la totalidad' ('Preludio a las eras imaginarias').

Proust's vast narrative is constructed as a 'cathedral,' as the narrator insists in *Le temps retrouvé*. And indeed the metaphor is not merely ornamental, for too many sections of the *Recherche*, separated by a considerable textual distance, are composed in such rigorous symmetry to one another that it is impossible to dismiss the metaphoric claim as extravagant. Similarly, the narrative construction of Lezama's text appears to be metaphoric in principle; it is certainly not impossible to read *Paradiso* as a tree, so that one may speak of an 'arborescent' structure unifying and conferring meaning to an otherwise chaotic text.

In his essay 'Mitos y cansancio clásico,' Lezama explores the temporal dimension of metaphor by juxtaposing the description of two paintings separated in time and conception: one, 'September,' an illuminated plate from the fourteenth-century *Book of Hours* of the duke of Berry, exhibits peasants harvesting, with a castle in the background; the other, 'The Knight of Da Fogliano,' a fourteenth-century painting by Simone Martini, represents the proud lord leisurely riding in the surroundings of his castle. Lezama's fertile imagination establishes a metaphorical relation between the two paintings, based on a common, apparently insignificant detail in both: an open door. This partial identity, added to the happy coincidence of a castle present in both paintings, triggers the metaphorical relation by unifying them into a single continuum: through that portentous door Da Fogliano happily rides out of his framed pictorial space into that of the plate, thus abolishing time and unifying space in the creative act of this metaphoric reading of the two paintings. The cultivated lands represented in Berry's *Book of Hours* have now become Da Fogliano's, while his riding acquires a new meaning: he seems to be surveying the work of the peasants, who have now become his serfs. This extraordinary dynamization of two static, originally unrelated paintings, has generated a potential narrative. Thus, from the metaphorical juxtaposition of the two a new, virtual painting has been created, while the passage from the one to the other has generated a virtual narrative dimension that each painting in isolation could not possibly have. Lezama claims that in such cases metaphor operates as the temporal factor that sets different cultural entities in motion and prevents them from remaining '*gelée* en su estéril llanura.'

In *A l'ombre des jeunes filles en fleurs*, Proust seems to travel in the opposite direction: as the train approaches Balbec, just as the sun is rising, Marcel delights in the contradictory landscapes that he can see from opposite windows; through one, the pink tones of the rising sun, through the other, dark night sprinkled with stars. By running from

Preface

one window to the other he experiences the very essence of metaphor: the identical in the midst of the different, the rapprochement of what is separate. The final pictorial metaphor freezes the sequence: 'je passais mon temps à courir d'une fenêtre à l'autre pour rapprocher, pour *rentoiler* les fragments intermittents et opposites de mon beau matin écarlate et versatile et en avoir une *vue totale* et un *tableau continu*' (italics mine). From motion, that is to say, from the 'temporal factor' inherent in narrative, Proust generates a metaphor of the simultaneous; a time sequence thus becomes a tableau, 'gelée,' as Lezama would say; and yet it does not lose the dynamic quality of the materials from which it was originally constructed, thus becoming a paradoxical, therefore metaphorical, tableau 'continu.'

Metaphor as a temporal dimension and, at the same time, claiming the simultaneous and instantaneous as its rightful domain, even daring to signify the intemporal! Lezama defines metaphor as the dynamic interaction between extension and the suddenness of revelation; extension, or the 'extensive world' ('mundo extensivo'), though spatial in nature, implies duration and progression (in the act of traversing it), while the suddenness of revelation is equated to the perception of the image resulting from a metaphoric relation ('el súbito'). Similarly, Proust claims that only through metaphor, as the equivalent of an experience of the convergence of different times, may one transcend time and escape contingency. Furthermore, he affirms that only metaphor may give 'une sorte d'immortalité au style.' But in fact, Proust conceives metaphor both as the instant in which all times converge, thereby abolishing succession, and as the 'spiritual equivalent' of experience, and therefore of time, of deployment, 'car on ne se réalise que successivement.'

Thus metaphor for Lezama as well as for Proust is both the simultaneous and the successive, the intemporal and the temporal, the cause and the effect ('causalidad metafórica,' as Lezama would say), the progressive and the sudden. Such extraordinary claims, coupled with profoundly original thinking about the way in which metaphor operates and means – apparently contradicting the current linguistic and rhetorical notions on the subject – and added to the extended use that both writers make of metaphor in their narrative works, result in a sort of multidimensional vision of the created fictional world.

These poetic meditations on metaphor initially led me to pose them as my starting point, as the bridge that would allow me to go from Proust to Lezama and back, almost metaphorically, proposing new readings of both. Nonetheless, since Proust and Lezama tend to define metaphor *metaphorically*, I felt the strong need for a metalanguage with which I could do full justice to their extraordinary insights, to their poetic 'theories' of metaphor, without falling myself into the vicious circle of a metaphorical interdescription. I therefore resorted to a semiotic and semantic theory of metaphor, hoping that this might prove, methodologically speaking, an effective foil against all those contradictory claims. And not only a foil but also a test, because, provided the local verbal specificity of metaphor could be transcended, such a descriptive instrument might even validate such claims: that, in one and the same operation, metaphor deploys a temporal dimension, parallel to the instantaneous quality of the effects of meaning that it produces; that only metaphor is capable of making different times converge into simultaneity thereby abolishing succession and, therefore, time.

My subsequent exploration of the semiotic and semantic possibilities of metaphor, as process, led me to the discovery of a *paranarrative* dimension, which I then called *metaphoric narration*: a virtual narrative line, resulting from metaphorical interactions of various kinds on different levels, and affecting all aspects of narrative in terms of both meaning and modes of representation of fictional time and space. Since this paranarrative dimension of metaphor, though encompassing it, is not restricted to the observable verbal texture of narrative, but rather constitutes a virtual dimension that must be *constructed* by the reader, I realized that it was necessary to go into a detailed theoretical description and mapping out of its various components and modes of operation. Furthermore, as the model was refined and minutely illustrated, I realized that it had gone well beyond the initial purpose of describing the peculiar effects of meaning produced by Proust's and Lezama's narratives – that the model was, in short, applicable to a larger narrative corpus.

I then decided to devote a substantial section of this work to the presentation and validation of the proposed model. I deliberately illustrated its different aspects using heterogeneous narratives in order to test the scope and reach of metaphoric narration. Obviously I would never propose this model as universal, nor is the paranarrative phenomenon of metaphoric narration observable in *all* kinds of narrative; it is merely the result of a long reflection on problems and questions posed by narrative texts. For, as so many critics and theoreticians have experienced, theoretical thinking always arises from problems posed by the critic about a specific text or texts, from areas of the text that call for different conceptual instruments in order

Preface

to do justice to their complexity, or to attempt a more comprehensive explanation. Both Proust and Lezama were always at the source of my explorations; Proust in particular, for in the *Recherche* all the possibilities of metaphoric narration are masterly realized. Although partly absent from the first part of the book, Proust is always at the back of the theoretical model and its detailed illustrations. Part 1, in fact, only prepares the ground for the extensive analyses of the *Recherche* that make up the whole of part 2.

Bestriding theory and criticism, my work could no longer be the originally planned comparative study of Proust and Lezama. That book remains to be written. Since the theory was paramount to the description of a vast dimension in the *Recherche*, so far virtually unexplored, I have devoted most of my efforts to that enterprise. Whether it is a success or a failure is for the reader to judge.

I wish to express my deep gratitude to Professor Dorrit Cohn, whose intensive and thoroughly involved reading of my work, in its avatar of a PHD dissertation, resulted in such penetrating remarks and objections that she invariably made me think more deeply and more rigorously. That Proust was once a revelation to me rather than just another author is largely due to Professor Richard Sieburth's inspired and inspiring lectures. I am also deeply indebted to Dr Margarita Quijano, who helped me generously through the whole process of writing and rewriting, revising and proof-reading, and whose comments often helped me to clarify my ideas. Last, but not least, I wish to thank Professor Mario J. Valdés for the interest he has taken in my work all along, and for his invaluable help and advice.

METAPHORIC NARRATION

Introduction

'Any form of contiguity,' says Jakobson, 'may be conceived as a causal series.'[1] In traditional narrative the relations of causality have always had a central role in the arrangement and design of narrative units. For this reason, Jakobson has repeatedly insisted that metonymical relations predominate in prose and metaphorical ones in poetry.[2] Although there are, he says,

> poems with a metonymic texture and prose narratives studded with metaphors (Biely's prose being a case in point) ... there is definitely a closer and more fundamental kinship between verse and metaphor and prose and metonymy. Poetry is based on associations by similarity; its effect is imperatively conditioned by rhythmic similarity, and rhythmic parallelism is enhanced by similarity (or contrast) in the images. Such attempts at calling attention by a deliberate similarity in the articulation of segments are unknown to prose. It is association by contiguity that gives narrative prose its fundamental impetus; narrative moves from one object to the next, by proximity, following causal or spatio-temporal trajectories, the passage from the part to the whole and from the whole to the part is nothing but a particular instance of this process.[3]

Starting from the fundamental premise that the essence of narrative is *transformation*,[4] and that the concatenation of such transformations, or 'events,' results in a narrative text, it could indeed be argued that

4   Metaphoric narration

narrative is a phenomenon of 'association by contiguity,' dominated by relations of causality, and/or by spatio-temporal relations subordinated to the former. Such a description of narrative entails a description of its basic *mode of signification*; to speak of *metaphoric narration*, therefore, would seem a sheer contradiction in terms. Yet if we look closely at the following texts in juxtaposition, two distinct forms of organization become apparent; thereby two radically different *modes of narrative signification* are implied.

> John got up and went to the door.
> 'I'm sorry, Veronica, if I've hurt you. You're very lovely, my dear, and I once loved you very much. Can't we leave it at that?'
> 'Good-bye, John. We're not leaving it at that. You'll find that out all right. I think – I think I hate you more than I believed I could hate anyone.'
> He shrugged his shoulders.
> 'I'm sorry. Good-bye.'
> John walked back slowly through the woods. When he got back to the swimming pool he sat down on the bench there. He had no regrets for his treatment of Veronica. Veronica, he thought dispassionately, was a nasty bit of work. She always had been a nasty bit of work, and the best thing he had ever done was to get clear of her in time. God alone knew what would have happened to him by now if he hadn't! ...
> He looked up sharply, disturbed by some small unexpected sound. There had been shots in the woods higher up, and there had been the usual small noises of woodlands, birds, and the faint melancholy dropping of leaves. But this was another noise – a very faint businesslike click.
> And suddenly, John was acutely conscious of danger. How long had he been sitting here? Half an hour? An hour? There was someone watching him. Someone –
> And that click was – of course it was –
> He turned sharply, a man very quick in his reactions. But he was not quick enough. His eyes widened in surprise, but there was no time for him to make a sound.
> The shot rang out and he fell, awkwardly, sprawled out by the edge of the swimming pool.[5]

> Fue entonces cuando Demetrio cometió una torpeza, al trinchar la remolacha se desprendió entera la rodaja, quiso rectificar el error, pero volvió la masa roja irregularmente pinchada a sangrar, por tercera vez

Introduction 5

Demetrio la recogió, pero por el sitio donde había penetrado el trinchante se rompió la masa, deslizándose: una mitad quedó aherida al tenedor, y la otra, con nueva insistencia maligna, volvió a reposar su herida en el tejido sutil, absorbiendo el líquido rojo con lenta avidez. Al mezclarse el cremoso ancestral del mantel con el monseñorato de la remolacha, quedaron señalados tres islotes de sangría sobre los rosetones. Pero esas tres manchas le dieron en verdad el relieve de esplendor a la comida. En la luz, en la resistente paciencia del artesanado, en los presagios, en la manera como los hilos fijaron la sangre vegetal, las tres manchas entreabrieron como una sombría expectación.

Alberto cogió la caparazón de los dos langostinos, cubrió con ella las dos manchas, que así desaparecieron bajo la cabalgadura de delicados rojeces. – Cemí, dame uno de tus langostinos, pues hemos sido los primeros en saborear su masa, para que cubra la otra media mancha –. Graciosamente remedó, con el langostino de Cemí ya en su mano, que el deleitoso viniese volando, como un dragón incendiando las nubes, hasta caer en el mutilado nido rojo formado por la semiluna de la remolacha …

Al mismo tiempo que se servía el postre, doña Augusta le indicó a Baldovina que trajese el frutero, donde mezclaban sus colores las manzanas, peras, mandarinas y uvas. Sobre el pie de cristal el plato con los bordes curvos, donde los colores de las frutas se mostraban por variados listones entrelazados, con predominio del violado y el mandarina disminuidos por la refracción. El frutero se había colocado al centro de la mesa, sobre una de las manchas de remolacha. Alberto cogió uno de los langostinos, lo verticalizó como si fuese a subir por el pie de cristal, hasta hundir sus pinzas en la pulpa mas rendida. El frutero, como un árbol marino al recibir el rasponazo de un pez, chisporroteó en una cascada de colores, estirándose el langostino contento de la nueva temperatura, como si quisiera llegar al cielo curvo del plato, pintado de frutas.[6]

The first text, from Agatha Christie's *The Hollow*, illustrates, point by point, Jakobson's description of metonymic relations in narrative prose. The contiguous appears in the form of a causal relationship; the reader will tend to associate, causally, John's argument with Veronica and his being shot, so that she will become the first suspect (the whole craft of detective novels also lying, among other narrative strategies, in the presentation of false relations of causality depending on relations of contiguity). The spatio-temporal relations drawn here are strictly subordinated to the causal: John's spatial position, the time that elapses between the argument and his murder, the description of the woods

6 Metaphoric narration

and its activities are all narrative *indexes*, as Barthes has called them (see chapter 3, n 20), which provide important information and/or delays for suspense effects; in short, information that feeds the causal chain of the main narrative *functions* (especially 'kernels'). Indeed Christie's narrative moves from one object to the next 'by contiguity'; it is a *transitive* narrative, calling attention to the causal chain. The reader, like the narrative itself, moves on, his attention centred on what happens next – who did it and why; he is never detained by the verbal texture of the narrative. It is the reference to the causal chain that is essential, for 'poetry is centred on the sign, while the pragmatic prose is mainly centred on the referent.'[7] Thus, the mode of signification of this kind of texts is predominantly *referential* – though the reference is not necessarily outside the text but in the fictional world the narrative creates.

By contrast, the second text, from Lezama Lima's *Paradiso*, is perfectly *intransitive*, centred on the poetic function; that is, it forces the reader to dwell on its verbal texture and on its peculiar organization, which is its only mode of signification. What happens next, though textually contiguous, does not build up a causal chain; it is simply a series of events in which the relations of causality are either played down or non-existent (after this dinner scene, Alberto has a few drinks at a café, quarrels with a Mexican guitarist, etc., the arbitrary series concluding with Alberto's purely accidental death).

The description of the beet stains, and the spatial relations established among fruit bowl, prawn, stains, and table are *not* subordinated to the narrative of 'events'; quite the contrary, this *is* the event: the description itself is narratively dominant. Because of narrative articulations that are of a purely metaphorical nature, Alberto's death is prefigured by the beet stains and the tablecloth, both elements interacting metaphorically with the handkerchief and the blood in Alberto's face (p 195). All four – beet stains, tablecloth, handkerchief, and blood – constitute the 'joints,' so to speak, in this metaphorical articulation. By the same kind of connections, the prawn, symbolic of involution, becomes identical with Alberto, a sort of metaphorical *alter ego*. In terms of the story as such, the family are unaware of Alberto's death at the end of chapter 7, yet the description of the prawn, closing that chapter, simultaneously develops the symbol and suggests Cemi's metaphorical awareness of his uncle's death: 'Pero él recordaba tan sólo la tibiedad de la mano que había cogido de las suyas el langostino para que se abrazase al pie de critstal del frutero. Le pareció de nuevo ver al langostino saltar alegre en la cascada de la iridiscencia desprendida por la bandeja con las frutas. Volvió de nuevo el frutero a lanzar una cascada de luz, pero ahora el langostino avanzaba, al refractarse los colores frutales, hacia un cementerio de coral.'[8]

If the reader of *Paradiso* merely moves from one object to the next, by proximity, the text will hardly make any sense. In order to generate a meaningful text, the movement must proceed by leaps, in search of similarities, telescoping narrative sequences that become meaningful due to an association, not by contiguity, but by similarity. Lezama's text does call attention 'by a deliberate similarity in the articulation of segments'; its narrative effect, and therefore its basic mode of signification, 'is imperatively conditioned by rhythmic similarity, and rhythmic parallelism is enhanced by similarity (or contrast) in the images.' Thus, narrative meaning in *Paradiso* is predominantly *metaphorical*, or poetic.

Therefore, my contention in this study is that in certain narrative texts the productive act of narration performs operations that are essentially identical – or at least homologous – to the process of metaphorization itself; that there is, in other words, a *narrative dimension* inherent in metaphorization that is liable to a semiotic transposition from the purely linguistic to the fictional domain. Accordingly, part 1 describes the semiotic and semantic mechanisms of the process in order to define the potential narrative dimension of metaphor. A model of *metaphoric narration* is then proposed, covering both the level of the manifestation in language and the level of the organization of the text. Illustrations are deliberately drawn from a broad, heterogeneous body of narrative texts, belonging to three different literary traditions.

Ricardou's work on metaphor as an organizing principle is one of the main sources for the model presented here.[9] The significant contribution of my own work, however, lies in the exploration of *verbal* metaphor as narratively significant. The theoretical model that I have proposed spans both the level of the manifestation in language (what Ricardou calls, rather contemptuously, 'expressive metaphor') and the level of the organization of the text (what he calls 'productive' metaphor, a general term inclusive of all his other categories). Contrary to Ricardou's summary dismissal of verbal metaphor, I believe that a description of the semiotic process of metaphorization uncovers its essential components, both as *verbal* and as *organizational* phenomena, and that the narrative dimension of metaphor is observable in the very components of the process, therefore observable both as a purely verbal and as an organizational *narrative dimension*.

8   Metaphoric narration

In part 2, once metaphoric narration has been defined and illustrated, I have explored its complex effects on narrative structure. For this purpose I have made extensive use of Gérard Genette's narrative theory, as expounded in 'Discours du récit' and complemented in *Nouveau discours du récit*. Illustrations for this second part have been drawn consistently from Proust's *A la recherche du temps perdu*. But if it is true that a systematic exploration of one single narrative text best illustrates the complex effects of metaphoric narration on narrative structure, it is no less true that an extensive application of this model of metaphoric narration on Proust's vast narrative results in a new and different reading of the text, even though a very partial one, as all critical readings are doomed to be.

PART ONE

METAPHORIC NARRATION

In part 1 of this study I intend to build a model of metaphor based mainly on the works of A.J. Greimas, the Liège Group (Group μ), François Rastier, Michael Riffaterre, Philippe Dubois, and Michel Leguern. The construction of a syncretic model of metaphor, however, entails a series of difficulties: on the one hand, given the breadth and heterogeneity of the work that has been done on metaphor, there is always the danger of incompatibility at the conceptual level, which might then put into question the validity not only of the model itself but also of the subsequent analysis of the function of rhetorical figures in narrative discourse; on the other hand, from the methodological point of view, using a syncretic model inevitably poses the problem of a homogeneous metalanguage. That is why, in spite of the heterogeneity of the works employed in the construction of the present model, the choice has been oriented towards the, perhaps partial, solution of these problems. Underlying the work of most of the semioticians and semanticists chosen are certain descriptive and operational concepts, such as *isotopy*, or *semes* and *sememes* as infralinguistic units of meaning.[1] I have found that these descriptive concepts not only provide the basis for a homogeneous metalanguage, but also, due to the emphasis on the infralinguistic level, it is possible to go beyond the stylistic specificity of metaphor in order to conceive it as a semiotic process. For, as Greimas has observed, 'it seems that rhetorical figures transcend the exclusive problem of natural languages: the fact that film making,[2] for example, consciously produces metaphors and metonymies shows that, at least in the frame of the generative process of discourse, figures point to a semiotic common root, therefore antecedent to any manifestation in a specific substance of expression.'[3] Furthermore, this very fact also points to the narrative dimension of the process.

Thus, conceived as a semiotic process, metaphor can be analysed on different levels. From this perspective, as it loses its purely stylistic specificity, metaphor gains a narrative dimension. Through the construction of a semiotic-semantic model of metaphor, I shall attempt to describe metaphor on two basic levels: lexematic (bound to the limits of the phrase or sentence) and transphrastic or discursive (extended, beyond the phrase, to a group of sentences or even to a whole text). Having described its mechanisms, I shall proceed to explore metaphor's discursive functions in narrative texts: first, metaphor as a generator of *virtual* narratives, and second, the *process* of metaphorization itself as a potential principle of organization and production of narrative meaning. Thus the narrative dimension of metaphor will be analysed at the level of the manifestation in language – which includes both the phrastic and the transphrastic modes of metaphorization – and at the level of the organization of narrative texts.

1 Metaphor within the boundaries of the sentence: the phrastic or lexematic level

Given a deliberately simple statement such as 'the ship ploughs the waves,' we notice that while 'ship' and 'waves' belong to the same semantic field, which might be called the aquatic field, the word *ploughs* clearly presents a semantic incompatibility, since it belongs to a different field, the 'agricultural,' to give it a name. The establishment of such semantic fields proceeds along referential and conceptual lines.[1] On the conceptual plane, any exhaustive definition of the so-called normal uses of 'ship' or 'waves' will isolate a series of generic *semes*,[2] which remain constant, such as /liquidity/, to focus on one only; or /agriculture/ in the many uses of 'ploughs.' On the pragmatic plane, a morphological analysis of the objects designated by 'waves' and 'ploughs' will also give us certain invariants. For 'waves': 'undulating conformations; a moving ridge or swell of water between two depressions.' For 'to plough': 'to make furrows in and turn up (the earth) with a plough, esp. as a preparation for sowing.' 'Furrow,' in turn, is morphologically defined as 'a depression in the earth, narrow in proportion to its length; a narrow trench made in the earth with a plough, esp. for the reception of the seed' (*Oxford English Dictionary*).

Since the subject 'the ship ploughs the waves,' given in isolation, with no other context, is clearly 'ship,' one may see that 'waves' is compatible since it implies the recurring seme, /body of water/; while 'ploughs' is an incompatible predication since it belongs not to the aquatic but to the agricultural domain. The notion of semantic compatibility pointing towards the univocal reading of a text corresponds to what I shall consistently call the *isotopy* of a text. 'Of an operational nature, the concept of isotopy initially designated the recurrence of classemes along the syntagmatic chain, which guarantees the homogeneity of discourse. From this definition, it is clear that a phrase containing at least two semic figures may be considered as a minimal context that makes the establishment of an isotopy possible.'[3]

According to the members of the Liège group (Group μ), two conditions, one positive the other negative, determine the establishment of an isotopy. If it is true that a recurrence of the same infralinguistic units of meaning, or semes (/temporal measurement/ in 'day and night,' for example), is necessary in order to establish an isotopic text, it is equally true that the *syntactic* relations at the level of the manifestation must not oppose other semes in a relationship of determination, such as equivalence and predication (cf 'day is night': an allotopic utterance).[4] While the first condition is fulfilled by a purely semantic rule, the second is a rule of composition of a logical nature. The Belgian rhetoricians define isotopy, then, as *'the property of limited sets of units of meaning entailing an identifiable recurrence of identical semes and an absence of mutually excluding semes in a syntactic position of determination.'*[5]

This is precisely what happens in metaphor: a lexeme or group of lexemes is opposed, at the level of the contextual semes, to the recurring classematic base constituting the rest of the utterance. In the statement under consideration, both 'ship' and 'waves' are isotopic and contribute to establish the main context; 'ploughs,' by contrast, is clearly non-isotopic, or allotopic, but it points to a virtual isotopy, the agricultural one. Given this rupture in the isotopic uniformity of the statement, a semantic manipulation or rearrangement of the semes of the terms involved will then be responsible for the production of metaphoric meaning. Now, the revaluation of the allotopic lexemes introduces one or more isotopies, so that the utterance may be read, simultaneously, on two or more isotopic paths. It is the pluri-isotopic potential of texts, activated by metaphorization, that marks the transition of metaphor from the purely lexematic to the discursive level (cf chapter 2).

With these considerations in mind I shall now define metaphor, as Leguern does,[6] in terms of an *isotopic breach*: metaphor is produced by the insertion, in a given text or utterance, of a word or group of words that are incompatible with the general isotopy of the context: the word *ploughs* in 'the ship ploughs the waves.' But if metaphor constitutes a breach in the general isotopy of the text, the breach may be of a semantic or of a logic nature. Thus metaphor may be brought about by the breach of *any* of the two conditions proposed by Group µ as ruling the establishment of an isotopy: 'day is night,' for example, is allotopic because the second condition, that of composition, is not fulfilled; without any other context the utterance is simply discarded as absurd, for no revaluation of allotopy seems possible. But even this utterance might become metaphoric in the appropriate context, thereby allowing for a semantic revaluation.

Given the essentially relational character of metaphor, the metaphoric meaning is not contained in the anomalous or allotopic lexeme itself, but rather in the relationship established between the 'given degree' and the 'constructed degree' of metaphor (the 'degré donné' and the 'degré construit').[7] The given degree is constituted by the interaction of both the isotopic and the allotopic lexemes; it is the complete utterance as it appears, though focused on the allotopic lexeme (*ploughs* in our example).[8] The constructed degree is not just a word that is substituted for the given degree but a complex of meaning determined by the context of the utterance in which the allotopic lexemes appear; the constructed degree entails the important semantic operation of *revaluation*, or rearrangement of the semes of the given degree, *controlled by the context*, in order to confer a semantically satisfactory meaning to the utterance. In our example, the constructed degree of metaphor could be paraphrased as something like 'the ship makes deep undulations in the water.'

The given and constructed degrees of metaphor correspond respectively – though very approximately – to I.A. Richards's concepts of 'vehicle' and 'tenor': the metaphoric utterance or text is given the value of a 'vehicle' carrying the metaphoric (i.e. the 'real') meaning or 'tenor,' so that the original utterance is considered simply as a means to an end. The term *vehicle* is inevitably valued negatively as that which may be discarded, or that which is subservient to what is 'important,' i.e. the 'tenor.' The terminology of the Belgian rhetoricians, by contrast, has the advantage of stressing the essentially operational and relational character of the process of metaphorization, thereby de-emphasizing the hierarchical value of the terms.

Metaphor, thus conceived as a rhetorical operation, consists in the initial perception of an allotopic lexeme and in its subsequent revaluation, regulated by the general context of the utterance,[9] for, as the members of Group µ observe,

14   Metaphoric narration

> The trope constitutes, as all rhetorical figures, a modification of the level of calculable redundancy of the code, a modification that is perceived due to a distributional impertinence. The impertinence is reduced thanks to the presence of an invariant induced by the context, in a phenomenon of *feed-forward* and *feed-back*. The invariant is, in the case of metaphor ... the intersection of semes of the given degree of the trope and of the class of its constructed degrees ... This invariant is given by the classemes or recurring semes ... We insist on the fact that the rhetorical operation defines not the trope itself but the *relationship* between the given and the constructed degrees, a relationship that opens what Genette has called 'the space of language.'[10]

Thus, in the example under examination, given the predominance of the marine isotopy over the agricultural one, the subject of the utterance being responsible for the primacy of the former, the revaluation of the allotopic lexeme *ploughs* is commanded by the aquatic context. Both the isotopic and the allotopic lexemes are confronted and subjected to a semantic manipulation that is regulated by the main context; a sort of semic *intersection*, a zone of shared meaning, is constructed out of the common attributes in both the isotopic and the allotopic lexemes ('waves' and 'ploughs,' in our example). If 'to plough' is 'to make furrows in the earth,' then the attributes of 'furrows' and 'waves' may be rearranged, by affixing them to a class of greater generality, in order to construct a semic intersection: /depression/ and /swells/ are among the different generic semes that are common to both. This, of course, does not account for the whole effect of meaning of this metaphor, simple as it is. It is clear, for example, that certain semes in 'ploughs' have been suppressed in the construction of the semic intersection, semes such as /narrowness/ or /sowing/, and that the suppression has been dictated by the context. For the construction of the metaphoric meaning, once the isotopic breach has been perceived, involves a twofold operation in order to devise a semic intersection: a semantic manipulation entailing a revaluation of semes, and an operation of addition and suppression of semes.

1   The semantic operation of addition and suppression

If on a very general plane a trope – and therefore metaphor – may be defined as a semantic modification, as a transformation or reorganization of the meaning of an utterance, this is due in part to the polysemic potential of words, but also to the fact that words are capable of being decomposed into smaller units of meaning or semes.[11]

Semantic decomposition is at the heart of the revaluation of the allotopic lexemes in tropes, for 'it is the manipulation of the arrangements of semes that will produce figures.'[12] There are rhetorical figures, such as synecdoche, in which semantic manipulation is relatively simple. Its usual definition is that of a trope in which the part is substituted for the whole ('roof' for 'house'), or the whole for the part ('the law' for 'a policeman'). It is evident that in the first case there is a sort of diminution and in the second an increment of meaning. A semic analysis reveals in the figure of synecdoche the simplest of semantic operations: that of suppression *or* that of addition of semes. Through this operation of addition and suppression, a semic intersection is constructed, bringing together all the similar semes, thereby restoring, or rather, conferring new meaning to an utterance initially perceived as allotopic.

Two types of semantic decomposition are proposed by the Liège group:[13] decomposition in mode π, or *referential*, and decomposition in mode Σ, or *conceptual*. In the former, an essentially morphological analysis, what is taken into account is the object designated by the word and the different 'parts' that shape it; in the latter mode of decomposition, what is brought into focus is the more abstract meaning (or meanings) of the word: conceptual decomposition operates on the semantic constitution of the word, whereas referential decomposition works on the morphological composition of the designated object. The word *tree*, for instance, may be decomposed referentially, according to its different 'parts' (trunk, *and* branches, *and* leaves, etc.), or it may be decomposed conceptually, according to its class (oak *or* birch, etc.).

In order to construct a semic intersection that may confer meaning to the utterance 'the ship ploughs the waves,' I have proceeded, in the absence of any other context, to a referential, therefore morphological, decomposition of the lexemes 'ploughs' and 'waves.' A similar operation is also possible with 'ship' and 'a plough,' by finding 'parts' that are similar in the two objects designated. It is from the morphological similarity of certain 'parts' in 'furrows' and 'waves' that a semic intersection has been constructed. But a different context might demand a decomposition in the conceptual mode, which might activate, or reinforce, the notion of *fertility*, associated then with a sea voyage, as part of the metaphoric meaning. Without this hypothetical context, however, the notion of fertility remains virtual and practically unfelt. It must be stressed that both conceptual and referential decomposition are, *stricto sensu*, semantic in nature, for what I have been calling 'parts,' or morphological constituents of the designated objects, are obviously an important aspect of the whole *meaning* of the terms.

Thus, many sememes may be decomposed in either of the two modes; which mode of decomposition is chosen in the rearrangement of semes, however, will thoroughly depend on the context in which they appear; so that we may speak of *both* referential and conceptual metaphor *and* referential and conceptual metonymy.

Michel Leguern, by contrast, bases his distinction between metaphor and metonymy solely on a radical opposition between referential and semantic manipulations. Metaphor, he claims, is based on a purely semantic transformation, whereas metonymy is the result of a 'referential glide' ('glissement de référence'). 'The metonymic relation is therefore a relation between objects; that is, between extra-linguistic realities; it is based on connections that exist in the reference, in the external world, regardless of the linguistic structures that may serve to express it.'[14]

But if this is true of such conventional metonymies as 'sail' for /vessel/; if it is true that only reference to external reality can give meaning to 'un sèvres' as china from Sèvres, or 'un Roquefort' as /cheese/, it is also true that other types of metonymy, especially poetic metonymy, may involve more complex semantic operations. Take, for example, these well-known lines from Yeats's 'Leda and the Swan': /A shudder in the loins engenders there / The broken wall, the burning roof and tower / And Agamemnon dead./

I will not pause to analyse the many synecdoches that make up this poetic metonymy: 'the broken wall, the burning roof and tower,' and the death of Agamemnon, all working synecdochically as 'parts' of the whole of the Trojan war and its aftermath; or the 'shudder' and the 'loins,' equally focused as 'parts' of the sexual act. But if knowledge of the whole of the Homeric epic and of the classical myth of Zeus's copulation with Leda is indispensable in the decoding of the metonymic relationship that Yeats establishes between the copulation and the Trojan war, there is also an undeniable semantic modification that *does* affect the very linguistic structures that express this relationship.

The copulation-generation-isotopy established in the first line is broken in the two subsequent lines. The verb *engenders* would require, in order to maintain the general isotopy of the context, a compatible object; that is, words containing compatible generic semes, such as

/human/ (or anthropomorphic divinity), or /animate/ and /life/. Instead of 'Helen and Clytemnestra, Castor and Pollux' as objects of 'engenders,' which the myth as our reference leads us to expect, what we have as predication is a series of sememes ('wall,' 'roof,' and 'tower') containing both generic and specific semes that are radically opposed to those in the 'engenders' of the copulation-isotopy (semes such as /construction/, /non-human/, /inanimate/ and /death/). The extralinguistic reality, or, to be more precise, the *intertextual* reality that functions as our reference – the myth and the Homeric text – provides a narrative sequence from which causal and temporal relationships may be drawn. This is the field that encompasses both the given and the constructed degrees of this metonymy. But the 'connections,' contrary to Leguern's observations, *do not* 'exist in the reference,' they are *created* by the poet – and therefore also created, conceptually and imaginatively, by the reader in the act of decoding.[15] Nowhere in the myth or in the Homeric text is Zeus's copulation with Leda posited as the ultimate cause of the Trojan war and of Agamemnon's death.

The 'effect-for-the-cause' upon which this metonymy is based is imaginatively created by the poet, and if the effect of the figure is that of a striking compression of time and of an instant telescoping and reorganizing of events, this is because the context triggers a decomposition of 'parts' of the reference that have been perceived as only peripherally connected. The syntactic structure – 'engenders' + 'the broken wall' – forces a rearrangement of these 'parts,' temporally separated by an enormous distance and *conceptually* incompatible, into a close semantic relationship of cause and effect: mythic time 'engendering' human time. And here, as may be seen, the line that divides metonymy from metaphor has become very thin indeed.

2 Conjunctive and disjunctive relations

One last important feature of metaphorization is that it establishes, *simultaneously*, both conjunctive and disjunctive relations; in other words, semantic relations of equivalence and of opposition are drawn among the different semes.

Initially the *generic* semes relate *disjunctively* due to the opposition of the allotopic lexemes to the general context of the utterance (the 'agricultural' as against the 'aquatic'). But the allotopic lexemes, because they belong to a different semantic or lexical field, carry with them semes belonging to other potential contexts, constituting a virtual isotopy (agriculture).[16] This virtual isotopy is emphasized if it is not a single word but a group of words that make up the given degree of metaphor. Although the allotopic lexeme has been detached from its virtual context, when introduced into the new one it still retains many of the generic semes that tie it to its original context, so that the incompatible lexeme preserves a virtuality of multiple readings that remain suspended, to a greater or lesser degree, by the discursive discipline. The effect of this potential multiplicity of readings is one of semantic richness and density.[17] The interaction of these two isotopies, the one organizing the main context of the utterance and the other virtual in the allotopic lexemes, results in a semic intersection constituted by semes shared by both semantic fields.

The semic intersection, which is the basis for the constructed degree of meaning in metaphor, is produced by means of a complex operation of suppression and addition of semes, as we have seen. It is at this level that the *conjunctive* relation takes place. But the selection of semes, added and suppressed in order to construct the semic intersection, is determined by the original context of the utterance. It is also at the level of the constructed degree of meaning in metaphor that a *disjunctive* relation, again, is simultaneously established, since those semes that have been suppressed or attenuated, due to contextual pressure, still retain their virtual meaning, a virtuality that affects metaphoric meaning as a whole.

In 'the ship ploughs the waves,' only those semes in 'ploughs' that are compatible with the context, and specifically with its correlate 'waves,' are retained, while others are suppressed or attenuated – /preparation for sowing/, for example. However, the suppressed semes do not wholly lose their meaning, for their virtual presence affects the production of metaphoric meaning as a whole. That is why the notion of potential fertility associated with a sea voyage, though attenuated, is still perceptible as a possible effect of meaning. '... if the part held in common is necessary as the conclusive evidence that establishes the proclaimed identity, the non-common part is no less indispensable for creating the originality of the image and for triggering the mechanism of reduction. Metaphor extrapolates; on the basis of a real identity indicated by the intersection of two terms metaphor affirms the identity of the totality of the terms. It extends to the *union* of the two terms a property that is, in fact, true only of their intersection.'[18]

This contamination, so to speak, of the two semantic fields by the semic intersection is what constitutes the complexity of metaphoric meaning. Out of the interaction between two isotopies, metaphoric

Metaphor within the boundaries of the sentence 19

meaning is created, encompassing the other two and deriving its *unique* and *local* existence from them.

The interesting work that Max Black has done on metaphor may be illuminating at this point. When we speak of metaphor, he says, we refer 'to a sentence ... in which *some* words are used metaphorically while the remainder are used non-metaphorically.'[19] In terms of the semantic theory I have been using, the words that are used metaphorically are those that fail to be indexed in the general isotopy of the text, the allotopic lexemes; while those that are used non-metaphorically constitute the primary isotopy. Black calls the metaphoric words 'the *focus*' of the metaphor, and the rest 'the *frame*.'[20] Metaphoric meaning is generated by the 'system of associated commonplaces' pertaining to the focus:

> The effect ... of ... calling a man a 'wolf' is to evoke this wolf-system of related commonplaces ... A suitable hearer will be led by the wolf-system of implications to construct the corresponding system of implications about the principal subject. But these implications will *not* be those comprised in the commonplaces *normally* implied by the literal uses of 'man.' The new implications must be determined by the pattern of implications associated by the literal uses of the word 'wolf' ... The wolf-metaphor suppresses some details, emphasizes others – in short, organizes our view of man ...
>
> We can think of metaphor as ... a screen and the 'system of associated commonplaces' of the focal word as the network of lines upon the screen ... that the principal subject is 'seen through' the metaphorical expression – or ... that the principal subject is 'projected upon' the field of the subsidiary subject.[21]

One observation is pertinent regarding Black's analysis: if it is true that the 'principal subject' or 'frame,' 'man,' is modified by the 'wolf-system of related commonplaces' (the wolf-isotopy, I might say), it is no less true that the principal subject ('man') *orients and determines* the revaluation of the allotopic lexeme or 'focus' ('wolf'), via the wolf-isotopy, *which is itself modified and reorganized by the principal subject, 'man.'* For it is highly questionable whether it is the 'literal uses' of 'wolf' (such as biological classification, anatomical features, living and eating habits, for example) that determine the 'new' view of man; one might say, conversely, that it is precisely the literal uses of wolf that are *attenuated* and that only those *compatible with the human-isotopy*, especially psychological or moral attributes, are highlighted. The

20 Metaphoric narration

operation of addition and suppression of semes (the suppression of some details and the emphasis of others, in Black's terminology), in order to construct a semic intersection, affects both the principal and the subsidiary subjects. The extension of the semic intersection to both principal and subsidiary subjects, modifying and organizing them, constitutes the constructed degree of metaphor, the metaphoric meaning itself. What is interesting is that the semes added to 'man,' from the 'wolf-system of related commonplaces' are not *inherent* but *afferent*. If /canine/, /carnivorous/, /rapacity/, or /predatory/ are inherent to 'wolf,' those that are selected (and notice that not all of them are) from this partial list to fit the context of 'man' become *attributed* meanings, socially codified, therefore afferent semes. It is significant that /canine/, for example, would not normally be selected in the decoding of 'man is a wolf.'

I shall now sum up some of the more salient features of the rhetorical operation that we know as metaphor. An utterance or text that the reader or listener perceives as metaphoric constitutes an interesting phenomenon of *isotopic rupture*. Unlike non-metaphoric statements in which meaning is more or less univocal, due to a semantic coherence underlying all its constituent terms, metaphor proposes the simultaneous coexistence of two or more isotopic paths. Nonetheless, there is always one isotopy that dominates the others, constituting the main subject.

A metaphoric utterance poses a word or group of words that seems to be incompatible with the main context; the rhetorical operation performed in order to confer to the utterance a rationally satisfactory meaning or meanings depends on a revaluation of the incompatible or allotopic words. This semantic revaluation is, in fact, an abstract manipulation of units of meaning of an infralinguistic nature in order to construct a set of units, drawn from the different semantic fields represented by the metaphoric and the non-metaphoric words, that may bear some similarity to one another. This set of units, or semic intersection, confers meaning to an utterance that might otherwise be discarded as absurd. It is to be noticed that the semantic manipulation of semes involved in this rhetorical operation depends, in turn, on a semantic decomposition of the terms that make up the utterance. A semantic decomposition, again of an abstract, infralinguistic nature, isolates semes that may relate *conjunctively* in order to construct the semic intersection responsible for the rational meaning of metaphor. But the semes that relate *disjunctively* also have an important participation, since they are responsible for the strong associated images characteristic of metaphor and that are an essential aspect of metaphorical meaning.²²

3   Poetic metaphor: an illustration

Since the metaphor I have been using as an illustration is one that has been worn out by use, a lexicalized metaphor, it would be illuminating at this point to examine a poetic metaphor in the light of the procedures outlined so far. I shall focus my attention on a few lines from stanza 52 of Shelley's 'Adonais.'

> The One remains, the many change and pass;
> Heaven's light forever shines, Earth's shadows fly;
> *Life, like a dome of many-coloured glass,*
> *Stains the white radiance of Eternity,*
> Until Death tramples it to fragments. (italics mine)

Although the text contains many other rhetorical figures, for the purpose of clarity and economy I shall restrict my analysis to those underlined.

The first two lines establish the general isotopy of the text with the recurrent macro-generic seme /abstraction/.²³ In this very general category, /abstraction/, are indexed most of the sememes of this fragment. Even though such words as 'many' are usually associated with the concrete rather than with the general, the context eliminates all the possible concrete terms that 'many' might qualify by turning into an abstract noun: '*the* many.' Furthermore, the procedure of capitalizing 'One,' 'Life,' 'Death,' and 'Eternity' does nothing but reaffirm the high level of generality imposed by the context. The abstraction-isotopy underlies the series of oppositions established by the poem: unity vs. multiplicity, mutability vs. immutability, mortality vs. immortality, and so on.

/Life, like a dome of many-coloured glass / Stains the white radiance of Eternity/ constitutes a major breach in the general isotopy of the text by opposing to it the recurring macro-generic seme /concreteness/ in words with greater referential potential, such as 'dome' or 'glass.' The metaphor is complex, for the allotopic lexemes activate, simultaneously, two virtual isotopies – which for the sake of brevity I shall call the purity/impurity-isotopy and the architectural-isotopy – both incompatible with the abstraction-isotopy.

22   Metaphoric narration

Let us examine first the central metaphor, /Life ... Stains the white radiance of Eternity/. A semic analysis of the verb *stain* reveals certain semes as invariant in all the sememes, or contextual meanings, especially features like /colour/, /impregnation/, /matter/, constituting the specific semes. Now /colour/ entails other specific semes: (a) /in patches or spots/ ('a spot or patch of colour different from the ground'; 'a mark or discoloration of the skin; a blotch or sore'; (b) /transparency of colour/ ('to colour tissue with some pigment so as to render the structure clearly visible'; 'to colour [glass] with transparent colours') (*Oxford English Dictionary*).

The seme /impregnation/ is often qualified by /contamination/: ('Of something dyed or coloured: to impart its colour to [something] in contact. Also in wider use [e.g. said of a chemical reagent], to alter the colour of [something] to which it is applied'; 'to damage or blemish the appearance of [something] by colouring a part of its surface; to discolour by spots or streaks of blood, dirt, or other foreign matter not easily removed') (*OED*).[24]

'Life and 'stains' are therefore semantically incompatible because the semes /matter/ and /colour/ are arbitrarily attributed to 'Life' as though it were capable of 'imparting its colour' or 'damaging' or 'blemishing' its syntactical object, namely 'Eternity' and its 'white radiance.' On the other hand, 'stains' and 'white' *are* semantically compatible in relation to each other, because the semes /colour/ and /contamination/ interact with the seme /purity/, afferent in the meaning of 'white,' thus activating the opposition purity vs. impurity. Now, if we remember that the recurrence of semes in at least two sememes produces an isotopic text, we may see that 'stains' and 'white,' in a syntagmatic relation, establish, by an afference that is local to the context, the virtual isotopy that I have called the purity vs. impurity-isotopy, or the contamination-isotopy, in which the specific seme /colour/ also qualifies the contamination.

Since the revaluation of allotopic lexemes is always regulated by the context, the allotopic phrase – 'stains the white radiance' – tends to be revalued in terms of the abstraction-isotopy in 'Life' and 'Eternity.' In order to reach the level of generality required, the more concrete semes are suspended (the suppression operation), while the more abstract are emphasized, i.e. /contamination/. Conversely, the abstraction-isotopy, represented by 'Life' and 'Eternity,' is affected by the contamination-isotopy, for 'stains' and 'white radiance' force 'Life' and 'Eternity' to be invested with more concrete features (the addition operation). Thus, 'Life' and 'Eternity' acquire a meaning of /colour/ and /mattter/ that

Metaphor within the boundaries of the sentence 23

they would not otherwise have, given the very high level of generality that the main context imposes. As T. van Dijk says, 'A main feature of the process of metaphorization is its RELATIONAL character. Strictly speaking there are no isolated lexemes serving as metaphors, although one may say that the specific selection of an ungrammatical lexeme in a given (co-) textual structure may bring about metaphorization ... the selection of a lexeme in a metaphorical process establishes additional relations with textual structures. Further, by its very relational character, metaphorization affects also the interpretation of the other lexemes of the collocation.'[25]

The simile 'like a dome of many-coloured glass,' introduces a different isotopy, the architectural-isotopy, to which 'stains' is also indexed, due to the semes /colour/ and /transparency/. Thus we have *two distinct meanings of the same word*, 'stain,' *simultaneously* active and greatly responsible for the complexity of the effect of meaning in this metaphor: 'stain'$_1$ /contamination/; 'stain'$_2$ /glass-colouring/, /transparency/. The architectural-isotopy, 'stain'$_2$, predominates over the contamination-isotopy, 'stain'$_1$. This is due to the different degrees of isotopic virtuality: 'stain'$_1$ is constituted by the shared seme /contamination/ in only two lexemes, 'stain' and 'white'; whereas 'stain'$_2$, a more complex phrase, has more lexemes with recurring semes – 'stains,' 'many-coloured glass,' 'dome,' 'white' – thus constituting a veritable sememic isotopy that points to a whole era of religious architecture, and to the spiritual values associated with it. Due to this semantic potential, aesthetic and spiritual values are attached to both sememes as afferent semes: 'stain'$_1$ is valued negatively /impurity/; 'stain'$_2$ positively, /beauty/.

If 'like a dome of many-coloured glass' is defined, on the level of the manifestation, as a simile rather than as a strict metaphor, the process of revaluation of these lexemes, perceived as allotopic, is not different from the process of metaphorization that has been described so far, for as van Dijk very aptly says, 'we actually might consider them [i.e. abbreviated comparisons] to be the DEEP STRUCTURE of a metaphor. The hypothesis harmonizes perfectly with the general conception of deep structures as explicit formulations of all relevant semantic or syntactic structures of a linguistic (surface) structure.'[26]

In order to reach the same level of generality of the context, certain specific semes in 'like a dome of many-coloured glass' are attenuated; other generic semes, such as /roundness/, /superiority/, and the like, are also attenutated; whereas semes such as /delimitation of space/ and, therefore, the more abstract /limitation/ are emphasized, so that there may be compatibility with the context. The same is true in the revaluation of 'many-coloured glass,' in which the more abstract seme /fragility/ is emphasized, again, in compatibility with the general opposition mortality vs. immortality that the poem establishes.

In 'Life, like a dome,' on the other hand, the more abstract characteristics that the general context has bestowed upon it are attenuated; 'Life' is invested with the concrete qualities of the simile that is syntactically placed in apposition to it; 'Life' adds afferent semes to its meaning, semes that are inherent to other sememes from a different semantic field. Thus, in this metaphor, two radically opposed movements take place simultaneously: one towards the general, the other towards the particular.[27]

This double movement is characteristic of the process of metaphorization, which covers a very wide range, from the most abstract to the most concrete levels of discourse *in one and the same operation*. 'Seized in the global generative process, the figurative level of discourse appears as an instance characterized by new installments – the setting of figures of content – which are added to the abstract level. From this perspective one may attempt to interpret *rhetorical figures* – such as metaphor – as *a specific structural relation spanning the abstract and the figurative levels of discourse*' (italics mine).[28]

Shelley's metaphor, in keeping with the abstraction-isotopy, emphasizes the limitations of life and its fragility; simultaneously, it evokes a very concrete image of *dirt* and, paradoxically, of *beauty* in the associations established connotatively between life and stained-glass; of form and colour projected onto a flat and anodyne 'Eternity,' which if unlimited is also evoked as *formless* and *colourless*, therefore given a negative value. Thus, the contamination-isotopy, though attenuated, does not remain unfelt, so that the peculiar dynamics of this metaphor is manifest in the simultaneous and contradictory values associated with both 'Life' and 'Eternity.'

In the first two lines, syntactic and prosodic parallelisms define the series of oppositions: mutability vs. immutability, mortality vs. immortality. A vertical reading outlines two alternate series: (a) 'the many change and pass,' 'Earth's shadows fly,' and 'Life ... stains ... '; (b) 'The One remains,' 'Heaven's light forever shines,' and 'white radiance of Eternity.'

Besides the more abstract oppositions already noted, the light vs. darkness opposition is also apparent, with all the culturally coded values attached to it. The negative value afferently attributed to 'shadows,' for example, is partly responsible for the activation of 'stain'₁. But at the same time, the simile 'like a dome of many-coloured glass' activates 'stain'₂, in which the opposition light vs. shadows is assimilated and transformed into an aesthetic synthesis of light and colour, with religious overtones. The synthesis is given a value that is culturally coded as positive, and that therefore necessarily reflects negatively on 'Eternity'; for in the system of oppositions established by the poem, 'Eternity' lacks the values associated with 'Life,' and vice versa. Furthermore, the stained-glass image, giving form and colour to a neutral eternity, suggests a religious aspiration that intensifies the positive values of this otherwise insignificant and ephemeral act of 'staining.'

As already observed, through a complex operation of addition and suppression, a semic intersection has been constructed from the semes shared by both the isotopic and the allotopic lexemes: /limitation/, /fragility/, /beauty/, /transitoriness/, /contamination/, and so on. But, especially in poetic metaphor, the incompatible semes are never thoroughly suppressed; their latency accounts for the effect of depth and density that metaphor produces. This virtual existence also accounts for the evoked image generated, which no verbal paraphrase can ever account for. 'That is the specific character of metaphor: in making abstraction of a number of features of meaning, at the level of logical communication, it emphasizes the features that have been maintained. By the introduction of a term, alien to the isotopy of the context, and at a different level from that of pure information, metaphor evokes an associated image perceived by the imagination, reverberating on the sensibility, without control from rational intelligence, for it is in the nature of the image introduced by metaphor to escape such a control.'[29]

Ricoeur elaborates on Leguern's notion of the associated image by redescribing it in terms of the Kantian concept of productive imagination: 'Treated as a scheme, the image offers a verbal dimension. Before acting as the recipient for faded percepts ['percepts fanés'], the image is the crucible for emerging meanings. Just as a scheme is the matrix for the category, the icon is that of the new semantic pertinence, born from the dismantling of semantic areas under the shock of contradiction ... the iconic moment involves a verbal aspect, in so far as it constitutes the apprehension of the identical amidst the different and despite the differences, but on a pre-conceptual mode.'[30]

The operation of revaluation of the allotopic lexemes in order to generate the metaphoric meaning is a logical operation that involves the suspension of those semes perceived as incompatible with the isotopy of the text. But, particularly in poetic metaphor, that is, creative metaphor, those incompatible semes – the ones blocking rational communication – are not completely deleted; they are precisely the ones that, at a transrational or at a preconceptual level, generate the associated image, as Leguern and Ricoeur observe.

Thus, the rhetorical perception of metaphor involves a complex, simultaneous operation, of which three stages may be artificially isolated:

(a) A first moment (irrational) occurs at the perception of the allotopic lexeme(s) in a given phrase that has already established an isotopic coherence.

(b) The intelligence immediately seeks to re-establish coherence and to assimilate the anomalous lexemes by revaluing them. By suppressing or suspending those semes that do not fit logically, and by emphasizing or adding others that bear similarity and are therefore compatible with the context, the intelligence does not discard the utterance or text as absurd but finds it metaphorically meaningful (a rational operation). A *conjunctive relation* is thereby drawn from the similar features that make up the semic intersection.

(c) The suspended semes, establishing a simultaneous *disjunctive* relation, remain virtual, though faintly perceptible in the case of poetic metaphor (in the case of lexicalized metaphor, they disappear almost completely), and constitute a complex image – a mental scheme that incorporates both abstract and concrete features and defies logical analysis or verbal paraphrase (a transrational phenomenon).

In Shelley's metaphor, there is a complex image that might be described, though inadequately so, as life in the guise of a Gothic church aspiring to *move* an otherwise immutable eternity by projecting onto it the shapes, the light, and the colour of its stained-glass. Paradoxically, life is also envisaged as the dirt that soils the purity of eternity. The intricacy and the essential irrationality of these coexisting images defy rational explanation, yet contribute to the single though complex effect of meaning.

2 Metaphor as a discursive phenomenon: the transphrastic level

As we have seen, in metaphor there is always a dynamic confrontation between two isotopies, one primary and the other secondary; the former underlying the main context of the utterance, the latter virtual in the allotopic lexemes. From this confrontation or interaction, the metaphoric meaning is produced. Unlike the semantic coherence of the virtual isotopy formed by the allotopic lexemes, which depends on previously established contexts, the resulting metaphoric meaning is local and unique, since its existence is completely subservient to the particular dynamics of a particular utterance. As Ricoeur has observed,

> Metaphor is then a semantic event produced at the intersection of several semantic fields. This construction is the means whereby all the words, taken together, gain meaning. It is then, and only then, that the metaphorical *twist* becomes, simultaneously, an event *and* a meaning, a significant event, an emerging signification created by language ...
>
> In a metaphorical utterance ... the contextual action creates a new meaning which has the status of an event, since it only exists in that particular context. But at the same time, one may identify it as the same, since its construction may be repeated. That is why the utterance of an emerging meaning may be held as a linguistic creation ... Only authentic metaphors, that is, living metaphors, are at the same time both event and meaning.[1]

28 Metaphoric narration

If allotopy in a metaphoric utterance is constituted by only *one* word, the degree of virtuality in the second isotopy will be greater, which is the case at the purely lexematic level of metaphor. Furthermore, because it is only one lexeme, its semic potential will point to many possible contextual meanings and therefore to as many isotopic paths; this, however, on a purely virtual level, which usually remains imperceptible. As soon as a second lexeme belonging to the same semantic field as the first is introduced, the second virtual isotopy becomes further defined, its potential actualized. As we have observed in Shelley's metaphor, 'stain'$_1$ – the contamination-isotopy – has a greater degree of virtuality (and is therefore *less* perceptible) than 'stain'$_2$ – the architectural-isotopy – because the isotopic path is made up of a smaller number of lexemes ('stains' and 'white').

In fact, the greatest potential for the dissemination of meaning, which is so characteristic of metaphor at the discursive level, lies in the activation of the second isotopy. For, once the second isotopy is defined, there may be an interplay, at different points of a text, between the two semantic fields, thus generating a whole constellation of metaphoric meanings but still producing only *one* complex effect of meaning. 'Metaphor develops its power to reorganize our vision of things when it is a whole domain that is transposed: sounds in the visual order, for example. To speak of the sonority of a painting no longer entails the emigration of an isolated predicate; it rather assures the incursion of a whole "kingdom" into foreign territory ... the organization in the foreign territory is *guided by* the use of the whole network from the original one.'[2]

What characterizes the metaphoric process at the discursive level is that as the links between the two fields are multiplied, the process may go beyond the limits of the sentence, considered as an independent syntactic unit, as a superior linguistic unit that is not itself constitutive of any larger unit. At the transphrastic level, the double existence of metaphor, paradigmatic and syntagmatic, is emphasized: the role of metaphor as a connector of isotopies is an essentially *paradigmatic* activity, but as the links between the two isotopies are multiplied, it also develops and deploys its *syntagmatic* character. 'We call *connector ... of isotopies* a unit of the discursive level which induces one or several different readings ... In the case of pluri-isotopy, it is the polysememic character of the discursive unit playing the role of connector which makes the superimposition of different isotopies possible. From the typological point of view, we may isolate, among others, the *metaphoric*

Metaphor as a discursive phenomenon   29

connectors, which allow the passage from an abstract (or thematic) isotopy to a figurative isotopy. The relation that brings them together is always oriented (that which is said on the second isotopy is interpretable on the first but not conversely).'[3]

Metaphor as a connector of isotopies produces a discursive phenomenon in which there is a constant *alternation* between allotopic and isotopic lexemes. As the allotopic lexemes are revalued by being indexed to a second isotopy, the phenomenon may be described as a constant *alternation of isotopies*. In English the name it has traditionally received is 'sustained metaphor,' but I now call it 'threaded metaphor,' after the French 'métaphore filée,' for I think it is a denomination that more effectively denotes the dynamics of this alternation. Michael Riffaterre defines threaded metaphor as 'a series of metaphors connected one to the other by syntax – they may be part of the same sentence or of the same narrative or descriptive structure – and by sense: each metaphor expresses a particular aspect of the whole thing or concept, which the *first* metaphor of the series represents' (italics mine).[4]

Riffaterre considers threaded metaphor a special code, since the various metaphors that constitute it are completely dependent for their meaning on the first metaphor of the series. For example, Shelley's 'Until Death tramples it to fragments' can be understood only in terms of the initial stained-glass metaphor. Both 'tramples' and 'fragments' reinforce the 'stain'$_2$ isotopy with the recurring seme /fragility/, thus contributing to the dominant character of 'stain'$_2$ over 'stain'$_1$. Each metaphor of the series is then seen as connecting both isotopies, a connection that not only operates the passage from the abstract to the figurative levels of discourse, but also enlivens different aspects of the same semantic field. The seme /fragility/, for example, virtual and only subliminally perceived in the initial metaphor, is actualized by the second metaphor.

What characterizes threaded metaphor, then, is that a series of distinct metaphors are drawn from the same field, thus constituting one isotopic path; and that in its textual development the series tends to be derived from a primary metaphor. But, as Philippe Dubois has observed,[5] the primary metaphor need not be, as Riffaterre suggests, the first; it does not even have to be explicit, for in some threaded metaphors it is the sum of the different metaphors that generates an implicit master-metaphor, encompassing all the others and without which the series would be devoid of meaning or perceived as isolated

30 Metaphoric narration

metaphors. Eliot's 'The Love Song of J. Alfred Prufrock' is a case in point:

> The yellow fog that rubs its back upon the window-panes,
> The yellow smoke that rubs its muzzle on the window-panes,
> Licked its tongue into the corners of the evening,
> Lingered upon the pools that stand in drains,
> Let fall upon its back the soot that falls from chimneys,
> Slipped by the terrace, made a sudden leap,
> And seeing that it was a soft October night,
> Curled once about the house, and fell asleep.

In this metaphoric description of 'the yellow fog,' the feline-isotopy (as opposed, say, to the canine) is not clearly defined by the first metaphor ('*rubs its back* upon the window-panes'), but gradually emerges from the cumulative effect of the subsequent metaphors.

An interesting feature of metaphor at the discursive level is that the potential semantic dynamism of the process of metaphorization is fully realized. Dubois perceives this semantic dynamism in terms of reversibility and of a semantic dissemination ('ensémencement sémantique') in a given text due to the specific discursive function of metaphor as a connector of isotopies. Dubois formalizes the mechanism as follows:

> it is enough that an utterance, coherent on one isotopy [1] (to which the units of discourse are indexed according to the syntagmatic chain ABCDEF) is suddenly connected to a second isotopy [2], due to the effect of metaphor [M] for a reactivation of the text to take place. The reactivation tends to inscribe on [2] the greatest possible number of discursive units from [1] and, therefore, to produce as many possible polysemic units that may function (or may be read) on both [1] and [2]; that is to say, there is a tendency to produce new, derived metaphors (M', M", M'").[6]

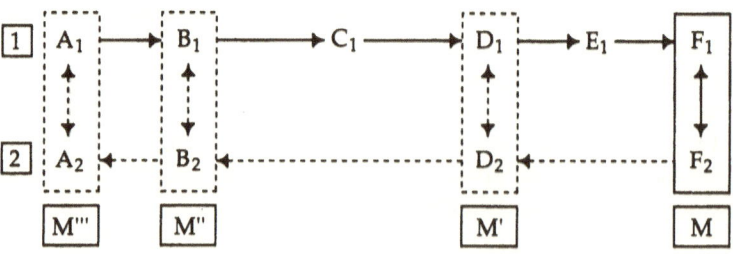

Metaphor as a discursive phenomenon

The reactivation of the text as described by Dubois corresponds to the operation of revaluation of allotopic lexemes. The revaluation at the transphrastic level may be *retrospective*, if the allotopic lexeme appears at the end of the text, as the diagram shows, and forces a revaluation of other words so far perceived as isotopic – that is, univocal. Due to the pressure of the introduced allotopic lexeme(s), many of the others may also undergo a revaluation, so that they may be indexed to and read on the second isotopy. Here is an example of semantic revaluation occurring at a terminal point:

> Under my window-ledge the waters race,
> Otters below and moor-hens on the top,
> Run for a mile undimmed in Heaven's face
> Then darkening through 'dark' Raftery's 'cellar' drop,
> Run underground, rise in a rocky place
> In Coole demesne, and there to finish up
> Spread to a lake and drop into a hole.
> What's water but the generated soul?
> (W.B. Yeats, 'Coole Park and Ballylee')

Here, as may be observed, the revaluation is no longer of isolated allotopic lexemes but of a whole text, first read as a coherent description of the world surrounding the poet. Due to the water-soul metaphor, a retrospective reading on a spiritual, rather than on a purely topographical isotopy, is activated.

Revaluation may also be *prospective* ('*proversive*'): when the allotopic lexemes of the primary or master-metaphor appear at the beginning of the text, their revaluation conditions and orients subsequent readings on a second isotopic path. This is the case in Shelley's threaded metaphor.

Thus metaphor, at the discursive level, projects onto the whole text essential features of its mechanism:[7] it emphasizes its *simultaneous* paradigmatic-syntagmatic nature by forcing a marked *vertical* reading alongside the usual *horizontal*, syntagmatic one. Back-reading ('rétro-lecture'),[8] activated by metaphor on the discursive level, plays on both axes: a sequential, therefore *syntagmatic*, reading is presupposed; at a given point, it is subverted by a rupture in the isotopic coherence of the text. Due to the semantic dynamism of metaphor, the revaluation of allotopy does not only take place locally, within the boundaries of the sentence, but retrospectively, at other points of the text, forcing a back-reading that is essentially a *paradigmatic* activity of selection and of searching for similarities. The reactivation of certain units of discourse in a given text does not necessarily occur at a terminal point; it may occur at any point of the text, thus giving way to a simultaneous prospective and retrospective reading. Or else the bi-isotopic text may be established from the beginning so that all the subsequent metaphors expand on the same semantic field intitially proposed by the first, and actualize as many aspects as possible from that second field connected to the first vertically by a series of metaphors.

An example of this is the famous 'baignoire' sequence in Proust's *Le côté de Guermantes* (II, 38–44).[9] In that narrative of an evening at the theatre, the first metaphor enlivens the whole semantic field of 'baignoire' as 'bath-tub,' a homonym that is completely alien to the theatrical context in which it appears, and that would remain unfelt were it not for the aquatic threaded metaphor that Proust forces upon the theatrical context.

To sum up and elaborate on Dubois's ideas, one may say that there are two fundamental moments in the rhetorical perception of a text. The first moment itself constitutes a complex, simultaneous operation in which, as has already been observed (p 26), three stages may be artificially isolated: (a) *perception of allotopy* in a given phrase, the isotopic coherence of which has already been established; (b) *revaluation* of allotopy through the operation of addition and suppression of semes or 'parts,' in order to construct a semic intersection; (c) *expansion of the semic intersection* to cover both fields, so that the suspended semes that have remained virtual, though still perceptible, contribute to evoke an associated image or mental scheme that incorporates both abstract and concrete features.

The second moment of the rhetorical perception, the one that marks the specific functioning of the mechanism at the discursive level, is the *prospective and/or retrospective reading*: 'Starting from the recognition of a double isotopy, the reader explores the whole text on that second isotopy with the purpose of indexing the greatest possible number of discursive units on to the new isotopy. These discursive units are thereby transformed into new rhetorical units.'[10]

A very important aspect of the process of metaphorization at the discursive level is the *temporal dimension* that characterizes the process: because metaphor is deployed in a syntagmatic chain that far surpasses the boundaries of the single sentence – the syntagmatic deployment necessarily implying succession – metaphor becomes a *temporal phenomenon*. At the lexematic level, as we have seen, the metaphoric effect of meaning is *instantaneous*; at the transphrastic or discursive

Metaphor as a discursive phenomenon

level, by contrast, the effects of meaning are of a *cumulative* nature, yet *single* in their global effect.

The temporal dimension of the process of metaphorization affects its mode of functioning. In fact, we have already identified two distinct modes:

(a) metaphorization at the discursive level may appear as a series of allotopic lexemes, all belonging to the same semantic field, interwoven with the isotopic lexemes (threaded metaphor, strictly speaking);

(b) this, however, is not always the case; metaphorization at the discursive level may also be brought about by a word, a group of words, or a phrase at the end of the text, or at any other point, constituting a breach in the general isotopy of the previous portion of the text. These terminal allotopic lexemes trigger a reactivation of other lexical units, earlier in the text, that may now be read on the second isotopy.

What is interesting in this second mode of functioning of metaphorization at the discursive level is that there is a clear *temporal shift* that allows both the literal and the metaphorical meanings to coexist, without mutually cancelling each other out. We noticed how in Yeats's poem 'Coole Park and Ballylee,' the metaphoric reading of the whole text on the spiritual isotopy does not cancel the previous reading on the topographic isotopy. The metaphorical reactivation of a whole text, then, constitutes an enrichment, an addition, without excluding the first, often literal, meaning. This is an exclusive feature of the process at the discursive level; at the lexematic level, by contrast, the decoding of the metaphorical meaning by means of the construction of a semic intersection excludes the literal or non-metaphorical meaning. The temporal dimension of discursive metaphor will be found to be essential in the narrative transposition of the process where it acts as an organizing principle (cf chapter 3, 2.1.2).

3 The narrative dimension of metaphor

To speak of the narrative dimension of metaphor may at first seem contradictory, especially given the traditional dichotomy between poetic and narrative discourses, and given the conventional but artificial assignment of metaphor to the former and metonymy to the latter.[1] But if it is possible to speak of metaphor and therefore of metaphoric narration, in terms of the structure of narrative, this is due to the fundamental operations and relations involved in the process of metaphorization itself:

(a) Metaphorization, as the elementary operation of semantic manipulation involving a rearrangement of semes, implies the essentially narrative operation of *transformation*;

(b) Because metaphorization brings two distinct semantic fields into close contact, it results in the confrontation between a primary isotopy and a second, virtual one, and, by extension, in the projection of different spatial coordinates and actors on to the primary ones of a given context.[2] Although *transformation* of a given state into a different one is the basic narrative component of *any* kind of discourse, the component is accentuated and rendered concrete, in the case of metaphor, by that projection of virtual spatial coordinates and actors different from the ones posed by the main context. It is this narrative potential of metaphor, completely dependent on the fundamental operations and relations involved in metaphorization, that I shall now proceed to examine.

The narrative dimension of metaphor may be analysed on two basic levels:

A on the level of the *manifestation in language*. The dimension remains purely virtual at the phrastic level and is actualized at the transphrastic level, especially in the shape of threaded metaphor and of the extended simile;

B on the *constructed* level of the *organization* of a narrative text. No longer a phenomenon of the manifestation in language, metaphor as *process* is structurally fundamental in the production of meaning of certain narrative texts.

Accordingly, to speak of metaphoric narration is to speak of special effects of meaning resulting from transformations characteristic of metaphorization, which may be either *observed* at the level of the manifestation in language or *constructed* from the mode of organization of the text. Therefore, metaphoric narration defines that class of narrative texts in which the process of metaphorization functions narratively on two basic levels: at the level of the manifestation in language and at the level of the organization of the text.[3]

Now, analysis distinguishes two levels in the functioning of *verbal* metaphor:

A.1 metaphor as an effect of meaning localized within the boundaries of an isolated sentence, that is, the *phrastic* or *lexematic* level. The narrative potential at this level is purely virtual and, therefore, barely perceptible;

A.2 metaphor as an effect of meaning transcending the boundaries of the sentence and thereby becoming a discursive phenomenon (threaded metaphor and the extended simile), that is, the *transphrastic* level. Here, the narrative potential becomes fully realized.

Thus, at the level of the manifestation in language and particularly in its discursive mode, the narrative function of metaphor is defined: (i) by the series of semantic transformations within a coherent semantic field, arranged in a relation of succession that may be both virtually chronological and causal. This is especially true of threaded metaphor; or (ii) by the same logic and chronologic relations of succession established among the various abstract 'events' outlined in the extended simile; or (iii) by the relation of succession established in a whole text that has been reactivated in order to be read, retrospectively, on a second isotopy. (For a more detailed description of this mode of metaphoric narration, see this chapter, 1, below.)

At the level of B, organization of the text, two aspects are also distinguished: metaphoric articulation and metaphoric construction of narrative sequences:

B.1 The process of metaphorization may determine the mode of *articulation* of two narrative sequences. By the term *articulation*, I mean the 'mode of jointing or junction'[4] of two sequences by means of specific units functioning as links or connectors between the two. In other words, because of the connecting role of certain units, two distinct narrative sequences interact in such a way that reading them in conjunction entails a process that is similar to that of the decoding of verbal metaphorization. 'Interaction' or 'confrontation' are terms that may sometimes be used synonymously, though they do not describe so precisely the process of junction entailing specific nexus to bring about the metaphoric linkage (cf this chapter, 2.1, below).

The modes of metaphoric articulation may be actual or virtual. In the *actual* mode, clear textual determinations link two sequences; both share the same textual space in continuity or contiguity. In the *virtual* mode, by contrast, the two sequences are textually discontinuous; there are no explicit marks to bring about the connection but, because of certain narrative units functioning as links in the connection – that is to say, a series of conjunctions and disjunctions in the second sequence that has been programmed to resonate with the first – both sequences are made to interact metaphorically by an act of retrospective reading. Metaphoric narration is therefore produced by the articulation of certain narrative units in a given sequence with other similar ones. In the virtual mode, the two articulated sequences are textually discontinuous; it is by means of retrospective reading and by the activation of certain units relating conjunctively and functioning as 'connectors of isotopies' that the articulation takes place.

The metaphorical articulation of two narrative sequences, whether actual or virtual, generates a virtual narrative that functions *paranarratively*; that is, a narrative with a purely virtual existence, developing parallel or alongside the main narrative; a virtual narrative thoroughly dependent on the interaction of specific sequences and on the local context of the main one.[5]

B.2 The *construction* of a narrative sequence may (a) narrativize a lexicalized metaphor underlying the main narrative as an implicit narrative program (cf this chapter, 2.2.1); (b) reproduce the network of the relations and operations that define the process of metaphorization itself (cf this chapter, 2.2.2); (c) be patterned upon the structure of another sequence serving as a model; both sequences may then be articulated metaphorically (cf this chapter, 2.2.3, and particularly the analysis of Cortázar's 'La noche boca arriba').

The diagram on page 37 proposes a spatial projection that classifies the various modes of metaphoric narration.

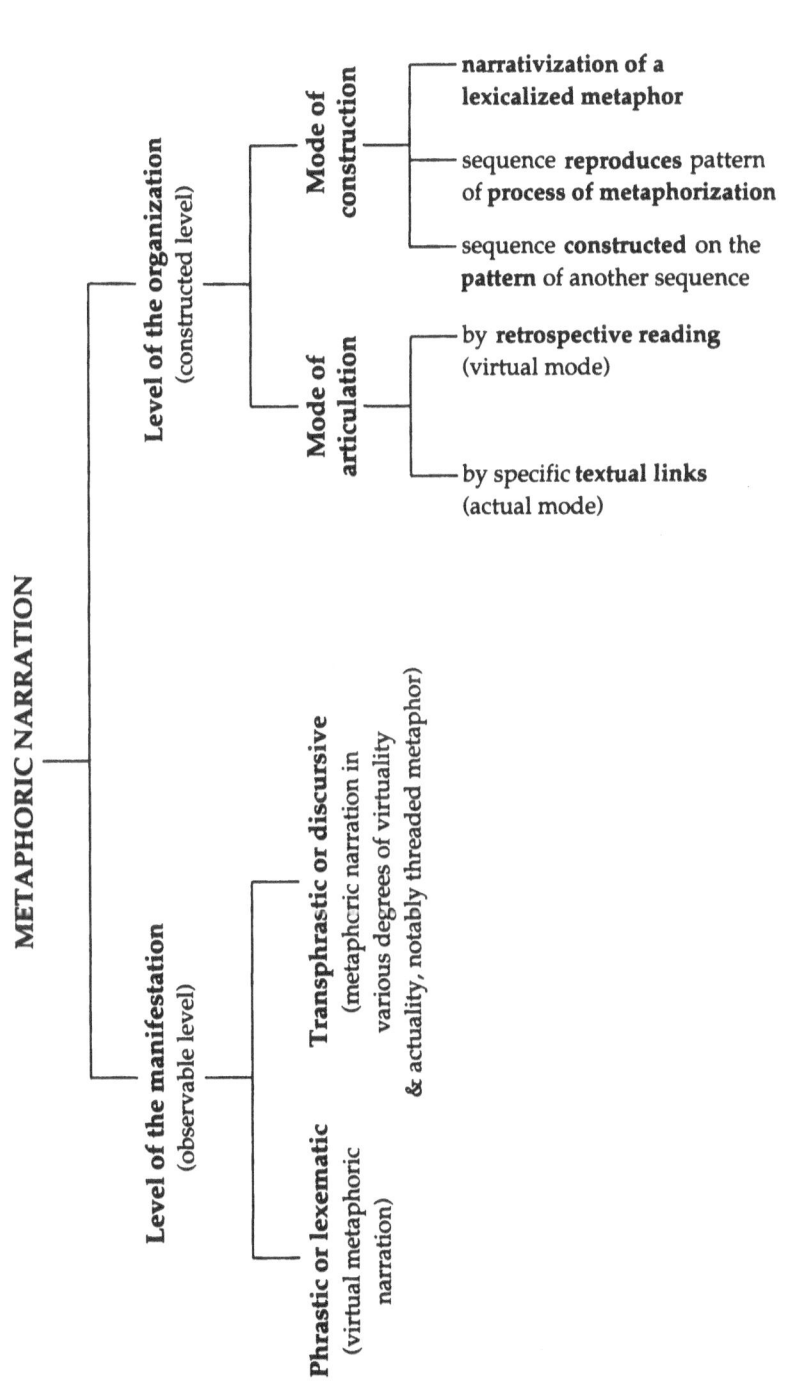

38   Metaphoric narration

1   Metaphoric narration: the level of the manifestation in language

So far, I have described the semantic functioning of verbal metaphor at both the phrastic and the transphrastic levels. Whether within the boundaries of the sentence or beyond, as a discursive phenomenon, the point of departure for my analyses has been the level of the manifestation in language (though metaphor is a particular form of the linguistic manifestation heavily depending on constructed degrees of meaning in interaction with manifested ones, in order to generate one single effect of meaning).

Threaded metaphor, as has been observed, multiplies the nexus between the two fields: a primary metaphor may generate a number of derived metaphors, or a series of linked metaphors may outline one master-metaphor that remains implicit. Because all metaphors thus connected belong to the same semantic field, constituting among themselves a coherent, though intermittent isotopic line, definite spatial coordinates are traced that are alien to those of the main context. The links, as we have seen, due to the temporal dimension of the process at the discursive level, may also be activated retrospectively by a terminal utterance belonging to a different semantic field. In both cases, however, we have a series of narrative and/or lexical units working as connectors of isotopies. The multiple metaphors constitute a *sequence* activating *different* aspects of a given field, therefore a *virtual temporal sequence* and a series of *transformations*. These, as we have seen, are the essential components of narrative: the transformation of a given state into a different one, operated in time.

In terms of narrative, then, threaded metaphor and the second, temporally displaced, mode of discursive metaphor may superimpose onto the primary isotopy the transformations, the spatial and temporal coordinates produced by a second isotopy, thus constituting a virtual narrative sequence with different degrees of autonomy. In other words, the syntagmatic nature of language manifested in an utterance or a written text necessarily implies sequential arrangement and therefore temporality. Now, if this temporal sequence of manifested language is reinforced by the operation of transformation implicitly established among the various metaphors activating different aspects of the same virtual semantic field, then threaded metaphor may become a veritable narrative sequence of varying degrees of virtuality. Thus, the metaphor from Shelley's 'Adonais' that has been examined proposes a paranarrative sequence that goes from the heroic cultural-religious act of 'staining' Eternity, to the eventual, ineluctable destruction of that stained-glass work produced by human limitations.

The narrative dimension of metaphor 39

As threaded metaphor is prolonged, the virtual narrative sequence becomes actual. Indeed it may be prolonged to such an extent that it will subvert the primary narrative sequence and take on a pre-eminent position in the attention of the reader. Since the fictional world of narrative is gradually built up by means of a succession of signs, the very sequential nature of signs in discourse, as Ricardou has so very aptly observed,

> determines a particular perspective whereby each of the descriptive details is interposed between the preceding one and the reader, thus hiding it to a certain extent. This process of concealment to which the successive order of signs gives rise, accounts particularly for the fact that if a description dares multiply its characters excessively, it ends by dissolving the object it initially attempted to construct. It also allows us to understand the phenomenon whereby any digression, even though it may have been presented as such, once prolonged beyond certain limits, tends to become the *main body* of the text [*corps principal*].[6]

The extreme prolongation of threaded metaphor may project a full-fledged secondary or ancillary narrative. As it interacts with the main one, a virtual narrative line with a paranarrative function is generated. The 'baignoire' sequence in Proust's *Le côté de Guermantes* is a case in point:

> En deçà, au contraire, de la limite de leur domaine, les radieuses filles de la mer se retournaient à tout moment en souriant vers des tritons barbus pendus aux anfractuosités de l'abîme, ou vers quelque demi-dieu aquatique ayant pour crâne un galet poli sur lequel le flot avait ramené une algue lisse et pour regard un disque en cristal de roche. Elles se penchaient vers eux, elles leur offraient des *bonbons*; parfois le flot s'entr'ouvrait devant une nouvelle néréide qui, tardive, souriante et confuse, venait de s'épanouir du fond de l'ombre; puis, *l'acte fini*, n'espérant plus entendre les rumeurs mélodieuses de la terre qui les avait attirées à la surface, plongeant toutes à la fois, les diverses soeurs disparaissaient dans la nuit. (II, 40) (italics mine)

What is striking about this passage is that the usual proportions in threaded metaphor have been inverted. As its name suggests, this discursive phenomenon is threaded; that is, metaphoric and non-metaphoric phrases alternate, with the predominance of the non-metaphoric. The primary isotopy remains strongly felt and is only intermittently broken by the appearance of the allotopic lexemes that interact with it. Since all the allotopic lexemes appearing at different points of the text tend to belong to the same semantic field, they establish a coherent isotopic line of their own, but this isotopy is *a mental construct that has no continuity in the manifestation*. If nonetheless the virtual isotopy is perceived as semantically *coherent* and *uninterrupted*, this is because it derives its continuity from the shared semantic filiation. In the manifestation, however, the second isotopic line is actually *intermittent* and *discontinuous*.

'Tel filet d'idée poétique qui chez André Chénier *découlerait* en élégie, ou chez Lamartine *s'épancherait* en méditation, et finirait par devenir *fleuve ou lac*, se *congèle* aussitôt chez moi et se *cristallise* en sonnet' (italics mine).[7] In this text from Sainte-Beuve, the allotopic lexemes are literally threaded, woven into his meditation on poetry. In the Proustian text under examination, by contrast, the reverse is true: it is the second isotopy that has displaced the first and has become dominant. But because the theatrical context has been strongly established from the beginning of the sequence, all the metaphors from the aquatic isotopy may still be revalued in terms of what Umberto Eco would call an 'entry' in the reader's 'encyclopaedia' of the world:[8] an evening at the theatre ('abîme' is still vaguely decoded in terms of the edge of the ground-floor box; 'galet poli' as a bald head, and 'disque en cristal de roche' as a monocle). Nevertheless, if this process of revaluation is still regulated by the original diegetic context, the aquatic isotopy, by virtue of its insistent syntagmatic presence, ends up imposing itself upon the reader, becomes, as Ricardou would say, 'corps principal': an evening in the theatre is thus paranarratively transformed into myth by the pressure of metaphorization.

'It may well be that the reference to everyday reality must be abolished so that another reference to other dimensions of reality may be released.'[9]

2   Metaphoric narration: the level of the organization of a narrative text

2.1 *Metaphoric articulation of narrative sequences*[10]

2.1.1 The actual mode of articulation

So far we have seen how threaded metaphor, featuring a given number of metaphors as connectors of isotopies, may function as a narrative sequence with a certain degree of autonomy. There are certain texts, however, in which meaning depends on the kind of interaction peculiar to metaphor, but where metaphor as such is absent at the level of the manifestation in language. These kinds of texts present, like threaded metaphor, a primary diegetic context to which is juxtaposed a complete narrative sequence with alien spatio-temporal coordinates and actors. The alien sequence may function as an isotopic breach of a diegetic kind; revaluation, as in ordinary metaphor, is determined by the main context. The interaction that takes place in order to produce meaning is of the same nature as that in metaphor, except that the connections between the two isotopies are not operated by single, intermittent metaphors; instead *the entire allotopic narrative sequence as a block* interacts metaphorically with the main narrative – certain features in the allotopic sequence, relating conjunctively with similar ones in the main narrative, act as the links in the metaphorical articulation of both. I shall illustrate this actual mode of metaphoric articulation with a passage from Lezama Lima's *Paradiso*: 'Baldovina se desesperaba, desgreñada, *parecía una azafata que, con un garzón en los brazos iba retrocediendo pieza tras pieza en la quema de un castillo, cumpliendo las órdenes de sus señores en huída*. Necesitaba ya que la socorrieran, pues cada vez que retiraba el mosquitero, veía el cuerpo que se extendía y le daba más relieve a las ronchas; aterrorizada, para cumplimentar el afán que ya tenía de huir, fingió que buscaba a la otra pareja de criados' (italics mine).[11]

The micro-narrative sequence proposed by the simile of the lady of the Queen's wardrobe, unlike threaded metaphor as it has been defined, is uninterrupted and coherent in itself. There is no alternation with the primary narrative isotopy, and there are no distinct, identifiable lexemes functioning as connectors of isotopies; rather, the whole sequence functions metaphorically *vis-à-vis* the main narrative sequence. Certain semes from key lexemes and certain narrative elements, similar in both sequences, are the ones that act as the joints in this metaphorical articulation: /extremely high temperature/, in both the burning castle and the feverish child; /social subordination/, shared by the lady of the Queen's wardrobe and Baldovina, the Cuban maid; /escape/, present in the double retreat of the metaphoric sequence and in Baldovina's frantic desire to escape.

The process of metaphorization is clearly at work in the articulation of both sequences: the shared semes and thematic elements, establishing a *conjunctive relation*, construct an intersection that gives both sequences a meaning that is rationally satisfying; simultaneously those aspects that are not shared, therefore relating *disjunctively* to the main context, generate not only an evoked image but, in this case, a veritable paranarrative sequence, independent from the main one, yet owing its local existence to its interaction with the main narrative.

Numerous are the elements relating disjunctively to one another, which are responsible for the intensity and autonomy of the 'burning castle' secondary narrative: the lady of the micro-sequence, for example, is heroically active in the saving of the child, while Baldovina is pathetically passive; in the micro-sequence it is the lord and lady of the castle who are in flight, whereas in the main narrative, Baldovina's masters are merely absent; it is she, Baldovina, who has a desperate impulse to escape. The subtle projection of Baldovina's fears and desires onto her masters is thus obliquely transferred to the secondary sequence. Baldovina's projection of fears onto others, with the associated overtones of evasion and cowardice, is part of the effect of meaning produced by metaphoric narration, an effect that is not to be located in either of the two narrative sequences; it emerges, paranarratively, from the metaphoric articulation of the two.

Another interesting aspect of the micro-sequence is that the lexemes *azafata* (lady of the Queen's wardrobe), *garzón* (infant), *castillo* (castle), and *señores en huída* (lord and lady in flight) are not only culturally but temporally marked; they outline a sort of cultural entity – another entry in the reader's encyclopaedia – that could be called something like 'war and defeat in medieval Europe.' Thus, clearly defined actors and specific time-space coordinates – which are completely alien to the context, and which would make no sense were it not for the metaphoric relation established between the two sequences – are superimposed on those of the main narrative: a military camp and a Cuban family in the twentieth century. Because of the prolongation of the simile, the superimposition is such that the narrative of the retreat in the burning castle becomes, for a moment, completely dominant and transforms this humble Caribbean maid, desperate and dishevelled, into a heroic lady of the court, saving a princely child – an ironic transformation, no doubt. The irony, in fact, is the effect of the enormous cultural and temporal distance between the two sequences thus identified by the simile structure. This is precisely what strikes the reader in the Lezamian simile: the extreme *arbitrariness* of the association.

In Proust's 'baignoire' sequence, though the distance between the two narrative isotopies is just as great, at least it is not thoroughly unmotivated: the degree of arbitrariness is reduced by the fact that there is a linguistic motivation in the polysemic nature of 'baignoire.' It is, as we have seen, a deliberate semantic game that Proust plays

The narrative dimension of metaphor   43

between the two completely different meanings of the word *baignoire*: a homonym for both bath-tub and ground-floor box. Therefore, the linguistic motivation that triggers the metaphorical paranarrative of the aquatic gods is to be found, specifically, in the homonymic nature of 'baignoire.'

In the Lezamian simile, by contrast, not only is the temporal distance between the two narrative isotopies unbridgeable, the cultural distance is just as great, while it is even further emphasized by the narratively unmotivated character of the simile. This distance, nonetheless, together with the extreme arbitrariness of the association, is cancelled at the level of textual production, for it is at that level, as Adam has observed about a poem by Breton, that the association has taken place; 'the arbitrary is reduced at the textual level of writing [écriture], released from the laws of denotation. This means that connotation and the isotopic fields take over the production of new relationships.'[12] The subversion of the laws of realistic representation weaves new threads that subtly connect aspects of reality never before interrelated. The novelty of the association, an effect that is typical of poetic metaphor, creates a new reference; a new dimension of reality has been called into existence by metaphor.

One observation to be made at this point is that the Lezamian simile under consideration proposes two juxtaposed narrative sequences, organized around completely different diegetic coordinates, the second one having no functional coherence or continuity in relation to the main one. Therefore, they can relate metaphorically only if they are to be read as meaningful; yet nothing at the level of the manifestation triggers the process of metaphorization. In fact, it is the very juxtaposition and the embedded simile structure that draw metaphoric relations. The discursive structure of the simile – 'like a' – explicitly brings about the articulation of the two otherwise incompatible sequences. Once the textual proximity has been brought about by the syntactic link of the simile, other semantic and narrative units function as nexus to connect the two sequences and generate the metaphoric meaning. Thus, because of these links, the two sequences may be said to be *articulated* metaphorically, the shared elements in both sequences having the same function as the 'connectors of isotopies' in threaded metaphor.

2.1.2 The virtual mode of articulation

In the Lezamian simile the connection is textual, that is to say, made

44   Metaphoric narration

explicit by syntactic links. In fact, even the mere juxtaposition of two texts may clearly imply an elided simile structure connecting both sequences; so that we may speak of juxtaposition itself as an actual textual determination that links two sequences in a metaphoric relation of analogy. Thus, the metaphoric articulation of two sequences is said to be *actual* when there are textual determinations linking them.

There are narrative texts, however, in which certain sequences, though textually *not* contiguous, are yet programmed to be read in conjunction. Again, a number of semantic, thematic, narrative, and/or diegetic similarities function as the links that connect the two sequences even though they may be separated by a considerable textual distance. Since the text does not explicitly mark the connection, it is the phenomenon of retrospective reading that brings about the metaphorical articulation. Reading both sequences in conjunction adds a new dimension of meaning to the second, just as it corrects, revalues, and enriches the meaning of the first. The result of such an interaction is a virtual narrative that functions paranarratively *vis-à-vis* the two sequences virtually articulated by an act of retrospective reading and by a kind of *intersection* – not unlike the one constructed in the decoding of verbal metaphor – *constructed* from lexic, diegetic, and/or thematic elements that are found to be similar in both sequences and that function as the nexus in the virtual articulation of the two textually discontinuous sequences. Since it is not an explicit textual mark, but the act of retrospective reading itself and the construction of a narrative intersection that are responsible for the articulation of the two sequences, one may speak of a *virtual* metaphoric articulation.

The Lezamian simile has provided us with a clear example of the actual mode of metaphorical articulation. For the virtual mode, I shall draw my illustrations from James Joyce's *Ulysses*, for it is a text heavily constructed on the principle of metaphoric articulation of narrative sequences. The virtual mode constantly makes significant, even symbolic, metaphoric connections between many of the episodes devoted to Stephen and those devoted to Bloom.

In the third episode, 'Proteus,' Stephen meditates on birth and death as he walks along the beach in Sandymount. His musings are prompted by two women, whom he fancies must be midwives, carrying a bag that he is sure must contain a 'misbirth with a trailing navelcord, hushed in ruddy wool.'[13] All the subsequent thoughts are inscribed in a context of motherhood and birth, with the sea as 'our mighty mother.' Suddenly, Stephen thinks of a humorous metaphor for the urge to establish a secret communication with his origins: a telephone. 'The cords of all link back, strandentwining cable of all flesh. That is why mystic monks. Will you be as gods? Gaze in your omphalos. Hello. Kinch here. Put me on to Edenville. Aleph, alpha: nought, nought, one' (43).

On this metaphorical telephone communicating with the origins of man, Stephen most appropriately dials a nil/one number: creation and dissolution. Throughout his meditation on birth, the other extreme, death, is always juxtaposed to it, as though it were the immediate and natural sequence. The misbirth becomes symbolic of this inexorable proximity: death in birth. Towards the end of the episode the contiguity is emphasized by the particularly striking alliteration 'allwombing tomb' (53). In Stephen's imagination, 'womb' and 'tomb' simultaneously *span* and *abolish* the distance between birth and death. Just as Stephen, in a fit of melancholy humour, has defined a pier as 'a disappointed bridge,'[14] similarly birth can only be conceived of as frustration, as a 'misbirth,' which indirectly describes his own attempted 'spiritual (mis)birth,' figured by his thwarted Parisian venture.

In the sixth episode, 'Hades,' Leopold Bloom attends a funeral ceremony. The doleful occasion engenders in his mind and imagination all sorts of lugubrious thoughts, but mostly his meditation on death seems to take the road towards resurrection: he continually imagines ways in which one could be reborn, or else he thinks of forms of thriving in death, of coming back to life. Throughout the episode, Bloom is constantly alive to all these possibilities; at one point he even startles himself by thinking that perhaps his friend, Paddy Dignam, is not dead after all: 'They ought to have some law to pierce the heart and make sure or an electric clock or *a telephone in the coffin* and some kind of a canvas airhole. Flag of distress ... ' (113) 'Have a gramophone in every grave or keep it in the house. After dinner on a Sunday. Put on poor old greatgrandfather Kraahraark! *Hellohellohello amawfullyglad* kraark *awfullygladaseeragain* hellohello amarawf kopthsth' (115) (italics mine).

It is interesting that Bloom hits on the same figurative device as Stephen, the telephone, in order to communicate with the living. What is different is the thematic direction: Bloom's telephone puts the dead in communication with the living, while Stephen's is the call of the living back to the origin. But, since the origin –significantly designated as *omphalos*, navel – is in birth and Stephen can conceive of birth only as a misbirth, communication is established from life to death. The difference also lies in the tone, half-serious in Stephen, highly comical in Bloom, especially because the figure is multiplied and extended to other forms of both simple and technological communication (flags of distress, a canvas airhole, electric clocks, gramophones, etc.).

For Bloom, death also offers the possibility of fertilization: 'It's the blood sinking in the earth gives new life ... Well preserved fat corpse gentleman, epicure, invaluable for fruit garden. A bargain. By carcass of William Wilkinson, auditor and accountant, lately deceased, three pounds thirteen and six. With thanks' (110).

If, as in Stephen's case, life and death are also contiguous in Bloom's imagination, the accent is on the former. Bloom even thinks, with some kind of morbid pleasure, about 'love among the tombstones. Romeo. Spice of pleasure.' This makes him conclude that 'in the midst of death we are in life. *Both ends meet*' (110) (italics mine). Such a conclusion is strongly reminiscent of Stephen's 'allwombing tomb,' except that the weight is differently placed: ironically the young man emphasizes death in a marine context of fertility and potential birth, while the older man can see only life and rebirth despite his mournful surroundings.

Bloom's insistence on life and regeneration is such that many of his imagined objects are either humorous, like the corpse of an epicure gentleman sold at a bargain, or gruesome, like the obese rat he sees wriggling itself in under the plinth. This latter scene starts a train of thoughts on death as nourishment: 'One of those chaps would make short work of a fellow. Pick the bones clean no matter who it was. Ordinary meat for them. A corpse is meat gone bad. Well and what's cheese? Corpse of milk' (116). Thus the cemetery rats thrive in death. Death as nourishment, in turn, promotes a strong and efficient 'underground communication' (116), thus closing the thematic cycle of life and death.

In these thematic, narrative, and figurative aspects that I have isolated from the two episodes, it will be noticed that there is a simultaneous, therefore *metaphorical*, interaction of conjunctive and disjunctive relations. However, since both narrative sequences are textually discontinuous, there are no specific syntactic links to bring about the conjunction; the sequences are, therefore, articulated metaphorically in the *virtual* mode. The phenomenon of back-reading, upon which this virtual articulation is based, is initially activated by the identity of the rhetorical figure employed: the telephone. Other diegetic determinations are also similar. Both Stephen and Bloom think about life and death at the same hour: eleven a.m. The subject of their musings is identical: life and death. In fact, all these similarities construct a kind of *narrative intersection*, on the basis of which

The narrative dimension of metaphor 47

metaphorization takes place, and which reveals that both sequences have been programmed to be read in conjunction. The effect of such a stereoscopic reading is that both are identified metaphorically as being the same yet different ('history repeating itself with a difference').

Nonetheless, and in the midst of these similarities making the narrative intersection possible, a series of *disjunctive* relations activate the radical oppositions between the two: the age of both protagonists, the degree of intellectual sophistication, their diegetic surroundings: the sea (birth, life) and the cemetery (death). At the very heart of a similar thematic development, symmetric oppositions are drawn ('symmetry under a cemetery wall'): in Stephen's monologue, death is emphasized despite the symbolic fertility of the marine context; in Bloom's, life, in spite of the cemetery and his friend's funeral. These symmetric oppositions differentiating the development of otherwise identical themes also entail a radical *tonal* opposition: essentially *dysphoric* in Stephen, paradoxically *euphoric* in Bloom (the paradox lies in the fact that 'Hades,' contrary to what one might expect, is perhaps one of the most hilarious episodes in *Ulysses*).

Thus, the virtual metaphorical articulation of both these episodes, despite the textual distance, depends entirely on a kind of stereoscopic reading of both, elicited by the conjunctive and disjunctive relations drawn among the various narrative, diegetic, thematic, and rhetorical points of convergence and divergence, thereby generating additional symbolic meanings, which the two sequences in isolation might not have. The stereoscopic reading of both sequences offers the reader a kind of metaphoric correction and complement to Stephen's meditations on life and death, while Stephen's sombre thoughts echo and colour the contradictorily comical thoughts that assault Bloom.

2.1.3 A mixed mode of articulation

There are instances in which the two modes of articulation, actual and virtual, may be mixed. This is the case, for example, in two sequences from Conrad's *Heart of Darkness*. At a point in Marlow's narrative, when he is looking for a job, an interesting temporal shift occurs: he is just about to cross the Channel on his way to Brussels in order to get his official appointment for a job in Africa, when a particularly long prolepsis breaks through the chronology of his tale, literally bringing Africa to Europe, the future to the present. The proleptic narrative – that is, the narrative of a segment temporally displaced from its chronological place in the story – breaks not only the temporal but the spatial narrative isotopies that the text has so far established:

48 Metaphoric narration

'I got my appointment – of course; and I got it very quick. It appears the Company had received news that one of their captains had been killed in a scuffle with the natives. This was my chance, and it made me the more anxious to go. It was only months and months afterwards, when I made the attempt to recover what was left of the body, that I heard the original quarrel arose from a misunderstanding about some hens ... Afterwards nobody seemed to trouble much about Fresleven's remains, till I got out and stepped into his shoes. I couldn't let it rest, though; but when an opportunity offered at last to meet my predecessor, *the grass growing through his ribs* was tall enough to hide his *bones*. They were all there. The supernatural being had not been touched after he fell. *And the village was deserted, the huts gaped black, rotting*, all askew within the fallen enclosures ...

'I flew around like mad to get ready, and before forty-eight hours I was crossing the Channel to show myself to my employers, and sign the contract. In a very few hours I arrived in a city that always makes me think of a *whited sepulchre* ...

'*A narrow and deserted street in deep shadow*, high houses, innumerable windows with venetian blinds, *a dead silence, grass sprouting between the stones* ...' (italics mine)[15]

These two sequences, it will be noticed, are narrated on the same diegetic plane – both Europe and Africa belonging to the same fictional universe of this narrative. Although the narrative of Fresleven's murder could easily become a totally different story, both sequences in fact belong to the same narrative level; that is to say, they are not two distinct stories but parts of the same story, even though this future incident in Marlow's life in Africa will not be referred to again. It is therefore not at the level of *narrative functions* (kernels or catalysts) but at the level of *indexes* – mainly themes and actors – that the metaphorical interaction between these two sequences takes place.[16]

The complex articulation of these sequences rests on a series of syntactical, rhetorical, and narrative links:

(a) *Syntactic and semantic links*. The strong syntactic and semantic parallelisms in 'the grass growing through his ribs' and 'grass sprouting between the stones' trigger a conjunctive reading of both sequences. Two different and unrelated semantic fields, that of 'ribs' and that of 'stones,' necessarily establishing disjunctive relations, are paradoxically forced to relate conjunctively due to their textual proximity, but particularly, due to the identical syntactic structure in which they appear. The partial semantic identity ('grass growing

The narrative dimension of metaphor 49

through' / 'grass sprouting between,' with the recurring semes /vegetal/, /interspersed growth/) highlights this conjunctive-disjunctive relation. The common elements constituting a sort of semic-syntactic intersection *contaminate* those that are dissimilar, so that 'stones,' due to this particular and unique metaphoric interaction, adds the afferent seme /death/ to its meaning.

(b) *Rhetoric and phonetic links*. The death overtones in 'stones' are emphasized by two elements: phonetic and rhetoric. There is a strong phonetic parallelism that makes the 'stones' of Brussels rhyme with Fresleven's 'bones,' thereby stressing their identity at the phonetic level, and, by contamination, suggesting a semantic identity. On the other hand, the analogy that Marlow makes between Brussels and a 'whited sepulchre' *modulates* the stones-death association, and constitutes a rhetorical link between both spaces, sharing its whiteness with that of the 'bones' in Africa, its lapidary nature with the 'stones' of Brussels. Furthermore, the intertext generated by the Biblical allusion reinforces the paradox growth-death. Christ said the scribes and Pharisees were 'like unto whited sepulchres which indeed appear beautiful outward, but are within full of dead men's bones, and all uncleanness.'[17] Marlow's analogy sums up the paradox at the heart of the Belgian colonial administration in Africa: in all appearance its mission is that of enlightenment and civilization, but in reality it is that of ruthless exploitation and destruction. The paradox, however, is not only apparent in the intertext generated by the Biblical allusion but also in the separate descriptions of Fresleven's bones abandoned somewhere in Africa, and of the desolate stones in Brussels: in both there is the same paradoxical growth in the midst of death – growth connoted not as rebirth but as concealment of corruption and death. The paradox is therefore generated paranarratively. Furthermore, both sequences are inserted in similar contexts of darkness and desolation: 'The village was *deserted*, the huts gaped *black*' vis-à-vis 'a narrow and *deserted* street in *deep shadow*, ... a dead silence.'

(c) *Narrative links*. Although a clear process of metaphorization is at work here, establishing conjunctive and disjunctive relations, contaminating the dissimilar with the similar as each of the sequences is semantically modified by its interaction with the other, nowhere in either description is metaphorization given locally or at the level of the linguistic manifestation. Neither 'grass growing through his ribs' nor 'grass sprouting between the stones' – strongly indicial as they may be – evince an isotopic rupture at the level of the manifestation. That 'stones' should become metaphoric is due to its *virtual metaphoric articulation* with 'bones' in the African sequence. This is also the result of a specific *narrative mediation*: the temporal figure of prolepsis; that is, the narrative is interrupted, at a given point in the story, in order to narrate events that belong to the future. The articulation of these two sequences, unlike that of the Lezamian simile, is not actual: there are no explicit syntactic connections that may be pointed to as responsible for the articulation. Yet, despite the chronological distance that separates both sequences *in the story*, it is not retrospective reading, as in the two sequences analysed from *Ulysses*, that is responsible for their conjunction. In this case, their proximity *is* textual due to the breach in the narrative discourse in order to include that future event. Therefore, the articulation is not purely virtual either.

Although there are no actual syntactic connections between the two, *prolepsis* as a narrative mediation is responsible for the textual proximity, thereby preparing the ground for the metaphorical interaction of similarities and dissimilarities that results in a virtual paranarrative sequence. Conrad, it seems, deliberately resorts to the narrative figure of prolepsis to explode the *here* with the *elsewhere*, to see the future fatally contained in the present. Given their textual proximity, the subtle syntactic and semantic parallelisms that he draws between the two sequences may then be read vertically, thereby activating the process of metaphorization that modifies and reorganizes their meaning.

Thus, the mediation of certain narrative figures, such as prolepsis, may be just as important in the metaphoric articulation of narrative sequences as syntactic determinations or paradigmatic reactivations of a text in retrospective reading.

2.1.4 Different forms of narrative isotopy in metaphoric articulation

As may be seen, the whole process of *metaphoric articulation*, whether actual or virtual, is homologous to the process of metaphorization itself as evinced in verbal metaphor. At the level of the organization of the text, however, no simple homologues may be drawn between metaphor and narrative. In *verbal metaphorization*, the confrontation takes place between a fully actualized semantic field (though we must not forget that this 'actual' character is still observable only at the infralinguistic level), constituting the main isotopic context, and a more or less virtual field implied in the allotopic lexeme(s). There is a clear relationship of *dependence* between the two: the virtual isotopy implied in the allotopic lexemes depends on the main context for the semantic revaluation that these lexemes undergo.

In *narrative metaphorization* this semantic confrontation may be replicated, but only when the articulation of the two sequences is *actual*, that is, when there are explicit textual connections or a textual juxtaposition. In that case, metaphoric narration, in its form of the extended simile and threaded metaphor, constitutes a secondary narrative sequence, directly depending on the main one, interacting with it conjunctively and disjunctively to generate a virtual paranarrative. By contrast, in the *virtual* mode of metaphoric articulation, both sequences are totally *independent*. Furthermore, the temporal dimension is of vital importance in this mode: there is a perceptible time shift between the two that affects the metaphorical articulation in interesting ways. The first sequence, though self-sufficient, is nonetheless revalued by the second; and yet despite the revaluation, the first *temporally unfolds and maintains both levels of meaning*: the non-metaphoric and the metaphoric.

In this latter mode, metaphoric narration as the virtual articulation of two narrative sequences is homologous to that second mode of functioning of discursive metaphor discussed in chapter 2, and illustrated with Yeats's 'Coole Park and Ballylee.' The temporal dimension is responsible for triggering a metaphoric reactivation of a text initially perceived as isotopic, so that it may be read on a second isotopy without losing its first meaning. The virtual mode of metaphoric articulation is analogous to this discursive peculiarity of the process. Initially, a narrative sequence is perceived as isotopic; the non-metaphoric meaning, at that point, is complete and self-sufficient (unlike the 'literal' reading of metaphor at the level of the manifestation, which is always perceived as allotopic unless there is a semantic revaluation). Subsequently confronted with a second sequence, the first undergoes a semantic revaluation in terms of the second that *adds* the metaphoric dimension of meaning without cancelling the previous, non-metaphoric one.

Metaphoric articulation of narrative sequences depends on their *diegetic status*; that is to say, on the kinds of transformations that the fictional universe may undergo in the metaphorical interaction. The diegetic status of the narrative sequences is determined by their narrative level.[18] A given story may constitute the main narrative or a metadiegetic narrative; that is, a totally different story embedded in the main one. Such is the case of all the stories contained in *The Canterbury Tales*, or of *Wuthering Heights*, to give just a couple of examples. In those narrative texts, there is always a first, all-encompassing story that serves as a frame for the other(s). Both the framing and the embedded narratives project totally different fictional worlds, so that the passage from the main to the embedded narrative entails a shift in narrative level from the diegetic to the metadiegetic.

Now, a given sequence may project, even though only momentarily, a completely different diegetic universe, which could almost become metadiegetic. This is especially true of narrated dreams, or of narratives that engage in the antecedents of secondary characters, so that they maintain a very tenuous connection to the main narrative line, to mention a few. These are secondary narratives, potentially metadiegetic, interacting metaphorically with the main one. (Cf pp 59–67 below, the analysis of Cortázar's 'La noche boca arriba,' in which the narrated dream is as important as the main narrative.) In these cases the metaphorical articulation of narrative sequences entails a change of narrative level as well. This, however, is not always the case. For a sequence may be so prolonged that it draws spatio-temporal coordinates with an abstract or virtual existence; nonetheless, they remain potentially narrative only, 'romans abstraits,' as Marcel Muller has called this narrative phenomenon in Proust.[19] They outline a diegetic universe of their own, without necessarily bringing about a shift in narrative level. Such a virtual diegetic universe may be called metaphorical and is opposed to the main, denotative one. This is the status of metaphoric narration in its form of sustained simile and threaded metaphor – metaphoric narration proposing a virtual *metaphoric diegesis* (cf the 'baignoire' sequence in Proust).

When the metaphoric articulation takes place between two sequences projecting different diegetic universes – whether on the same or on a different narrative level – there is a confrontation between two different diegetic universes, a confrontation that in itself may be homologous to that of two isotopies in verbal metaphor. Similarities between elements are abstracted in order to construct a network of conjunctive relations. Thus, the dynamic interaction among elements relating disjunctively is already *given* in the confrontation of two different diegetic universes, while the conjunctive relations are an *abstract construction*.

Alternatively, two sequences made to interact metaphorically by an act of retrospective reading may belong to the same diegetic universe; the metaphorical articulation is then triggered by similar diegetic elements that seem to be merely repeated (cf the image of the telephone in *Ulysses*). In that case the conjunctive relations are already *given* in the diegetic replication of elements; conversely, it is the disjunctive relations that are *constructed*. Thus, the conjunctive rela-

The narrative dimension of metaphor

tions are *given* at the diegetic level, but *constructed* at the level of themes. The differences, working in a similar manner to that of the allotopic lexemes in verbal metaphor, are to be found in the characters and themes, not in the diegetic universes presented. In that case, it is not the whole diegetic universe that functions allotopically, as in the actual mode of articulation (cf the Lezamian simile), but the thematic and actorial shifts in sequences with a predominantly similar or even redundant diegetic context. In Proust's *Recherche*, for example, the Vinteuil sonata sequence (I, 345ff) undergoes a reorganization in its narrative and symbolic meanings due to a paradigmatic interaction with the Vinteuil septet sequence (III, 373ff). The similarities in the external stimuli that trigger the meditation on music and in the many paths that both Swann and Marcel pursue during the course of their contemplative act – that is to say, those elements, relating conjunctively – bring these two sequences together by the mediation of retrospective reading. But if it is the *given* similarities in the narrative functions – even to the extreme of event replication – that are responsible for the initial confluence, it is the *constructed differences* in actors and themes that generate the interaction resulting in a metaphoric reading of these two sequences as different, and therefore narratively significant, stages in spiritual evolution.

From what has been said, it is evident that the concept of isotopy must be *relativized* when transposed to the narrative domain. The homology is not to be found in a one-to-one correspondence between an isotopic text and a diegetic universe; the constructed homologue of isotopy may shift, depending on the diegetic status of the two sequences. Therefore, we might isolate at least five forms of what may be called narrative isotopy; metaphoric narration would effect a rupture in the narrative isotopy of a given sequence by forcing a metaphorical reading of that sequence with another, whether textually contiguous or not:

(a) *Diegetic isotopy*. A narrative sequence may constitute a rupture by projecting a whole other diegetic universe. Thus we may say that the Lezamian simile constitutes a major breach in the diegetic isotopy of the main narrative.

(b) *Temporal isotopy*. Temporal coherence is based on chronology. Any rupture in chronology is potentially metaphoric. It must be remembered, however, that a breach in the temporal isotopy of the text, by itself, is not enough to trigger metaphorization; simultaneous conjunctive and disjunctive relations must be established for that breach to become metaphorically significant (cf above, the proleptic sequence in Conrad's *Heart of Darkness*). There are several kinds of temporal ruptures: (i) temporal breaks in the continuity of the story, or anachronies, which may be of two kinds: analepsis and prolepsis; that is, narratives dealing with segments of the story occurring before the narrative in process (analepsis or flashback) or later in story time (prolepsis); (ii) embedded narratives (on a metadiegetic level) resulting from prolonged anachronies, (iii) a virtual temporality suggested by metaphoric narration itself (extended simile and threaded metaphor). In chapter 5, I discuss at length the effect of metaphoric narration on the temporal structures of narrative.

(c) *Spatial isotopy.* Any rupture in the representation of a spatial reality is also potentially metaphorical. There are three kinds of spatial ruptures: (i) anachronies also entail a break in spatial coherence; another space is confronted to the one in the main context (cf Proust's experiences of involuntary memory); (ii) arbitrary, unexpected spatial juxtapositions; (iii) a virtual space is conjured when gnomic discourse resorts to similes or metaphors drawing spatial coordinates that are very concrete; in this case, there is a partial break that involves a break in narrative level (extradiegetic). Unlike the breach in the diegetic isotopy of a text, a spatial rupture may occur within the same diegetic universe. This is the case in arbitrary spatial juxtapositions; at the level of narrative discourse, different places may be brought into a contiguity that is non-existent in the diegetic universe (cf Robbe-Grillet's *Dans le labyrinthe*).

(d) *Functional isotopy.*[20] A sequence establishing a specific pattern of interrelations between a given number of narrative functions may be replicated, thereby becoming the main context against which differences in actors and/or themes are played off. Virtual paranarratives are thus generated. Or else, the same pattern of narrative functions may be replicated in the second sequence, with a given number of functions placed in a disjunctive position – the disjunctive narrative functions will then trigger metaphorization. (Cf Cortázar's 'La noche boca arriba.')

(e) *Thematic isotopy.* As Barthes has observed, semes sharing similar semantic fields may be organized in thematic fields. The recurrence of such predominantly connotative units of meaning not only outlines a thematic field but may constitute a veritable thematic isotopy, subject to ruptures of potential metaphoric significance.[21]

An important observation to make is that in both the actual and the virtual modes of metaphorical articulation there is *redundancy*:[22] the second sequence is almost a repetition of the first; it is only the degree

The narrative dimension of metaphor 55

of abstraction that varies. When the two sequences have the same diegetic status – that is, when they belong to the same diegetic universe – there is a closer resemblance between the specific fictional events; when the status is different, although difference is still emphasized, there is, nonetheless, replication in the abstract pattern, in the network of interrelations among the otherwise different diegetic elements. But in both cases a phenomenon that may be validly called *metaphorization* occurs: a revaluation of one sequence, determined by the context of the other, takes place, affects the narrative significance of both and is triggered not by differences and similarities in isolation, but by the simultaneous interplay of both. The conjunctive relations act as connectors of isotopies in the metaphorical articulation.

2.2 *Metaphoric construction of configuration of narrative sequences*

At the level of the organization of a narrative text, metaphoric narration may be generated by the virtual or actual articulation of two narrative sequences. Metaphoric narration may also be brought about by the way in which the narrative elements of a given sequence are arranged into a particular form or shape, that is to say, by the particular *configuration* of a narrative sequence.

2.2.1 Lexicalized metaphor as an implicit narrative program

A narrative sequence may be so constructed that it activates a dead metaphor. The phenomenon may be described as both the *literalization* and the *narrativization* of a lexicalized metaphor. The following sequence from García Márquez's *Cien años de soledad* is a case in point:

> Tan pronto como José Arcadio cerró la puerta del dormitorio, el estampido de un pistoletazo retumbó en la casa. Un hilo de sangre salió por debajo de la puerta, atravesó la sala, salió a la calle, siguió en un curso directo por los andenes disparejos, descendió escalinatas y subió pretiles, pasó de largo por la Calle de los Turcos, dobló una esquina a la derecha y otra a la izquierda, volteó en ángulo recto frente a la casa de los Buendía, pasó por debajo de la puerta cerrada, atravesó la sala de visitas pegado a las paredes para no manchar los tapices, siguió por la otra sala, eludió en una curva amplia la mesa del comedor, avanzó por el corredor de las begonias y pasó sin ser visto por debajo de la silla de Amaranta que daba una lección de aritmética a Aureliano José, y se metió por el granero y apareció en la cocina donde Ursula se disponía a partir treinta y seis huevos para el pan.

56   Metaphoric narration

> – ¡Ave María Purísima! – gritó Ursula.
> Siguió el hilo de sangre en sentido contrario ...²³

At the level of the manifestation in language, it will be noticed, no isotopic rupture is evinced in this narrative. The lexical choices favour items with a strong referential function: doors, streets, street corners, chairs, walls, etc; the spatial relations are carefully traced and described by means of logic-linguistic concepts that match similar spatial descriptive models that have been constructed in the extratextual reality: the blood turns *right, around* the corner, then *left*; it turns in a *straight angle* in front of the house; it traces *curves*, goes *under* chairs, and so on. Thus the progress of the blood is factually described, tracing its spatial trajectory throughout the city in minute detail, with no isotopic rupture, no superimposition of other space-time isotopies. But in fact, the whole narrative sequence is a 'realistic' narrativization of a very well-known lexicalized metaphor in Spanish: 'el llamado de la sangre' ('the call of the blood') – indeed, José Arcadio's blood *calls* his mother to witness his death. Yet, despite the realistic treatment, the effect of the sequence is highly fantastic. This is because 'le fantastique de l'écriture,' as Ricardou would call this textual phenomenon,²⁴ is the direct result of both the literalization and the narrativization of this lexicalized metaphor. Thus, at the level of the organization of the text, the implicit dead metaphor proposes a *virtual narrative program*. It is the manifest narrativization of that program, however, that makes the reader aware of the implicit metaphor underlying the construction of the narrative sequence; in the same operation, a dead metaphor has been reanimated.

2.2.2 The process of metaphorization as the constructive principle in certain narrative sequences

A second mode of metaphoric construction is the *narrativization* of the *process of metaphorization* itself. Metaphor is used as a principle of organization and as an implicit narrative program. This is a common practice in Proust's *Recherche*: the episode of the Petite Madeleine, for instance, narrativizes the confrontation between two semantic fields in terms of two different experienced times and spaces linked by a common sensation, a perfect narrative homologue of the semic intersection.²⁵

Another instance of this phenomenon is observable in Lezama's *Paradiso*.²⁶ In chapter 7, for example, a game that Rialta and her

The narrative dimension of metaphor   57

children are playing is described in terms that are highly reminiscent of those that Lezama has used elsewhere in his essays to define, poetically, the process of metaphorization: what he calls the dialectics of the fixed, resistant matter, and the ascent/descent dynamics – 'the impossible duality.' That impossible duality, the interaction between resistant matter and an ascending or descending movement, 'miraculously' results in an image. Likewise, the ascent/descent dynamics may be expressed in the distance that separates one object from another (the 'fixed, resistant matter'), distance itself relating creatively to the objects that it both separates and conjoins, thus generating an image. 'Images as interpositions born from the distance between objects. The distance between persons and things creates another dimension, or a sort of entity of non-being, the image, that completes the vision or unity of those interpositions. For it is undeniable that between the jug and the ivory bough there is a network of images, communicated by the poet when he conceives them within a *coordinate of irradiations*'.[27]

This poetic description of the process of metaphorization perfectly agrees with the semantic-semiotic model presented here: the confrontation of two different semantic fields ('persons' and 'things') establishing conjunctive and disjunctive relations in the space outlined by that in-between construction, the semic intersection (cf the 'distance between objects'), which achieves unity by extending the process of identification to both domains, thereby generating an image, that is, a scheme or mental construct akin to sensory perception, particularly of the visual kind, a meaningful image for which the suppressed semes are responsible (cf chapter 1, 3).

Now, Lezama's narrative presentation of the process is very similar to the arguments expounded in his essays.

> Rialta no quería romper el círculo formado por sus hijos entregados absortos al juego de yaquis. Se sentó en el suelo con ellos, penetrando en el silencio absorbido por el subir y descender de la pelota. El cuadrado formado por Rialta y sus tres hijos, se iba trocando en un círculo. Hicieron los infantes un pequeño movimiento para darle entrada a la madre, afanosa de llegar a esa isla, apoyada en un círculo cuyos bordes oscilaban, y en una vertical trazada por los puntos móviles de la pelota, que se lanzaba hacia un pequeño cielo imaginario, y después se hundía momentáneamente en las losas, que parecían líquidas láminas, pues la fijeza de las miradas sobre la suma de su cuadrado las iba trocando en un oleaje *ad infinitum*.
>
> Violante había llegado al número siete ... Rialta había comenzado a

58 Metaphoric narration

> lanzar la pelota, su absorto anterior la ayudaba a la coincidencia entre la ascensión de la pelota y el semicírculo de la mano para recoger los yaquis. La mirada de los cuatro absortos coincidía en el centro del círculo. La concentración de la voluntad total en las losas y en el ritmo de la pelota, fue aislando las losas, dándoles como líquidos reflejos, como si se contrayesen para apresar una imagen. Un rápido animismo iba transmutando las losetas, como si aquel mundo inorgánico se fuese transfundiendo en el cosmos receptivo de la imagen ...
>
> ... El contorno del círculo se iba endureciendo, hasta parecer de un metal que se tornaba incandescente. De pronto, en una fulguración, como si una nube se rompiese para dar paso a una nueva visión, apareció en las losas apresadas por el círculo la guerrera completa del Coronel, de un amarillo como oscurecido, aunque iba ascendiendo en su nitidez, los botones aun de los cuatro bolsillos, más brillantes que su cobrizo habitual ...[28]

The circle formed by the four people and the jacks on the hard floor, interacting with the rhythmic rising and falling of the ball, irradiates fragmentary images until the unified vision of the dead Colonel's tunic is ecstatically perceived. The instantaneous character of this hallucination is similar to the vague, elusive nature of the associated image in metaphor, the unique product of a unique interaction. Here, the image results from the *spatial position* of the mother and children, and the circular figure they draw, in relation to the physical space of the tiled floor, as a background, and the jacks. The potential morphological similarity between the jacks and the buttons on the Colonel's tunic elicits a peculiar narrative process that is highly reminiscent of metaphorization. This narrative *and* metaphoric articulation of actors, spaces, and objects thus results in a symbolic image of unity; of a family capable of collectively hallucinating the missing father to achieve this impossible unification. But the ingredients used and the interrelations described closely parallel the various phases of the process of metaphorization as we have described it: (a) *a confrontation between two distinct semantic fields* narratively figured by the mother and children set against the floor and the jacks, in an attempt of the living to call the dead back; at a more abstract level, there is a clear opposition between the animate and the inanimate. (b) The confrontation sparks a simultaneous interplay between *disjunctive relations* (the human group vs. the objects) and *conjunctive relations* (the semic/narrative intersection constructed by the similarities between the jacks and floor, on the one hand, and the Colonel's tunic and buttons, on the other; the image

The narrative dimension of metaphor 59

of the Colonel as the symbolic projection of his family's intense desire for union). (c) The result is also similar to that process: a *rationally satisfactory meaning* and an *associated image* that defies all rational explanation.

2.2.3 The metaphoric configuration of a narrative sequence on the pattern of another

Thus far, we have examined the role of metaphor in the organization of the text in terms of a *virtual narrative program* proposed either by a lexicalized metaphor or by the process of metaphorization itself. The third mode of metaphoric construction of narrative sequences varies slightly from the other two: it is no longer an underlying narrative program that organizes the construction of a narrative sequence, but the *configuration* of a narrative sequence; that is, *the particular arrangement of its parts*, which may then serve as the model, a sort of 'blueprint' to be used in the construction of another narrative sequence. The second sequence will replicate the pattern of the first, with significant differences that are responsible for triggering a metaphoric reading of both sequences in conjunction, despite their textual discontinuity.

Because of the similarities of such a derivative structure, and the dissimilarities that make up the second sequence as distinct from the first and not merely its verbatim duplication, both sequences will also tend to be articulated metaphorically (in the manner described in this chapter, 2.1). Cortázar's short story 'La noche boca arriba,' for example, is entirely constructed on this double principle of metaphoric articulation and configuration of narrative sequences.

In Cortázar's story, a man riding on his motorcycle has a serious accident on the road and is taken to hospital, where he is subjected to X-rays, treatment, and an operation (though this is only an inference the reader makes, since the word *operation* is never used). As evening falls, feverish and parched with thirst, he falls into a dream. At this point the dream sequence runs parallel with the hospital sequence, alternating with it at an increasingly faster pace until the distance between both realities is closed, *diegetically* as well as *textually*, especially in the syntactic fusion that occurs towards the end of the story. The dream sequence is built entirely on the basis of the first sequence with a few sememes and a great number of narrative elements working just like connectors of isotopies in threaded metaphor, except that these lexical and narrative elements do not appear as allotopic in their local contexts. Again, the temporal dimension is responsible for the shift apparent in both meanings: the metaphoric and the non-metaphoric. All these elements acting like 'joints' in the articulation are made to function metaphorically in a retrospective manner, by the configuration of the second sequence.[29]

In his dream, the motorcyclist becomes a Motec, a member of a pre-Hispanic tribe at war against the Aztecs. As he runs along the road, he is caught by the enemy, taken to the pyramid, where he is bound while his turn comes to be sacrificed by the high priest. The Motec is finally sacrificed, exactly at the moment in which the perspective on reality is drastically reversed and the dreamer becomes the dreamed.

Two key lexemes are central in the fusion of these two realities: 'calzada' ('main road') and the pair 'motociclista-moteca.' 'Calzada,' as against 'carretera,' 'camino,' 'calle,' or 'avenida,' is a strongly marked lexeme; it specifically denotes the roads in ancient Rome or those that used to link the Great Tenochtitlan with other tributary kingdoms. In modern México, only those ancient roads still bear the name of 'calzada' (Calzada de Tlalpan, Calzada México-Tacuba), while the rest are ruled by the prevailing system of denomination (carretera, avenida, calle, etc.). So that, already from the very beginning of the story, at its most 'realistic' stage, and by the very choice of the word *calzada*, Cortázar subtly situates his contemporary man in the temporal and cultural zone of the Motec. This gravitation towards pre-Hispanic reality is emphasized by the partial phonetic identity ('mot') between 'motociclista' and 'moteca.' The phonetic identity, however, is very subtle, for the word *motociclista* as such is never used: the protagonist of the story is only referred to as 'the man' or 'he,' but since his one and only activity before he is taken to hospital is riding a motorcycle, his being a 'motociclista' is obvious, even though the name itself remains implicit.

At the level of kernels, and making abstraction of catalysts, indexes, and informants, there is a striking *functional* identity in the structure of both sequences:[30] 'to travel in the open along a road,' 'to deviate, fatally, to the left,' 'to be trapped/have an accident,' 'to lose consciousness,' 'to be lifted, face up, by others,' 'to be taken indoors,' 'to be manipulated by others,' 'to be tied down, face up,' 'to be operated on/sacrificed.'

Other functional narrative elements interact both conjunctively and disjunctively, and this is what brings about metaphorization. There is *light* in both sequences, for example, but set in radically opposed contexts: for the motorcyclist it is morning and the sunlight is refracted by the buildings; for the Motec it is night and there is a reddish glow in

The narrative dimension of metaphor 61

the sky. For the motorcyclist, light is indexed positively – the green light that gives him right of way, and the bluish light in hospital that soothes him from the nightmare; for the Motec light is indexed negatively – the reddish light in the sky as the Aztecs' torches are ominously reflected in the horizon, as a conflagration ('Como si el cielo se incendiara en el horizonte, vió antorchas moviéndose entre las ramas, muy cerca'); this, he knows, can only mean war. At the end of the story, both green and red lights and fire converge into what becomes the Motec's dream – 'que el sueño maravilloso había sido el otro, absurdo como todos los sueños; un sueño en el que había andado por extrañas avenidas de una ciudad asombrosa, con luces verdes y rojas que ardían sin llama ni humo.'[31] At this point, incidentally, the temporal gravitation has been reversed: the road is no longer referred to as 'calzada' but as 'avenida'; it is the Motec now that gravitates towards the temporal and cultural zone of twentieth-century man.

Many other elements relate conjunctively and disjunctively in the manner described for the light motifs. Both men move along the road, but for the motorcyclist it is bordered with trees and gardens, for the Motec with marshlands. Both men are manipulated by others, but the motorcyclist is treated gently, signs of sympathy are multiplied and constantly stressed; the Motec, by contrast, is manipulated brutally as a preparation for sacrifice; in both men, the focal point, acting as a connector of narrative isotopies, is the right arm in pain.

In the midst of this constant interplay of similarities and dissimilarities, there are central thematic elements that establish relations of radical opposition, which give each of the two sequences its distinct value, thus constructing two very different diegetic universes. The *accidental*, purely contingent nature of the experience is constantly stressed in the first, while its *fatal determination* is emphasized in the second. This gives way to another opposition: *absent-mindedness vs. alertness*. The motorcyclist, relaxed and immersed in the pleasure of the ride, is unaware of what is coming to him, whereas the Motec is fully alert and painfully aware of his destiny. Another insistent opposition is that between *well-being* and *malaise*. In the waking sequence, in spite of the seriousness of the accident, most adjectives and adverbs qualify the events positively, all functioning as indexes of well-being: a *soft* stretcher, a *golden* broth, an arm *comfortably* suspended from a pulley, and so on. The experience of pain is notably attenuated and often negated, the hospital smell is significantly *not* qualified. In the dream sequence, by contrast, everything is qualified negatively, especially smells, indexed as nauseating. All these oppositions, given in the

62   Metaphoric narration

linear unfolding of the narrative, set these two sequences at radically opposite poles; but because of their functionally constructed *identical configuration*, they are forced to interact and articulate metaphorically.

If the waking sequence constitutes the blueprint for the construction of the dream sequence, there are, nonetheless, a number of displacements, points of coincidence and of non-coincidence, which become metaphorically significant too. In many of the functional elements that relate in simultaneous conjunction and disjunction, there are interesting time shifts and coincidences at both temporal levels: diegetic and discourse times. For both the motorcyclist and the Motec, for example, an external agent *lashes* their bodies: fresh wind makes the motorcyclist's trouser legs flutter; branches strike the Motec's trunk and legs. It is significant that Cortázar uses similar verbs in both descriptions: 'un viento fresco le *chicoteaba* los pantalones' (157) (literally: 'a fresh wind *lashed* his trousers'); 'ya no podía dar un paso sin que las ramas de los arbustos le *azotaran* el torso y las piernas' (161) (literally: 'he could no longer walk without having branches from shrubs *whip* his trunk and legs'). Again, the motorcyclist experiences this particular contact with the external world as pleasurable, the Motec as an ominous sign.

Despite their functional identity, there is a significant shift in the diegetic time of these events: the wind lashes the motorcyclist before the accident, before the fatal deviation to the left, while the branches whip the Motec after he has deviated to the left and gone astray in the marshes: what is purely contingent for the one becomes determinant for the other. For the Motec, this becomes a sign that he has stepped into the sacred time of the Aztecs and is now trapped. For the motorcyclist, *as dreamer*, this time shift confers significance to an event previously experienced as non-significant, thereby giving the lie to his vision of the world as pure contingency: what is read as an *accident* on the waking plane is rewritten as *fate* on the oneiric plane. For the Motec, *as dreamer*, on the other hand, the oneiric dimension liberates him from fate; the time shift and the substitution of a fresh breeze for branches constitute a metonymic displacement that expresses a compensatory oneiric experience of pleasure.[32]

The points of coincidence in the two diegetic times – that is, the motorcyclist's and the Motec's story times – are equally significant. It is precisely these points of coincidence that reveal the dream as a *configuration* based on the scheme of the waking sequence. In terms of discourse time, however, the two sequences are notably displaced, the second also starting on the road, in the open, but well after the first has moved indoors to the hospital, thus transforming the diegetic opposi-

The narrative dimension of metaphor 63

tion day/night into a *metonymic* displacement (the dream, though re-enacting the 'accident' in similar terms, borrows it night environment from the point of its narrative inception in the waking sequence, at night, in the hospital). But as the dream unfolds, it moves to close the distance between the two fictional worlds. There is a crucial point of coincidence, *loss of consciousness,* in which all times begin to converge: the metadiegetic time of the dream,[33] the diegetic time of waking reality and discourse time (we might also include 'mythic' time as the result of this multiple convergence). Loss of consciousness occurs for both men at exactly the same diegetic point in each sequence – as the motorcyclist strikes his head against the pavement; as the Motec is caught by the Aztecs. But it is precisely at this point that discourse time operates the convergence, for on the plane of *narration*, the Motec's loss of consciousness occurs precisely at a point when the narrator shifts to the waking man puzzling over his own loss of consciousness earlier that day, the textual gap perfectly coinciding with the narrated gap of consciousness and with the anamnesic efforts of the motorcyclist to recover that gap in time. When the narrator resumes the story of the Motec, it is at the moment when he is coming to and finds himself bound onto a cold slab. From this point the two diegetic times begin to coincide and the narration begins to gravitate towards the Motec's world as the prevailing reality. From this point, too, the anaphoric ambiguity of the pronouns is emphasized and maintained, thus bringing about the complete fusion of the two men. Syntax also carries out this fusion by means of constant double referents or antecedents: 'Como dormía de espaldas, no lo sorprendió la posición en que volvía a reconocerse' (164).[34] The reference here points back to the motorcyclist in the hospital, who was the subject of 'sleeping on his back' in the previous paragraph, but it also points forwards to the Motec, who is just coming to from his own loss of consciousness and 'recognizes himself again,' also on his back, in a dungeon of the Aztec's sacrificial temple.

Although rhetorical figures as such have a notably low incidence in this story, there is a series of lexical items that connect both fictional worlds and that function just as connectors of isotopies do in threaded metaphor. This is the status of 'calzada,' as we have seen, and of the partial phonetic identity between 'motociclista' and 'moteca' (mot). The very few similes that appear in the story have precisely this connective function. For instance, the man in hospital is 'thirsty as if he had run for miles,' a simile that obliquely connects the motorcyclist with the running Motec. A more interesting connector is 'cielo raso' ('ceiling'). Its status either as lexicalized metaphor or catachresis is very difficult to determine, for 'cielo raso' is the only precise term in Spanish to refer to the ceiling, though there is the alternative 'techo' (but primarily 'techo' means 'roof'), while there are other importations such as 'plafón' from the French 'plafond' to fill up the absence of a specific term. Now, 'cielo raso' literally means 'clear sky,' but this literal meaning, because of the catachretic nature of the term, is never felt in normal usage. Owing to the metaphoric configuration of the dream sequence in terms of the waking sequence, this lexicalized metaphor is strikingly reanimated and works to connect both worlds metaphorically: as the Motec is carried, face up, through a narrow passage to the top of the pyramid, he dreads the moment when he will reach the open sky, for it will open into death. The focus of his anguished perception is the low, oppressive ceiling, significantly referred to as 'techo.' Its correlate in the waking sequence, again indexed positively, is the protective 'cielo raso' of the hospital room. This 'cielo raso' metaphorically fuses, in a sort of semantic triangle, the hospital ceiling, the low ceiling made of live rock and the open sky to which it will inexorably give access. It is indeed a 'cielo raso,' a 'clear sky,' the Motec is coming to in the end – a return to the open that fatally signals the end of his life, just as it signals, simultaneously, a radical revaluation of the story: what has so far been read as a dream becomes waking reality and vice versa.

At this point of reversal the extraordinary dynamism of the process of metaphorization is remarkably heightened. It is precisely the reversal of the planes of reality that activates in the reader's consciousness the perception of metaphor as the structuring principle of this story. As the dreamer becomes the dreamed, an instantaneous retrospective reading takes place, reorganizing the significance of *all* the events in the motorcyclist sequence. It is then, and only then, that 'calzada' gains metaphoric significance and becomes a connector of narrative isotopies; it is only then that the implicit 'motociclista' resounds on the explicit, textual 'moteca,' and that the reanimation of 'cielo raso' as metaphor occurs. In this process of retrospective reading, the reader will attempt to index as many narrative units of the so far supposed 'waking' sequence onto the 'dream' sequence to produce virtual narrative sequences that function paranarratively. A simultaneous double reading will lead to the interpretation of the dream in terms of the motorcyclist's world and vice versa. The text has so far encouraged the first; when the narrative permutation occurs, the second reading is stimulated alongside the revaluation of the first as

The narrative dimension of metaphor

dream and no longer as waking reality. Such a stereoscopic reading, triggered by metaphor, generates paranarrative sequences that are no longer realistic, but rather virtual worlds produced by a text that has been made to function metaphorically: what Ricardou would call 'le fantastique de l'écriture.' In turn, the metaphoric configuration of the Motec sequence results in a text the verbal surface of which will also become metaphoric at the level of the manifestation in language: '... ahora sabía que no iba a despertarse, que estaba despierto, que el sueño maravilloso había sido el otro, absurdo como todos los sueños; un sueño en el que había andado por extrañas avenidas de una ciudad asombrosa, con luces verdes y rojas *que ardían sin llama ni humo, con un enorme insecto de metal que zumbaba bajo sus piernas* ...' (166) (italics mine).[35]

The new doubly metaphoric reading of the story that the Motec himself initiates is an invitation to the reader to *rewrite* the rest from the Motec's initial and partial reading of his dream.

It may be noticed at this point that this description of the reactivation of the text corresponds point by point to the mechanism of threaded metaphor. Metaphor has a potential semantic dynamism that is fully accomplished at the discursive level; Philippe Dubois, as has already been noted, conceives this semantic dynamism in terms of reversibility and of a semantic dissemination due to the work of metaphor as a connector of isotopies. If a text, coherent on one isotopy, is suddenly connected to a second isotopy, due to the insertion of an allotopic term or utterance (cf Yeats's 'Coole Park and Ballylee'), an instant reorganization of the text takes place in which the reader tends to inscribe on the second isotopy as many units from the first as possible. In this reactivation of the text, due to the semantic dissemination produced by those polysemic units outlining a second isotopy, there is also a potential reversibility that some texts may execute: the second isotopy may be metaphorically projected on the first, just as the first may be read metaphorically on the second. This apparently contradicts Greimas's definition of 'connector of isotopies,' which I have already quoted: 'the metaphoric connector,' he says, 'assures the passage from an abstract (or thematic) isotopy to a figurative isotopy. The relation that brings them together is always oriented (that which is said on the second isotopy is interpretable on the first but not conversely).'[36] Nevertheless, the non-reversible character of these relations depends, in my opinion, on an opposition in the level of generality of the two isotopies that relate metaphorically. But if both isotopies are on the same *figurative* level – or, in terms of my narrative homologue, if both isotopies are diegetic, even though each one may pose a different diegetic universe – the potential for reversibility exists, as Dubois has theoretically shown it with the following line from Desnos:[37] 'une neige de seins,' which could be read both on the 'Cosmos' or on the 'Anthropos' isotopies; that is, if the snow, particularized as flakes, constitutes the subject of the utterance (the 'Cosmos' isotopy), it could be metaphorized as a woman's breasts. In that case the semic intersection would be constructed from the morphological similarity (i.e. /roundness/ and perhaps the afferent seme /softness/?) in snowflakes and breasts. Conversely, if the subject is breasts (the 'Anthropos' isotopy), it might be metaphorically qualified as snow; in which case the semic intersection would be constructed by isolating common semes such as the inherent /whiteness/ and/or the afferent /purity/ or /softness/; or /coldness/, which would be an inherent seme in snow and an afferent seme in breasts.

Cortázar's story fully *actualizes* the theoretical potential reversibility inherent in metaphorization. Since the configuration of the second sequence on the basis of the first entails a series of narrative units mirrored in their narrative functions and in their distribution, these units effectively act as connectors between the two narrative worlds, as links in the metaphorical articulation of the two sequences (articulation being usually the necessary consequence of the metaphoric configuration of one sequence on the pattern of another). In 'La noche boca arriba,' the *narrative connections* are multiplied and made to operate at various levels: they link *temporal* isotopies (contemporary and pre-Hispanic, on the one hand; on the other hand, the 'night' motif links the two diegetic times: the motorcyclist's accident happens early in the morning, the Motec's early in the evening; both are operated on/sacrificed at night); they also link different *spatial* isotopies ('calzada' and 'cielo raso' play this role of connectors of spatial isotopies), different *functional* isotopies ('the fatal deviation to the left,' 'being carried face up,' among others), or two *thematic* isotopies (the accident on the road interpreted as either fate or contingency; the abundance of indexes connoting a protective or a hostile world, etc.). All of these connections, though establishing conjunctive relations, are, at the same time, based on a radical disjunctive relation between the two diegetic isotopies.

In the metaphorical articulation of the two sequences, some of these narrative units evince their connective role in the course of a first reading; others are activated only by a retrospective reading. Owing to their connective role, these narrative units gain a dimension of

The narrative dimension of metaphor 67

meaning that turns them into polysemic rhetorical units, even though the particular lexemes that make them up do not relate rhetorically to the local context of each sequence in isolation. Since both sequences, on the other hand, trace distinct spatial and temporal isotopies – though simultaneously relating conjunctively due to the many shared elements – and constitute different diegetic universes, their similar level of figuration allows them to interact metaphorically in a *reversible* manner: the Motec's world as a metaphor of the motorcyclist's and vice versa.

Thus, the configuration of a narrative sequence on the basis of another also activates essential aspects of the process of metaphorization, particularly at the discursive level: (a) a bi-isotopic (or pluri-isotopic) text instituted by a series of units functioning as connectors of isotopies, thereby *articulating* both, and thereby activating their own polysemic and rhetorical potential; (b) an expansion of meaning due to the mutual contamination of two interacting fields; (c) a double reference, in which denotative reality is attenuated to give way to another reality paranarratively constituted; (d) a potential reversibility that poses either isotopy as the primary one on which the other may be read metaphorically; and, finally, (e) the discursive time shift that allows both 'readings' of a text to coexist without cancelling each other out – the introduction of the second isotopy at a given point of the text immediately triggering a retrospective reading in order to give meaning to the previous text also on the second isotopy.

4 Metaphor and metaphoric narration: an illustration

As an illustration of the process of metaphorization, let us examine a text on various levels of functioning. Given the phrase 'chasseur arborescent' ('arborescent hunter'), and in the absence of any immediate context, we still perceive the phrase as allotopic, due to the kind of semantic relation that the two lexemes establish. Since the relation is not paratactic but hypotactic, 'arborescent' is classematically incompatible with 'chasseur'; furthermore, since 'arborescent' is placed in a syntactic position of determination in relation to 'chasseur,' it is also syntactically incompatible, thus breaking the two rules that Group μ has proposed as essential for the establishment of an isotopic text. The very word *arborescent* is metaphorical in its semantic constitution: one of its specific semes draws a relation of analogy with 'tree': ' "*tree-like*" in growth, in general appearance or in the arrangement of parts' (*Oxford English Dictionary*). In the absence of any immediate linguistic co-text,[1] the reader or listener is forced to resort to pre-textual contexts, usually of a culturally coded nature. 'Readings' of this phrase are extraordinarily numerous, because there is no co-text to orient the process of decodification and thereby to limit the number of possible interpretations. Here are a number of empirically gathered readings or interpretations of this unusual collocation. I shall try to trace, analytically, the intuitive paths that may have led to them:

Metaphor and metaphoric narration

(a) 'a man with many branches growing out of his body'
(b) 'a man with arms like branches'
(c) 'a man disguised as a branch'
(d) 'a man with a deer head'
(e) 'Man realized in all his potential'

In (a), 'a man with many branches growing out of his body,' the process seems to have taken the path of amalgamation of 'parts,' referentially decomposed and recomposed. This is the *literalization* of the figure, which opens into that 'fantastique de l'écriture' for which the irrationally evoked image is always responsible.

Interpretation (b), 'a man with arms like branches,' seems to follow the same process of referential decomposition, except that here there is a slight attempt at compatibility, which might have been influenced by conceptual decomposition, too: bringing into focus arms and branches as /lateral extensions of a main body/, the proliferation of branches in (a) is here reduced to only two for the sake of compatibility with two arms.

In interpretation (c), 'a man disguised as a branch,' a decomposition in the referential mode is still presupposed, but it seems to be balanced by a strong conceptual decomposition as well. The semic intersection in (c) is built from 'parts' referentially decomposed, /branch/, and with semes conceptually decomposed, /concealment/ and, implicitly, /immobility/.

Interpretation (d), 'a man with a deer head' is an interesting phenomenon that points, even more explicitly than the others, to the highly culturally coded context to which the reader must resort. In what may be called the 'hunting frame,'[2] there are usually, among other components, trees, guns, traps, particular animals, etc. (This may also be called the lexical field of hunting.) In the frame of hunting (which could be European or native American) to which this interpretation obviously refers, the deer is one of the possible animals metonymically included. In this frame, *branches* from trees and deer *antlers* have been metaphorically identified before, while there are other cultural frames, pictorial and ritual, that have habituated us to this identification.[3] Thus, proceeding along the mode of referential decomposition, interpretation (d) bases its process of decoding upon another metaphor, already constituted, which is culturally coded in turn, and reads 'chasseur arborescent' as a metaphor of a metaphor: 'a man with a deer head.'

In the four interpretations so far examined, only (c) and (d) have

70 Metaphoric narration

included other semes in 'chasseur' besides the generic /human/ and /vegetal/, but because of the referential character of the constructed intersection, the evoked image is still very strong. It is interesting to notice that it is usually the *referential* component in the process of revaluation that accounts for the evoked image in its varying degrees of irrationality. By contrast, interpretation (e), 'Man realized in all his potential,' seems to have been arrived at purely by a process of *conceptual* decomposition: all referential 'parts' have been attenuated, all other semes in 'chasseur,' generic or specific, have been suspended except /human/; the very central seme /vegetal/ in 'arborescent' has also been suspended in order to reach a very high level of abstraction in semes like /multiplicity/, /abundance/, which both the numerous branches from a tree and the *rich, varied potential* of man share. Another seme shared by both fields is that of /growth/, a seme arrived at, evidently, by the conceptual mode of decomposition. An interesting feature is that in this interpretation, the evoked image is practically unfelt, or at least a very secondary place is allotted to it, given the dominance of the conceptual over the referential semantic decomposition that has been carried out in order to give 'chasseur arborescent' this very abstract meaning.

The path that the decodification of a metaphorical utterance may take largely depends on the mode of decomposition chosen, and on the semes or 'parts' that are singled out to construct the semic intersection. Now, it is usually the immediate verbal co-text that limits and determines which semes will be focused and what semantic mode of decomposition will be chosen. Even in such cases interpretations are never univocal, but because of co-textual determinations, their number is limited – the tendency being to complementarity rather than to exclusion in the kind of interpretations offered. In the absence of any orienting co-text, however, as in the case under examination, the reader will tend to refer to pre-textual contexts of a cultural or personal nature, which have a greater degree of arbitrariness and which are responsible for the disparity and for the uncontrolled proliferation of interpretations.

I shall now put our 'chasseur' back in his original context: Proust's *A l'ombre des jeunes filles en fleurs*.

> À côté des voitures, devant le porche où j'attendais, était planté comme un arbrisseau d'une espèce rare un jeune chasseur qui ne frappait pas moins les yeux par l'harmonie singulière de ses cheveux colorés que par son épiderme de plante. À l'intérieur, dans le hall qui correspondait

Metaphor and metaphoric narration 71

au narthex, ou église des catéchumènes, des églises romanes, et où les personnes qui n'habitaient pas l'hôtel avaient le droit de passer, les camarades du groom 'extérieur' ne travaillaient beaucoup plus que lui mais exécutaient du moins quelques mouvements. Il est probable que le matin ils aidaient au nettoyage. Mais l'après-midi ils restaient là seulement comme des choristes qui, même quand ils ne servent à rien, demeurent en scène pour ajouter à la figuration ... Mais le chasseur du dehors, aux nuances précieuses, à la taille élancée et frêle, non loin duquel j'attendais que la marquise descendît, gardait une immobilité à laquelle s'ajoutait de la mélancolie, car ses frères aînés avaient quitté l'hôtel pour des destinées plus brillantes et il se sentait isolé sur cette terre étrangère ... Le *chasseur arborescent* en concluait qu'il n'avait rien à attendre de la marquise et, laissant le maître d'hôtel et la femme de chambre de celle-ci l'installer avec ses affaires, il rêvait tristement au sort envié de ses frères et conservait son immobilité végétale. (I, 706–7) (italics mine)

This passage inaugurates the series of promenades with Mme de Villeparisis. The first apparent effect of co-textual determinations is that the meaning *hunter* in 'chasseur' is practically suppressed, while the hotel context activates the meaning *footman*. These, however, are not two sememes of the same lexeme, for unlike the 'stain' of Shelley's 'Adonais,' in which the same semic nuclear figure may be co-textually actualized as /glass painting/ or /contamination/, the word *chasseur* is an identical formal cover for two distinct and unrelated semic nuclear figures. Therefore these are two homonyms rather than two sememes of the same lexeme. Homonymy increases the semantic *distance* between meanings, in contrast with the *hypotactically related* sememes of the same lexeme. In a given context, the excluded sememes remain in a state of latency that may be easily activated; in the case of homonyms, by contrast, the exclusion is radical, unless in a veritable *tour de force*, as in Proust's 'baignoire' sequence, both meanings are forced to coexist in the same text. In the 'chasseur arborescent' sequence, the *hunter* meaning is never suggested until the end of the series of promenades, due to certain graphic devices, obviously used for emphasis, and to the metaphorical articulation with the Hudimesnil trees sequence, as will be seen later. It must be noted that none of the empirically gathered interpretations resorts to the hotel context. It seems that in the absence of definite co-textual structures, and due to the established contiguity of trees and hunters in the 'hunting frame,' the hunting context was naturally favoured.

72 Metaphoric narration

The metaphor 'chasseur arborescent' does not appear isolated in the text but as part of a discursive structure: it is one of the last in the series of metaphors and similes with the same semantic filiation that compose the text, and around the same object of description – the footman.

The function of threaded metaphor in this text is not just ornamental but *constitutive*. The footman's physical appearance is never described factually, never given a denotative reality that the metaphor could then be said to embellish. From the very beginning the footman's identity is referred to exclusively in vegetal terms; his plantlike nature is effectively highlighted, not only by the subject-verb inversion but, particularly, by the delayed appearance of the subject of the sentence ('jeune chasseur'), due to the interposition of the simile: 'à côté des voitures ... était planté comme un arbrisseau d'une espèce rare un jeune chasseur ... ' The shrubby tree is established here as the diegetic referent that all other descriptive elements will qualify and refer back to: 'nuances précieuses' refers back to 'son épiderme de plante,' while the 'taille élancée et frêle' of the young footman is also read on the tree isotopy, evoking not the image of the footman but that of a tree. It is therefore a *metaphorical diegetic universe* that acts as the referent of this fictional creature: the 'chasseur.'

Many similes and metaphors single out a number of semes such as /immobility/, /rarity/, /fragility/, /slenderness/, and so on, semes that are then concentrated in the metaphor that crystallizes the series: 'chasseur arborescent.' Thus the series of similes and metaphors builds up the text around which the 'chasseur arborescent' metaphor grows; it also provides the ground for its decodification, since all of the previous metaphors and similes emphasize certain semes and therefore, in a cumulative manner, orient the interpretation of 'chasseur arborescent.' The metaphor is particularly striking, not only because it culminates and crystallizes the effect created by all the others, but because it grows out of the text: being both metaphor and textual reality, the threaded tree metaphor *institutes* the footman and *makes him arborize*.

The footman continues to grow, treelike, at the end of the series of promenades, when the narrator redescribes him, playing once more on the vegetal-isotopy, and adding more details to the portrait of this rare plant. 'Nous apercevions déjà l'hôtel, ses lumières si hostiles le premier soir, à l'arrivée, maintenant protectrices et douces, annonciatrices du foyer ... Seul "le chasseur," exposé au soleil dans la journée, avait été rentré, pour ne pas supporter la rigueur du soir, et emmailloté de lainages, lesquels, joints à l'éplorement orangé de sa chevelure et à la fleur curieusement rose de ses joues, faisaient, au milieu du hall vitré, penser à une plante de serre qu'on protège contre le froid.' (I, 723)

In the metaphoric description of the footman, a virtual paranarrative line is traced, coexisting with the main diegetic space and time co-ordinates (the Grand Hotel at Balbec and the promenades with Mme de Villeparisis). This is the 'story' of a rare, hothouse 'arbrisseau,' transplanted to alien soil, exposed to the roughness of the weather, yet eventually protected indoors against the cold. The pseudo-temporal sequence imposed on the iterative narrative of the series of promenades stresses the narrative aspect of this threaded metaphor. Although they stretch over a long period of time – weeks perhaps – the promenades are narrated in such a way that they shape *one* super-promenade, so to speak: the series begins with Marcel waiting for the 'marquise' in the morning, and ends with their return in the evening. This gives the illusion that a one-day promenade has been narrated, instead of several over a longer period of time. The different parts of the day are used as an organizing principle that results in a sylleptic arrangement of the various events that take place during the promenades.[4]

The threaded metaphor that gives existence to the footman frames the whole series, so that it participates, paranarratively, in the double temporal determination that characterizes the promenades: one day in the life of a rare plant – day and night, heat and cold, exposure and protection – and at the same time, the story of its exile over an indefinite period of time. The effect of this metaphor is at once *fragmented* and *unified*. Its effect as a unified metaphor depends on the identical semantic filiation of all metaphors and similes generated around the footman; each one in the constellation takes the others as referents, actualizes different aspects of the semantic field left virtual by other metaphors, or expands on aspects already elaborated on at other points of the text – operates, in short, the series of transformations that gives threaded metaphor its narrative character. But if the *semantic* effect is unified, the *syntagmatic* unfolding of this threaded metaphor is textually fractured by the interposed narrative of the promenades. This textual rupture, however, has the double effect of introducing an extratemporal dimension, and of reinforcing the temporal dimension that characterizes the process of metaphorization at the discursive level, which, in consequence, activates the narrative potential of this metaphoric description.

74 Metaphoric narration

At the level of syntax, 'le chasseur arborescent' appears as a phenomenon of isotopic rupture restricted to the boundaries of one sentence – 'le chasseur arborescent en concluait qu'il n'avait rien à attendre de la marquise' – but its whole effect of meaning transcends the local lexic and syntactic structures in which it appears: semantic connections are drawn with other points in the text, making this particular metaphor one in a constellation with the same semantic filiation. Much of the otherwise 'daring' effect of this metaphor is attenuated by the similes and metaphors that prepare the ground and orient its decodification, thus 'naturalizing' it, making it seem less arbitrary, less daring. In fact, the discursive structures that support this metaphor make it appear as the necessary result of a text that has built up all the needed diegetic references around it, so that if in isolation the 'chasseur arborescent' metaphor might appear fantastic or arbitrary, it has been naturalized by having been made to refer only to the text that generates it; by having been made to grow and feed, so to speak, in familiar soil.

The footman sequence, however, is not merely a metaphoric frame to embellish the series of promenades with Mme de Villeparisis. It appears to have yet another metaphoric narrative meaning that no longer depends on the *linguistic manifestation* but on the way it is *articulated* with the central sequence of the series: Marcel's experience with the trees of Hudimesnil. Unlike the metaphoric articulation operated in 'La noche boca arriba,' in which the links are greatly multiplied until they become a network of echoes and correspondences, the 'chasseur arborescent' sequence is made to resonate very subtly and delicately with the Hudimesnil trees episode, because of the *very sparse points of articulation* that relate these two sequences metaphorically. The central place that the Hudimesnil trees episode (I, 717–19) has is evident not only from its diegetic content, but also from its structure and position in the series. It is the only really *singulative* event; other events, such as the incident with the fisherwoman, are also narrated singulatively, but they are narratively dependent on the iterative mode that prevails in the series. Though singulative events in nature, they function as *representative* of other similar events that must have occurred during the promenades; their status is typical rather than unique.

Not so with the Hudimesnil trees. The uniqueness of the episode is marked in various ways: (a) no narrative transition prepares for it as for the others; (b) the irrupting quality of the episode is signalled by a marked elliptic end of the previous sequence; (c) the shift in the verbal

Metaphor and metaphoric narration 75

tense from the imperfect to the past, therefore a shift from iterative to singulative narrative, is yet another mark of its singularity; (d) the position of this episode is climactic: towards the end of the series. Its diegetic content also makes it stand out from the rest: it is one of those supreme moments of happiness that must be decoded if life is to be found meaningful. The episode is patterned on the model provided by other similar experiences of bliss. Because of Marcel's intense activity of analogizing, all these other experiences are explicitly made to interact metaphorically with one another.

Furthermore, the Hudimesnil trees sequence is also articulated metaphorically with that of the footman. There are a number of thematic elements and diegetic determinations that relate conjunctively and disjunctively in the two sequences, expanding the meaning of both, and functioning as the nexus, or links in this metaphorical articulation: the *theme* of exile, the *opposition* between movement and immobility, the *spatial* dynamic relation between the inside and the outside. In the footman sequence there is movement within and immobility without – the other bellboys inside the hotel are all activity, even though pointless activity,while the footman outside is marked by his immobility and his 'exteriority,' so to speak (in the text, the word *extérieur* is graphically marked by quotation marks). His exterior position is both physical and spiritual, for he feels 'isolé dans une terre étrangère.' A similar network of relations is drawn in the Hudimesnil sequence. Marcel, as observer, is in movement, while the trees are stationary: *movement inside, immobility outside*. In both sequences immobility is represented by trees, metaphorical in one ('chasseur arborescent'), diegetic in the other (the 'real' trees of Hudimesnil). But if spatial and kinetic determinations constitute a clear-cut opposition in the footman sequence, they establish a reversible, dynamic, and therefore more complex relationship in the Hudimesnil sequence: the boundaries between inner and outer space are effaced, movement relativized. The very dynamism of Marcel's perception is transferred to the trees: it is the trees, though actually immobile, that are described as though they were in motion, when in fact it is the observer who is in movement: 'Cependant ils venaient vers moi ... Dans leur gesticulation naïve et passionnée ... Je vis les arbres s'éloigner en agitant leurs bras désespérés ...' (I, 719).

The external nature of the trees is also relativized, for in this experience of bliss they cease to be merely external objects; they are 'mimed' within; they become signs to be decoded: the trees as correlates of consciousness – 'Ce plaisir, dont l'objet n'était que pressenti, que j'avais à créer moi-même ... je bondis plus avant dans la direction des arbres, ou plutôt dans cette direction intérieure au bout de laquelle je les voyais en moi-même' (I, 718). To go in pursuit of the world is in the end to go in pursuit of the self.

> Car si on a la sensation d'être toujours entouré de son âme, ce n'est pas comme d'une prison immobile: plutôt on est comme emporté avec elle dans un perpétuel élan pour la dépasser, pour atteindre à l'extérieur, avec une sorte de découragement, en entendant toujours autour de soi cette sonorité identique qui n'est pas écho du dehors, mais retentissement d'une vibration interne. On cherche à retrouver dans les choses, devenues par là précieuses, le reflet que notre âme a projeté sur elles; on est déçu en constatant qu'elles semblent dépourvues dans la nature du charme qu'elles devaient, dans notre pensée, au voisinage de certaines idées ... (I, 86–7)

Each sign, hunted and decoded, is a new shoot, a sign of inner growth. *Paranarratively*, Marcel himself becomes a 'chasseur arborescent.' As long as those signs, fortuitously presented by the external world, are not *read* properly, Marcel experiences an intense feeling of estrangement: 'les environs de Balbec vacillèrent et je me demandai si toute cette promenade n'était pas une fiction, Balbec, un endroit où je n'étais jamais allé que par l'imagination, Mme de Villeparisis, un personnage de roman et les trois vieux arbres, la réalité qu'on retrouve en levant les yeux de dessus le livre qu'on était en train de lire et qui vous décrivait un milieu dans lequel on avait fini par se croire effectivement transporté' (I, 717).

This pursuit of the self, narratively represented by the vehicle in movement, leads to a metaphoric identification between Marcel and the footman; the identification is reinforced by certain diegetic elements. The most striking is perhaps the gradual *personification* of the Hudimesnil trees. At first Marcel's own movement is transferred to the trees, next they are internalized; the crossed displacements result in an interesting personification: 'Je vis les arbres s'éloigner en agitant leurs bras désespérés.' Finally, from personification we pass on to an identification: the trees become one of the deepest, truest dimensions of Marcel's self, 'toute une partie de toi-même.' If, initially, the contemplated object receives its movement from the contemplator, if it is brought inside to live as an image, eventually the contemplator himself is metaphorically transformed into a tree. Marcel's conversion is considerably accentuated by the metaphorical existence of the treelike

Metaphor and metaphoric narration 77

footman. Furthermore, the footman is wrapped and protected against the cold in the same way as Marcel so often is.

Another interesting aspect of this spiritual pursuit is that it activates the /hunting/ meaning in 'chasseur.' It is significant that in the description of the footman that closes the series of promenades, the words, like 'extérieur,' are graphically stressed by quotation marks – 'le chasseur' (I, 723) – as if to suggest the /hunting/ meaning. But by then, with the strong resonance from the Hudimesnil trees, 'chasseur arborescent' has been charged with a stronger paranarrative meaning, transforming the footman into a metaphoric *alter ego* of Marcel. Marcel is truly a 'chasseur arborescent,' for the trees have now moved within himself; but as he has failed to read them, exile has also moved within. Like the 'chasseur,' Marcel feels 'isolé sur cette terre étrangère': exiled from himself.

PART TWO

METAPHORIC NARRATION AND NARRATIVE STRUCTURE

In part 1 of this study I used a semiotic-semantic descriptive model of metaphor in order to map out the different constituents of a potential narrative dimension inherent to metaphorization. The key descriptive and operational concepts defining the process were also found susceptible to narrative homologizing: *transformation* gives metaphor its distinctive narrative potential, while *isotopic interactions* and the simultaneous interplay of *conjunctive* and *disjunctive* relations account for the role of metaphor as an organizing and constructive principle in certain narrative texts. Accordingly, metaphoric narration was defined as that class of texts in which the process of metaphorization functions *narratively* on two basic levels: that of the manifestation in language, and that of the organization of the text.

The narrative function of metaphor may be variously activated: (a) by a series of semantic transformations within a coherent semantic field, arranged in a logical and chronological relationship of succession; (b) by the same kind of succession established among the abstract 'events' outlined in the extended simile; (c) by the particular semantic connections linking two different segments of a text, whereby the text re-enacts processes and semantic transformations proper to metaphor.

Therefore, metaphoric narration may be conceived as a paranarrative dimension to be located in *verbal* metaphor, or in the organization of the text as a *productive principle* of a semiotic rather than of a purely linguistically manifest nature. Paranarratives of varying degrees of virtuality are generated.

My purpose in this second part is to explore the metaphoric dimension of narrative. This shift in perspective will allow us to sound the effects of metaphoric narration on narrative structure. Given the complex interactions and semantic manipulations that characterize metaphor, both in its encoding and decoding phases, and given its predominantly relational nature, metaphorization may be seen as a semiotic activity that signals itself as language, as discourse, as production of meaning, thus refusing to play up to the illusion of referential transitivity. What Michael Riffaterre has said about the literary work in general is particularly pertinent for metaphoric narration and its deferred referential function: 'Every literary work constitutes a system. In the semantics of that system, the relations between the words of the text prevail over, or even replace, the relations that those words maintain with things.'[1]

As I said in part 1, it is only at the discursive level that the narrative potential of metaphor is actualized; thus, metaphoric narration appears as both a *discursive* and a *narrative* phenomenon. That is why an essentially relational narrative theory, describing not one or the other but the various relations between discourse and narrative content, is a more appropriate instrument to trace the many and subtle effects of metaphoric narration on narrative structure. For this reason, I have chosen Gérard Genette's theory as the organizing principle of part 2.[2]

My own model will now be subordinated to Genette's narrative theory. I believe that at the crossroads the ground for exploration may be fertile; perhaps at the crossroads new light may also be shed on Proust's *A la recherche du temps perdu*.

If part 1 contains illustrations drawn from a very heterogeneous body of narrative texts, part 2 is devoted exclusively to the *Recherche*, because of the very wide range for exploration that Proust's text provides for this particular topic. For metaphoric narration, as I have insisted all along, is not restricted to narrative texts where metaphorization is apparent only at the level of the manifestation in language, such as many of Rubén Darío's short stories (cf 'El rubí'). Metaphoric narration may be observed even in texts devoid of rhetorical figures, where it becomes an active principle *at the level of the organization of the text* – Robbe-Grillet's *La jalousie* or García Márquez's *Cien años de soledad* are perfect examples of narratives in which the incidence of *verbal* metaphors is very low, yet metaphorization as process accounts for much of their narrative organization and meaning.

Proust's *Recherche* is, then, a particularly interesting text, because metaphoric narration spans both its *manifest* and its *organizational* levels. Moreover, the central role played by metaphor in the narrator's *gnomic discourse* provides a special opportunity for examining the effects of metaphoric narration on narrative voice, perhaps the most elusive area of study in this domain. For these reasons, metaphoric narration seems to me a subtle and far-reaching tool with which to analyse certain aspects of Proust's vast work that have not been sufficiently highlighted by Proustian criticism; conversely, the *Recherche* is an ideal testing ground for the theoretical model proposed in this study.

In keeping with my methodological choice, three main categories organize this second part: the temporal structures of narrative, narrative modulations, and narrative voice.[3] These correspond closely to Genette's tripartition in 'Discours du récit': Time, 'Mode' ('mood') and Voice. For the second, I prefer the concept of 'narrative modulations' that Genette uses in *Nouveau discours du récit*, because it is less ambiguous than 'mode' and is more descriptive of the processes involved in that aspect of the narrative reality.

Each section of this second part is headed by a critical summary of Genette's concepts, which are subsequently used as guiding principles in my analysis. My summaries, however, are not exhaustive;[4] I restrict myself only to what may be pertinent to my topic. I also follow Genette in isolating three rather than two aspects of the narrative reality:[5] (a) *narrative discourse* ('récit') is defined both as 'discours narratif' and as 'texte,' discourse functioning as the *signifier* of narrative; (b) *diegesis* ('diégèse') or story ('histoire') – Genette uses both terms indistinctly – is defined as the *narrative content* or *signified* of narrative; therefore, the adjective *diegetic* always denotes 'that which is related or belongs to the story';[6] (c) *narration* ('narration') is defined as the productive narrative *act*.

It is important that we keep in mind the purely relational principle of Genette's theory, for it is in the analysis of relations, rather than of content or isolated areas, that he believes full justice is done to the complex narrative reality. That is why story and narration, as he says, 'do not exist for us except through the mediation of narrative discourse [*récit*]. But reciprocally, narrative discourse can only be such if it tells a story, otherwise it would not be narrative (as, let us say, Spinoza's *Ethics*), and if it is uttered by someone, otherwise it would not in itself be a discourse (as, for example, a collection of archaeological documents). As narrative, it lives in its relationship to the story it tells; as discourse, it lives in its relationship to the act of narration that utters it.'[7] This careful delimitation of *récit* emphasizes its double nature, as *discourse* and as *narrative*, and therefore justifies the central place it has in Genette's theory: 'out of the three levels ... that of narrative discourse is the only one directly available to textual analysis, itself the

82 Metaphoric narration

only instrument of examination at our disposal in the field of literary narrative, and especially of fictional narrative.'[8]

Genette's description of '*récit*' as narrative discourse provides a useful conceptual parallel to my own theory of metaphoric narration in which both aspects, discursive and narrative, have been emphasized. With these initial definitions and specifications in mind, I shall now proceed to examine the effect of metaphoric narration on the temporal structures of narrative.

5 Metaphoric narration and the temporal structures of narrative

A narrative text, as many semioticians have observed,[1] is founded on a temporal duality.[2] The story told has a chronology and duration of its own similar to human duration and chronology. This fictional temporality constitutes *diegetic* or *story* time. Narrative discourse is also temporally determined. Even if this is, in fact, a pseudo-time, the very principle of *succession*, from which no verbal narrative can escape, accounts for the particular arrangement of narrative sequences, thus establishing the definite *textual succession* we call discourse time. Textual succession, however, does not necessarily coincide with the chronological order that the diegetic time establishes. But whether chronological or textual, succession characterizes both diegetic and discourse times. Therefore, two successive temporal lines traverse the narrative text, informing the *order* of events, both by their position in the text and by their diegetic chronology. Another aspect of time is its *duration*. Since events in diegetic time imitate real human time, one may speak of the duration of fictional events by giving them explicitly temporal measurements – hours, days, years. But in fact, diegetic events have a duration that eventually depends on the space allotted to them in the narrative text. Strictly speaking, the duration of discourse time should be that of its reading, but its subjective variables are too great to be a reliable measure. Genette has therefore resorted to a spatio-temporal equation – the extension of the text – which in terms of diegetic duration results in the notion of speed or *tempo*,[3] whereby

84   Metaphoric narration

purely conventional relations of concordance or discordance may be drawn between both diegetic and discourse times. One last aspect of this double temporality of narrative is its capacity for repetition. Here concordant or discordant relations of *frequency* are established between discourse and diegetic times: how many times an event 'happens' in diegetic time; how many times it is 'told' in discourse time.

Relations of concordance strengthen the tendency in the reader to assimilate both times; while relations of discordance evince perceptible ruptures that create *temporal figures* of narrative significance and with specific functions. It is precisely on these temporal figures that the impact of metaphoric narration may best be observed.

1   Order

Genette calls *anachronies* temporal ruptures brought about by a discordant relation between the order of events in diegetic time and their order in discourse time. There are two main anachronies:[4]

(a) *Analepsis*, in which the main narrative is interrupted to recount an event that happened, in diegetic time, *before* the point of its inception in the narrative discourse ('flashback' in film terminology);

(b) *Prolepsis*, in which the main narrative is interrupted to narrate, or refer to, an event diegetically *posterior* to the point of its inception in the text.

It must be observed that the concept of 'main narrative' is completely relative to the segment where the rupture occurs, so that an analeptic or proleptic sequence itself may act as the main narrative against which another anachrony may be played off.[5]

Analepses or prolepses have a completing function when they provide information (at an earlier or later point in discourse time) about events elided or left aside by the narrative discourse at their appropriate diegetic time; they have a repeating function when they feature narrative information already given (analepsis), or announce events that have not yet 'happened' in diegetic time (prolepsis). The *repeating analepsis* is a narrative device whereby 'the text remembers its own past.'[6] The *repeating prolepsis* has the function of an advance notice ('annonce'); its iteration may be used as a device to generate suspense. Advance notices, says Genette, should not be confused with hints ('amorces'), 'simple markers without anticipation, even an allusive anticipation, which will acquire their significance only later on and which belong to the completely classic art of "preparation" ... Unlike the advance notice, the hint is then, in principle, at its place in the text, only an "insignificant seed," and even an imperceptible one, whose importance as a seed will not be recognized until later, and in a retrospective manner.'[7]

As temporal figures resulting from ruptures in the coincidence of diegetic and discourse times, anachronies usually signal themselves and the moment of rupture by explicit marks: introductory phrases, such as 'two years earlier,' 'as we shall see before long,' and the like; temporal adverbs signalling an earlier or a later time; shifts in grammatical tense; or sophisticated narrative games with the very relationship between the two temporal determinations, such as using the 'dead times' in the story to open up an analeptic sequence. The antecedents of all the characters in Maupassant's 'Boule de suif,' for example, are given while the travellers are silent and the coach moves steadily on without anything else 'happening' in diegetic time.

Now, metaphoric narration, especially at the transphrastic level of the manifestation in language (threaded metaphor) and at the level of the organization of the text (particularly in its form of the extended simile), weaves a virtual temporal order that may trouble or resonate with the corresponding temporal relation between diegetic and discourse times. Being a discursive phenomenon, metaphoric narration also exists as pure discourse time (since it takes up a given textual space) with *no* corresponding diegetic time, for the diegetic time of metaphoric narration is completely *other*. This status of metaphoric narration as pure discourse time has also an important effect on the narrative tempo, as we shall see later.

Metaphoric time – to give a name to this virtual temporality – is constituted by the relation of succession established among the different semantic transformations of threaded metaphor, or among the abstract, pseudo-events, of the extended simile; often the sequence is even doubled by consequence, thus establishing a virtual causal line as well. Metaphoric time, thus embodied in abstract events or transformations within a given semantic field, outlines a pattern of narrative functions (in the Barthean sense) that may interact metaphorically with the main narrative in various ways. One form of interaction may be perceived in the relations of order: (a) metaphoric narration itself may function as an anachrony with a completely different diegetic status; or (b) an ordinary anachrony may furnish the material for metaphoric narration, resulting from the interaction of that particular temporal figure with the main narrative.

An important observation to make about these forms of *metaphoric anachrony* is that such distinctions as heterodiegetic and homodiegetic,

86 Metaphoric narration

or internal and external anachronies, are no longer pertinent, since the diegetic status of metaphoric anachronies is completely *other* than that of the main narrative. Furthermore, metaphoric narration, when it functions as an anachrony, does not signal itself as such; it needs no marks of any kind since metaphoric time has no direct relationship with the main diegetic time – for it constitutes a sort of *metaphoric diegesis* – and therefore cannot be said to come before or after. But, though strictly speaking metaphoric time has no before or after in terms of diegetic time, it may nonetheless act as an anachronic sequence that affects the narrative in particular ways.

1.1 *Metaphoric narration as prolepsis and analepsis*

The first pages of the *Recherche* abound in similes that have a clear proleptic function, even though they do not bear the usual proleptic marks. To illustrate this potential anachronic function of metaphoric narration, I shall quote the sequence concerning the sick traveller, juxtaposed to the narrative of the fretful sleeper of the beginning pages.

> J'appuyais tendrement mes joues contre les belles joues de l'oreiller qui, pleines et fraîches, sont comme les joues de notre enfance. Je frottais une allumette pour regarder ma montre. *Bientôt minuit*. C'est l'instant où le malade qui a été obligé de partir en voyage et a dû coucher dans un hôtel inconnu, réveillé par une crise, se réjouit en apercevant sous la porte une raie de jour. Quel bonheur, c'est déjà le matin! Dans un moment les domestiques seront levés, il pourra sonner, on viendra lui porter secours. L'espérance d'être soulagé lui donne du courage pour souffrir. Justement il a cru entendre des pas; les pas se rapprochent, puis s'éloignent. Et la raie de jour qui était sous sa porte a disparu. *C'est minuit*; on vient d'éteindre le gaz; le dernier domestique est parti et il faudra rester toute la nuit à souffrir sans remède.
>
> *Je me rendormais*, et parfois *je n'avais plus que de courts réveils d'un instant*, le temps d'entendre les craquements organiques des boiseries, d'ouvrir les yeux pour fixer le kaléidoscope de l'obscurité, de goûter grâce à une lueur momentanée de conscience le sommeil où étaient plongés les meubles, la chambre ... (I, 4) (italics mine)

This sequence is particularly rich in narrative significance. In relation to the main sequence of the insomniac narrator, the 'Intermediary Subject' as Marcel Muller calls him,[8] it produces a virtual paranarrative

Metaphoric narration and temporal structures 87

that is of a clear metaphorical nature, as we shall see presently. Because of their textual proximity, the mode of articulation of these two sequences is actual (cf chapter 3, 2.1.1), for although there are no explicit marks to link them, the juxtaposition itself has the value of an elided or implicit simile structure ('Bientôt minuit. / C'est l'instant où le malade ...'). At the same time, due to a series of detailed descriptions that appear superfluous at this point, the sick-man sequence is also articulated *virtually* with many other sequences in the *Recherche*. In its virtual mode of articulation, this piece of metaphoric narration has a *completing proleptic function*, with a number of peculiarities that set it off from the ordinary type of proleptic sequence: it has no explicit marks (introductory phrases, etc.); it is both an *advance notice* and a *hint*; it is neither homo- nor hetero-diegetic but *metaphorically* diegetic, so to speak.

For a more detailed analysis of these peculiarities, let us turn first to the *actual* mode of articulation of these sequences. The status of the sick man is doubly metaphorical: he is the narrator's *alter ego*; he is also the metaphorical extension of the traveller who figured in a prior passage, who, in turn, is another metaphorical extension of the Intermediary Subject: 'le sifflement des trains ... *me* décrivait l'étendue de la campagne déserte *où le voyageur* se hâte vers la station prochaine; et le petit chemin qu'*il* suit va être gravé dans son souvenir ...' (I, 3) (italics mine).

The whole sick-man sequence as a block constitutes a breach in the diegetic isotopy of the main narrative. Nonetheless, this completely different diegetic universe presents a series of abstracted narrative functions that interact metaphorically with the main sequence, that constitute, in other words, the 'joints' in this actual metaphorical articulation: in both sequences the actor believes it is dawn already, when in fact it is only midnight. To be precise, what is identical is that both actors need to find out what the time is and find it is midnight. In the main narrative, however, the narrator does not explicitly say he thinks it must be morning, but the sequence of narrative functions – especially 'waking up' and 'finding it is midnight' – becomes strongly coloured by a similar one in the metaphoric sequence where confusion and disappointment are added: it is only midnight and not dawn as the sick man had thought. Thus the narrator's gestures acquire a connotative dimension of meaning for which the metaphoric sequence *alone* is responsible.

The *disjunctive* relations, based on the difference of diegetic universes, produce very interesting effects of meaning. It must be noted that in the main sequence, the intermittent waking during the night is not connoted negatively; quite the contrary, the positive, pleasurable qualifications are stressed throughout: darkness is qualified as 'douce et reposante pour mes yeux' (I, 3); pillows are 'pleines et fraîches ... comme les joues de notre enfance'; the consciousness of sleep projected onto the furniture is qualified as joy-giving, 'de goûter ... le sommeil où étaient plongés les meubles.' By contrast, in the metaphoric sequence, playing on the illness isotopy, a *tonal* isotopic path is traced: the disphoric tone that colours the second sequence is opposed to the euphoric that characterizes the first. Anguish pervades this narrative sequence: 'crise,' 'secours,' 'l'espérance d'être soulagé,' which is then thwarted; 'souffrir,' 'rester toute la nuit à souffrir sans remède.'[9] One effect of the interaction between the two is that, as in the case of the time confusion, the main sequence is strongly tainted with the suffering of the illness sequence, so that even at this early point, and despite the positive connotations in the main narrative, the equation is obliquely established between sleep-insomnia and illness-suffering.

This paranarrative contamination of the main sequence is one of the effects of metaphoric narration. As we saw in chapter 1, 2 the phenomenon of semantic extension and contamination is characteristic of metaphorization. ' ... if the part held in common is necessary as the conclusive evidence that establishes the proclaimed identity, the non-common part is no less indispensable for creating the originality of the image and for triggering the mechanism of reduction. Metaphor extrapolates; *on the basis of a real identity indicated by the intersection of two terms, metaphor affirms the identity of the totality of the terms*. It extends to the *union* of the two terms a property that is, in fact, true only of their intersection' (italics mine).[10]

Because of the phenomenon of contamination, therefore, illness, suffering, and insomnia, in a context of travelling (though at this point patently absent from the main narrative of the Intermediary Subject), become henceforward irremediably associated with Marcel. At this point, the interesting proleptic function of this piece of metaphoric narration becomes apparent.

The metaphoric diegetic universe of the sick traveller, made up of train rides, unknown hotels, menacing bedrooms, illness, and crises that make him bedridden, is a virtual, abstract universe at this point, acting paranarratively; later it will be *actualized* in the diegetic universe of the main narrative. An important feature of this metaphoric diegetic universe is that, when actualized, it will not be *replicated* in all its details, but rather *implicated* and referred to in an oblique manner. Balbec is one of the actualizations of this virtual diegesis. Marcel's suffering in the new, unfamiliar bedroom *is* developed with all the details that are absent from the early metaphoric narration, but the actual *nocturnal* crises that force Marcel to his bed during his stay at Balbec are never narrated directly, only alluded to: 'Le médecin de Balbec appelé pour un accès de fièvre que j'*avais eu*' (I, 704) (italics mine); 'de plus en plus souffrant, j'étais tenté de surfaire les plaisirs les plus simples à cause des difficultés mêmes qu'il y avait pour moi à les atteindre'[11] (I, 787). At the very end of *A l'ombre*, a long analeptic sequence goes back to those early days in Balbec. Once more, references to Marcel's illness abound without any narration of his actual sufferings *at night*: 'ma grand'mère, sur l'ordre du médecin, me força à rester couché dans l'obscurité' (I, 953); 'Je me recouchais; obligé de goûter, sans bouger, par l'imagination seulement, et tous à la fois, les plaisirs des jeux, du bain, de la marche ...' (I, 954). Those endless nights of anxiety, of being bedridden with illness and 'accès de fièvre' are never described, but they all refer back to that virtual diegetic world established at the very beginning, the abstract world where the sick traveller lives.

Thus we may legitimately see in the early sick-traveller sequence a sort of *metaphoric prolepsis* with a completing function; the specific narrative information given here, paranarratively, is later on omitted *paraliptically*[12] – that is, even though the corresponding diegetic segments are accounted for by the narrative discourse, this particular information of Marcel's nights at Balbec is left aside. Because of its virtual mode of articulation, depending on an act of retrospective reading and on the series of conjunctive elements acting as links, this proleptic sequence might be classed as a hint ('amorce'); it is however far too long to be considered as 'an insignificant seed' or as an imperceptible detail. The vividness of its descriptive detail, the strong narrative accent of its abstract 'events,' its very extension – all of these features force themselves on the reader's attention. Though it may, in a first reading, appear superfluous at its place in the text, the sequence later acquires metaphoric significance, to the extent of constituting a real *advance notice* ('annonce'), a veritable proleptic sequence with a completing function.[13]

The fact that so much specific narrative information – made up of diegetically disembodied actors, spaces, and actions – should be conveyed proleptically by metaphoric narration contributes to the antirealistic or antimimetic effects of this text. This effect is enhanced by the fact that the sick man exists purely in discourse time. In fact, such proleptic pieces of metaphoric narration are in keeping with the explicitly avowed antimimetic poetics of the *Recherche* ('On cherche à se dépayser en lisant' III, 888). 'Ce que nous appelons la réalité est un certain rapport entre ces sensations et ces souvenirs qui nous entourent simultanément – rapport que supprime une simple vision cinématographique, laquelle s'éloigne par là d'autant plus du vrai qu'elle prétend se borner à lui ...' (III, 889).

The sick-man sequence acts metaphorically at the level of the *organization* of the text, since metaphorization is not apparent in the verbal texture of either the main or the secondary sequence. Textual juxtaposition and similarity in the pattern of narrative functions, set against the dissimilarity in the diegetic universes, trigger metaphorization; but because of similar conjunctive-disjunctive relations established with later narrative sequences, the virtual metaphoric articulation acquires a proleptic function of a metaphoric nature.

Turning now to metaphorization *at the level of the manifestation in language*, we find that verbal metaphors may likewise have an anachronic function. An important difference is that verbal metaphor can play that role only when it has become a stylistic constituent of *repetitive* narrative (cf this chapter, 3.2 below). Therefore, verbal metaphor can only have a repeating function. A case in point is the recurring astronomic images initially used to describe the young girls at Balbec. The group of girls is metaphorized as a 'lumineuse comète' (I, 791). As he looks at one of them, Marcel wonders 'du sein de quel univers me distinguait-elle?', for her look has been transformed into 'le rayon noir émané de ses yeux' (I, 794). The girl turns out to be Albertine.

In the long, explicitly analeptic sequence that closes *A l'ombre*, Marcel, recalling those early days, uses the same trope: 'des yeux qui ... avaient croisé mes regards *comme des rayons d'un autre univers* ...' (I, 950) (italics mine). Late in *La prisonnière*, meditating on the essential impenetrability of Albertine, Marcel reverts to a variant of those original metaphors: 'comme si j'eusse manié une pierre qui enferme la salure des océans immémoriaux ou *le rayon d'une étoile*, je sentais que je touchais seulement l'enveloppe close d'un être qui par l'intérieur accédait à l'infini' (III, 386) (italics mine).

At this point there are no explicit analeptic marks; in fact, the sequence itself is not primarily analeptic. But because 'le rayon d'une étoile' is a close variant of the recurrent metaphors associating

Albertine's mystery with the first days of their acquaintance,[14] and because of the marine context that frames this, like so many other metaphors, the sequence has also an analeptic function. Furthermore, due to the constant evocation of the sea in connection with all the metaphorical transformations to which she is subjected, wherever she may happen to be at other moments of the *Recherche*, Albertine ends up symbolically containing the whole of Balbec within herself. Thus all these transpositions have an analeptic function of a metaphoric kind, and strongly contribute to that effect of unity of place that several critics, notably Poulet and Genette, have observed in Proust's narrative.[15]

1.2 The analeptic sequence as a constituent of metaphoric narration

A repeating analeptic sequence may be used in order to bring into direct contact thematic aspects, or diegetic constituents, otherwise thought to be unrelated at the level of the story. Mme Swann's spring salon provides an interesting and complex example of this.

> Et la vérité totale des ces semaines glaciales mais déjà fleurissantes, était suggérée pour moi dans ce salon, où bientôt je n'irais plus, par d'autres blancheurs plus enivrantes, celles, par exemple, des 'boules de neige' assemblant au sommet de leurs hautes tiges nues, comme les arbustes linéaires des préraphaélites, leurs globes parcelés mais unis, blancs comme des anges annonciateurs et qu'entourait une odeur de citron ... Il me suffisait, pour avoir la nostalgie de la campagne, qu'à côté des névés du manchon que tenait Mme Swann, les boules de neige (qui n'avaient peut-être dans la pensée de la maîtresse de la maison d'autre but que de faire, sur les conseils de Bergotte, 'symphonie en blanc majeur' avec son ameublement et sa toilette) me rappelassent que l'Enchantement du Vendredi Saint figure un miracle naturel ... et, aidées du parfum acide et capiteux de corolles d'autres espèces dont j'ignorais les noms et qui m'avait fait rester tant de fois en arrêt dans mes promenades de Combray, rendissent le salon de Mme Swann aussi virginal, aussi candidement fleuri sans aucune feuille, aussi surchargé d'odeurs authentiques, que le petit raidillon de Tansonville. (I, 634-5)

The explicit analeptic mention of Combray here, a perfume 'qui m'avait fait rester tant de fois en arrêt dans mes promenades,' makes this analepsis *repetitive*, especially since it evokes at least two specific hawthorn sequences (I, 112-14; 138-9). But this evocation is *iterative* as well, since it encompasses all the many similar episodes, whether already narrated or not — the explicit syntactic marks of iterative narrative being the adverbial phrase 'tant de fois,' and the pluperfect 'avait fait rester.' But if the analeptic sequence is formally iterative, the whole constellation of religious connotations ('miracle naturel,' 'Vendredi Saint'), and metaphors ('blancs comme des anges annonciateurs'; the whiteness of the salon metaphorically qualified as 'virginal'), make this analepsis refer back more concretely to the first hawthorn episode (I, 112–14): 'C'est au mois de Marie que je me souviens d'avoir commencé à aimer les aubépines. N'étant pas seulement dans l'église, si sainte, mais où nous avions le droit d'entrer, posées sur l'autel même, inséparables des mystères à la célébration desquels elles prenaient part, elles faisaient courir au milieu des flambeaux et des vases sacrés leurs branches attachées horizontalement les unes aux autres en un apprêt de fête ...' (I, 112).

In this earlier sequence, the flowers are set in a religious context that favours their association with the Virgin ('le bouquet d'étamines, fines comme des fils de la Vierge'). But the harmonious relationship between the flowers and the Virgin is immediately contaminated by the appearance of Mlle Vinteuil. The intermediary stage between the sacred and the profane is constituted by the metaphoric transformation of the flowers into girls, whereby Marcel incorporates the outer world of the flowers into his inner world of imagination and desire: 'en essayant de mimer au fond de moi le geste de leur efflorescence, je l'imaginais comme si ç'avait été le mouvement de tête étourdi et rapide, au regard coquet, aux pupilles diminuées, d'une blanche jeune fille, distraite et vive. M. Vinteuil était venu avec sa fille se placer à côté de nous' (I, 112).

With Mlle Vinteuil's appearance the flowers have been contaminated; thereafter they will be described, no longer in a purely religious, but in a vaguely erotic context: 'Quand, au moment de quitter l'église, je m'agenouillai devant l'autel, je sentis tout d'un coup, en me relevant, s'échapper des aubépines une odeur amère et douce d'amandes, et je remarquai alors sur les fleurs de petites places plus blondes sous lesquelles je me figurai que devait être cachée cette odeur, comme, sous les parties gratinées, le goût d'une frangipane ou, sous leurs taches de rousseur, celui des joues de Mlle Vinteuil' (I, 113). The movement towards the profane culminates in the simile, 'cette intermittente odeur était comme le murmure de leur vie intense dont *l'autel vibrait ainsi qu'une haie agreste visitée par de vivantes antennes ...*' (I, 114) (italics mine).

Metaphoric narration and temporal structures 93

Later, all these diegetic and metaphoric elements will be taken up again in the Tansonville episode (I, 138-9) to create interesting effects of meaning of a purely metaphorical nature, but also to connect, *analeptically*, these two early hawthorn sequences with the sequence of Mme Swann's salon. The triple connection is, of course, not explicit but made through metaphoric narration. In the two hawthorn sequences, the recurrent elements are the flowers associated with the Virgin, their mixed perfume, the flower-girl transformation, the altar-hedge-insect simile – which works, in fact, exactly like *reciprocal metaphor*[16] – and the metonymic juxtaposition of a 'real,' that is, diegetic girl.

> Je le trouvai tout bourdonnant de l'odeur des aubépines. La haie formait comme une suite de chapelles qui disparaissaient sous la jonchée de leurs fleurs amoncelées en reposoir; au-dessous d'elles, le soleil posait à terre un quadrillage de clarté, comme s'il venait de traverser une varrière; leur parfum s'étendait aussi onctueux, aussi délimité en sa forme que si j'eusse été devant l'autel de la Vierge, et les fleurs, aussi parées, tenaient chacune d'un air distrait son étincelant bouquet d'étamines, fines et rayonnantes nervures de style flamboyant comme celles qui à l'église ajouraient la rampe du jubé ou les meneaux du vitrail et qui s'épanouissaient en blanche chair de fleur de fraisier. (I, 138)

According to Genette, with '*repetitive* analepsis, or "recalls," we no longer escape redundancy, for in these the narrative openly, sometimes explicitly, retraces its own path. Of course, these recalling analepsis can rarely reach very large textual dimensions; rather, they are the narrative's allusions to its own past.'[17] This is exactly what happens in the passage quoted above, except that there are no explicit marks recalling the earlier episode as a series of events. What is repeated here, with important variations, is the *system of metaphoric relations*. It is metaphorization, therefore, that marks this particular sequence as analeptic (as in the case of the astronomic images associated with Albertine that we examined in this chapter, 1.1 above). Its function is not simply to recall but to interact metaphorically with the previous hawthorn sequence. The dialogue between both becomes an *extended reciprocal metaphor*, for if in the first the altar is metaphorized as a hedge swarming with insects, in the second an actual swarming hedge (i.e. diegetic) is metaphorized as an altar and extensively described in terms of ecclesiastical architecture.

As in the first sequence, a 'real' girl appears after the description of the flowers: Gilberte. Although hints of Gilberte's probable homosexu-

94 Metaphoric narration

al involvement with Léa and with Albertine herself are not revealed till much later (III, 695 and III, 376 respectively), the metaphoric articulation of these two hawthorn sequences already identifies Gilberte with Mlle Vinteuil, and therefore with homosexuality. This trait in the latter will soon be revealed (I, 159ff) and has already been intimated at by her description: 'avait l'air d'un garçon,' 'la figure hommasse' (I, 113). Thus the metaphoric articulation of these sequences contaminates Gilberte with Mlle Vinteuil's doubtful sexuality by *metaphoric extension* (metaphor 'extends to the *union* of the terms a property that is, in fact, true only of their intersection'). In the virtual mode of articulation of these two sequences, the very important theme of contamination begins to be developed paranarratively. Furthermore, this metaphoric contamination of Mme Swann recalls Swann's suspicions on the subject and prepares for future revelations about Odette's doubtful sexuality: Elstir's portrait of her as 'Miss Sacripant.'

The analeptic sequence in Mme Swann's spring salon refers back to the complex paranarrative contamination in the already virtually articulated hawthorn sequences. As it interacts metaphorically with the description of the salon itself, the anachrony develops the theme of contamination and adds a whole ironic dimension to both Mme Swann and the recalled hawthorn sequences.

In the incredibly beautiful – because incredibly idealized – transformation of Mme Swann into a flower (see particularly I, 636–41), there is a series of tonal deflations. The final irony is the product of an intricate weaving of meanings radiated from such diegetic elements as flowers, girls, and chapels. At one end of the tapestry is the system of connotations in the hawthorn episodes identifying the flowers with the Virgin; at the other end is the consistent and systematic associations of Mme Swann with flowers, culminating in her spectacular metaphorical transformation into a flower. But Mme Swann is not only associated with and transformed into a flower, she is insistently, though obliquely, associated with the Virgin by the description of her 'boudoir' as the 'coeur du Sanctuaire' (I, 509), as a 'chapelle mystérieuse ...' (I, 526), so that the apparently innocent qualification of Mme Swann's salon as 'virginal' points back, metaphorically, to that identification, flowers = virgin, as well as to its semantic extension: whiteness = purity. But the qualification inevitably extends, metonymically, to Odette herself, thus producing the intensely ironic effects of meaning: cocotte = virgin!

Genette has observed that 'the most persistent function of recalls in the *Recherche* [is] to modify the meaning of past occurrences after the event, either by making significant what was not so originally or by refuting a first interpretation and replacing it with a new one.'[18]

In the light of my previous analysis of Mme Swann's salon, I believe Genette's observation must be qualified. When metaphoric narration is involved in the production of these temporal figures, either because it plays the role of a repeating analepsis or because an analeptic sequence is articulated metaphorically with the main narrative, the function of this kind of anachrony is quite different. *Modifying* the meaning of an earlier event, or *replacing* an earlier interpretation with another are statements that have two important implications: (a) one meaning or interpretation is *cancelled out* by the other; (b) the modification is *explicitly* brought about by means of gnomic discourse ('interpretation'). In metaphoric narration, by contrast, there is no such exclusion or cancellation when the mode of articulation is virtual, nor is the modification brought about by the narrator's gnomic discourse but rather by the metaphoric interaction itself. As I have insisted all along, in the virtual mode of metaphoric narration, the first sequence *temporally unfolds* and *maintains* both levels of meaning – the non-metaphoric and the metaphoric. The semantic and narrative revaluation of the first sequence in terms of the second adds the metaphoric dimension of meaning without cancelling the previous non-metaphoric one. This is also, as we saw in chapter 2, one of the modes of functioning of metaphorization at the discursive level: the time shift involved is responsible for the maintenance of both the metaphoric and the non-metaphoric meanings in the phenomenon of the reactivation of the text due to the introduction of an allotopic utterance at a terminal point.

In all the examples of repeating analepses that we have examined, their function is not merely to recall the text's own past, nor do they primarily cancel the previous meaning or replace one interpretation with another; rather they add a dimension of meaning *that is not on the same level* – diegetic or discursive – as that of the previous meaning (Odette's metaphoric-metonymical virginity, for example). These metaphoric repeating analepses have also the function of developing, paranarratively (and therefore virtually), important themes of the *Recherche*, like that of contamination (the two hawthorn sequences articulated with the sequence of Mme Swann's salon), or that of the unification of space (the recurrent evocations of the sea and the astronomic metaphors that describe Albertine, or the fusion of diegetic space achieved metaphorically by the analeptic sequence that brings Combray and its flowers into the Parisian salon).

96 Metaphoric narration

What has also become apparent in the preceding analysis is the important role that the repeating analepsis plays in the virtual mode of metaphoric articulation. As we saw in chapter 3, 2.1.2, the two sequences are textually discontinuous, usually without any explicit marks to make the connection between the two. Nevertheless, there is a series of elements in the second sequence that are programmed to resonate with the first, a series of elements acting as 'joints' in this phenomenon of metaphorical articulation of narrative sequences: *at the level of the manifestation in language* these elements may be constituted by recurring metaphors or other forms of intratextual relations, such as direct quotations from the earlier sequence; *at the constructed level of the organization of the text*, a pattern of narrative functions, abstracted from the events that are specific to the second sequence, may relate conjunctively to the first. All these elements, related conjunctively and programmed to resonate with the first sequence, have therefore a clear analeptic function, since they act as 'recalls' of an earlier time (both diegetic and discursive times). Thus, metaphoric narration, in relation to narrative anachronies, adds a completely different dimension of meaning to the narrative – different because it exists in a different domain from that of diegetic time.

2   Narrative tempo (duration)

Narrative *tempo*, as we saw earlier, defines the proportional relation between the fictive duration of events in diegetic time and the amount of space allotted to them in the narrative text. This conventional relation of *speed* between diegetic and discourse times constitutes the rhythms of the narrative text.

Genette isolates four distinct *narrative movements*:

(a) *Scene*. A conventional relation of *concordance* between both durations defines an isochronous narrative: the diegetic duration of events is roughly equivalent to their textual extension in narrative discourse. The scene tends to be a more or less detailed narrative of events; often it privileges dialogue as the most dramatic – therefore scenic – form of narration.

Relations of *discordance* between the two durations, or anisochronies, give rise to the other three narrative movements:

(b) *Pause*. No diegetic time whatsoever corresponds to a given segment in the narrative discourse. This is the status of descriptions in which no character's consciousness or act of contemplation are involved, and that constitute a 'stop' in diegetic time.

Metaphoric narration and temporal structures

(c) *Summary*. Events have a much longer duration in diegetic time than the space given to them in the narrative discourse: ten years of a character's life, for example, are disposed of in two or three lines.

(d) *Ellipsis*. A given diegetic duration has no 'place' in the narrative discourse. No account is given of those ten years, not even summarily.

These four basic narrative tempos are not clear-cut or mutually excluding; rather they relate one to the other as a series of gradations between two constant forms of duration: at the two extreme poles are the *pause* and the *ellipsis*. In the former, *diegetic time is nil*, while discourse time has a variable extension; in the latter *discourse time is nil*, while diegetic time is assumed to have some variable duration. In both extremes, the proportional relation is constant, one of the two conventional durations being nil. In the other two narrative movements, covering the distance between the two extreme poles, the relation is *variable*: a summary may be more or less detailed, that is, closer to a scene if more detailed or closer to the ellipsis if more succinct; a scene may also be narrated at greater or lesser length, closer to the pause if it abounds in descriptive detail, or closer to the summary if the details are scarcer.

Here I have deviated from Genette, who does not see in the scene a 'form with variable tempo.' He defines it simply as: '*scene*, most often "in dialogue," which, as we have already observed, realizes conventionally the equality of time between narrative and story ...'[19] This notation, however, 'most often "in dialogue,"' given as in passing, is clearly not enough to describe the complex status of the scene, especially since Genette himself proceeds to demonstrate that *descriptions* in Proust do not constitute a *pause* but are in fact the narrated perceptions of the hero and therefore events narrated in scenic form. Now, obviously these narrated perceptions are not couched in a dialogic but in a descriptive form. If dialogue were the only criterion to define scene, then indeed the form of that movement would not be variable, dialogue constituting the *invariant* (just as nil diegetic time is the invariant in pause, and nil discourse time the invariant in ellipsis). But if dialogue is not the sole criterion, then the amount of descriptive detail with which a scene may be narrated is necessarily variable, thus making the scene, like the summary, *a form with a variable tempo*. In fact, we could speak of the scene as a narrative movement having the qualities of a *tempo rubato*; that is, within a given conventional tempo – in this case the hypothetical isochrony between discourse and diegetic durations – slight accelerations and/or decelerations may be allowed, without the original tempo losing its identity for the changes.

98 Metaphoric narration

It is the variability of the descriptive dimension that gives the scene this quality of a *tempo rubato*.

These different narrative movements, as in music, from which the analogies have been drawn, are responsible for the different 'speeds' or 'tempos' that a narrative may have, thus imprinting it with particular rhythmic patterns. A narrative in which descriptive pauses abound tends to be perceived by the reader as slow; whereas summaries and ellipses tend to give the reader an impression of acceleration.

Genette has brilliantly demonstrated how in Proust, contrary to the views held by many, descriptions do not constitute a pause, because the object or sight described is always an event rather than just description for description's sake.

> ... Proustian narrative never comes to a standstill at an object or sight unless that halt corresponds to a contemplative pause by the hero himself ... and thus the descriptive piece never evades the temporality of the story.
>
> ... In fact, Proustian 'description' is less a description of the object contemplated than it is a narrative and analysis of the perceptual activity of the character contemplating ... A contemplation highly active in truth, and containing 'a whole story.'
>
> What we are compelled to conclude, therefore, is that description, in Proust, becomes absorbed into narration, and that the second canonical type of movement – the descriptive pause – does not exist in Proust, for the obvious reason that with him description is everything *except* a pause in the narrative.
>
> ... Absence of summary, absence of descriptive pause – on the roster of Proustian narrative, then, only two of the traditional movements still exist: scene and ellipsis.[20]

An important observation that Genette makes in his revision of 'Discours du récit' – *Nouveau discours du récit* – is that it is *focalization* that turns a description into an event: 'narrativization by focalization.'[21] Although I fully agree with Genette that description in Proust has a central narrative function, the very real fact of the Proustian slow tempo is still not accounted for. If it is true that in Proust all description is event and therefore there is no standstill in diegetic time, why is it that most readers would label Proustian narrative 'slow'? One possible answer is implied in Genette's own comments: 'the halt corresponds to a contemplative pause by the hero himself'; that is to say, the diegetic

Metaphoric narration and temporal structures 99

time itself is full of pauses and is therefore slow. Nevertheless, it is in our experience as readers that we perceive the differences in narrative tempo solely through narrative discourse. If ten diegetic years are accounted for in three lines, the reader is not left with the impression of a ten-year duration, but of a perceptible acceleration in the narrative. Therefore, what seems to matter in narrative tempo is not the fictional duration of the event, but the *pace of narration*.

Another important reason for the impression of slowness in Proust's narrative is description itself, *despite its narrative function*. By its very nature, the descriptive mode affects the narrative tempo because, as Genette himself has observed, it 'dwells on the objects and beings considered in their simultaneity, and [because] it contemplates the processes themselves as spectacles'; therefore, description 'seems to suspend the flow of time and contributes to unfold the narrative in space.'[22]

Two other possible explanations may be offered for the perceptible slow tempo in Proustian narrative:[23] (a) the extremely frequent 'interruptions' in the narrative, giving way to long tracts of gnomic discourse; (b) metaphoric narration, existing as pure discourse time, projecting its own metaphoric time, and therefore duration, onto the diegetic time.

2.1 The role of metaphoric narration in narrative tempo

Genette has observed that it is not description alone that makes a pause in the narrative;[24] there are other kinds of pauses, which he calls 'digressive,' and which belong to the gnomic discourse. Their narrative status is very different, for they are extradiegetic and belong to the domain of reflection rather than strict narration. Unlike the descriptive pause, one cannot say that the *narrative* discourse makes a standstill in diegetic time; rather narrative discourse itself is interrupted to give way to another kind of discourse, the gnomic. The effect of such 'reflexive digressions' on narrative tempo is, however, undeniable. Yet, since this kind of pause cannot be measured against diegetic time (as discourse time can), Genette proposes to name the effect of such digressive pauses a *rallentando*, thus making the 'reflexive digression' the fifth narrative movement.

The possibilities of these *rallentandos* are many and complex, for, particularly in Proust, 'reflexive digressions' are not always, as their name suggests, reflexive in an abstract manner. Very often, the narrator's gnomic discourse is cast in the language of vivid and concrete metaphors – just as vivid as those in the narrative – often reaching such an extension as to draw whole micro-diegetic universes. At times it is very difficult indeed to determine whether a piece of metaphoric narration belongs to the *gnomic* or to the *narrative* discourse. The blurring of frontiers here is not without narrative consequences, as we shall see.

I shall first examine a piece of metaphoric narration that clearly belongs to the narrative rather than to the gnomic discourse: the description of the tombstones at the church of Saint-Hilaire. 'Ses pierres tombales, sous lesquelles la noble poussière des abbés de Combray, enterrés là, faisait au chœur comme un pavage spirituel, n'étaient plus elles-mêmes *de la matière inerte et dure, car le temps les avait rendues douces et fait couler comme du miel* hors des limites de leur propre équarrissure qu'ici elles avaient dépassées *d'un flot blond, entraînant à la dérive* une majuscule gothique en fleurs, *noyant* les violettes blanches du marbre ... (I, 59) (italics mine).

Let us first analyse the constituents of this striking metaphor, before we go on to examine its effects on narrative tempo. The Proustian metaphor imbues with new life an old cliché – 'time flows'[25] – by means of a series of complex transformations. The rich polysemic potential of the lexeme *douce* is the point of convergence for a double metaphoric isotopy,[26] thus making this threaded metaphor *pluriisotopic*: 'douce'$_1$ (soft) is part of the hardness/(softness) isotopy of the main context; 'douce'$_2$ initiates the process of metaphorization, by activating the sweetness/(bitterness) isotopy subsequently actualized by the honey metaphor. The *simultaneous* interplay of both sememes in 'douce,' /sweet/ and /soft/, brings about a triple transformation: (a) from hard to soft; (b) from solid to liquid (honey); and (c) from bitter (implicit in the destructive force of time) to sweet (time as honey). In turn, the second transformation, from solid to liquid, generates the aquatic isotopy due to the seme /liquidity/ in honey.

There is a dynamic reciprocity in this double isotopy – hardness/(softness), sweetness/(bitterness). From the pont of view of *reception*, that is, from the perspective of a syntagmatic reading and decoding, 'douce'$_2$, /sweet/, is not perceived until the honey simile appears; before that, 'douce' has been decoded as /soft/, in keeping with the hardness/(softness) isotopy established by the main context, 'matière inerte et dure,' present both in the passage quoted above and in the previous lines describing the destructive effects of countless years of countless peasant women walking, even if ever so softly, on the stone porch of the church – 'comme si le *doux* effleurement des mantes des paysannes entrant à l'église et de leurs *doigts timides* prenant de l'eau bénite, pouvait, répété pendant des siècles, acquérir *une force destructive, infléchir la pierre ...*' (I, 59) (italics mine). From the point of view of *production*, however, one might not unreasonably speculate that it was the polysemic potential of 'douce' itself that initially suggested the honey metaphor – a beautiful example of the productive and creative powers of language ('It would be more illuminating ... to say that the metaphor *creates the similarity* than to say that it formulates some similarity antecedently existing').[27]

The activation of the meaning /sweet/ is therefore startling and delightful because unexpected. The honey isotopy also activates the so-far virtual and hardly felt connotations of bitterness associated with the destructive force of time, in the first part of the description. In the second part, the threaded metaphor quoted above, it is no longer the destructive force of time and its bitterness that are emphasized but its sweetness and creative powers of transformation.

Once the honey metaphor has been launched, certain semes other than /sweetness/ begin to interact with yet another semantic field: liquidity. If 'miel' activates 'douce'$_2$ /sweet/, 'couler' activates /liquidity/ in the same lexeme ('miel'). In turn, this seme of /liquidity/ will multiply its connections in the same field until a very subtle but radical *transfer* is made, within the network of the same threaded metaphor, *from honey to water*. The connectors of isotopies are multiplied, at first encompassing both honey and water ('couler,' 'flot blond'), but eventually excluding honey altogether ('entraînant à la dérive,' 'noyant'). In this golden flow, time achieves its work of creation by transformation, 'introduisant un caprice de plus dans la disposition de ces caractères abrégés, rapprochant deux lettres d'un mot dont les autres avaient été démesurément distendues' (I, 59).

Now, all the connectors of isotopies that have woven this threaded metaphor have also drawn among themselves clear relations of *sequence* and *causality* – even a relationship of *gradation* – that may be easily abstracted into a pattern of narrative functions: 'flowing,' 'overflowing,' 'flooding the banks,' 'setting adrift,' and finally 'drowning.' Such a sequence establishes a virtual or metaphoric time that is superimposed onto the diegetic time of the contemplative pause.

The description of the tombstones does not correspond to a standstill in the diegetic time but to a contemplative pause by Marcel; yet the first impression is not that of a static pause, diegetic or otherwise, but of *active movement*, of time actually passing. That time, however, far exceeds that of the moment of contemplation. But the movement in this passage does not belong to the story, *it is a purely discursive effect*. If the two durations, diegetic and discursive, may be conventionally labelled isochronous – since the contemplative pause is narrated in scenic form (only two of the traditional movements still existing in Proust: the scene and the ellipsis) – then metaphoric narration provides a sort of rhythmic counterpoint that troubles the isochronous relation of duration in this scene. In fact, the rhythmic counterpoint is both metaphoric and thematic. As *pure discourse time*, this threaded metaphor establishes its own duration by signalling itself as discourse, by forcing the reader to dwell on its intricate semantic transformations, by the instantaneous character of surprising simultaneous effects of meaning, and so on. As *metaphoric time*, the virtual sequence of narrative functions, setting the static in motion, also establishes a duration that is definitely *other* than that of the contemplative duration. Finally, *time as theme* makes both the metaphoric and the diegetic times converge (since it is a description of the effects of time on man-made works); thus its duration expands well beyond the metaphoric and the diegetic.

The same effect is apparent in the sick-traveller sequence examined in this chapter, 1.1 above; its duration far exceeds that of diegetic time. The Intermediary Subject in the main narrative wakes up, realizes it is close to midnight, and then goes back to sleep – sometimes waking up again for *short periods of time*. From this last notation, and from all the pleasurable connotations in the main narrative, we assume that when he first wakes up it is also for a short period. The sick-traveller sequence, by contrast, makes the waking time last the whole night ('il faudra rester toute la nuit à souffrir sans remède'). Thus the metaphoric sequence blows up the time between the two diegetic markers, 'Bientôt minuit' and 'Je me rendormais,' far beyond the limits of diegetic time. Furthermore, for a moment the sick-traveller sequence contaminates the first by making it seem as though the Intermediary Subject has spent the whole night awake between those two diegetic markers.[28] This disproportionate duration is underlined by the sequence of actions – even though of an inner, spiritual nature – in the metaphoric sequence, and their pointed absence in the main narrative; crises, hopes, speculations, self-delusion, anguished anticipations ...[29]

The sick-traveller sequence is pure *narrative discourse time*, because it has no direct relations with the corresponding diegetic time, only with a ghostly metaphoric time. Therefore, if it exists as discourse without a corresponding diegetic time, this sequence *does constitute a pause*. Its status, however, is very different from that which Genette calls a

Metaphoric narration and temporal structures 103

'descriptive pause.'[30] Since metaphoric narration exists as discourse time with no corresponding diegetic time, we might call this kind of pause *a metaphoric, paranarrative pause with a rallentando effect*. But if these pieces of metaphoric narration constitute a *rallentando* in terms of diegetic time, in terms of their own metaphoric diegesis they are full of action, establishing narrative sequences of their own. All this activity constitutes a strong rhythmic counterpoint to the relatively static moments in diegetic time – a contemplative pause in the one, a waking pause in the other. So that, in fact, the complex effect of these two instances of metaphoric narration may be described as an *accelerando within the frame of a rallentando*.

The same effect is apparent in many of the digressive pauses in Proust, which differ so little from the paranarrative pauses just described that often it is only by the formal frame of gnomic discourse that they can be distinguished. The formal syntactic and discursive marks that clearly set off gnomic from narrative discourse are:

(a) the choice of grammatical tense; gnomic discourse always uses the timeless present of reflection and generalizations,[31] while narrative discourse resorts to the past when the narrator's position *vis-à-vis* the events he narrates is ulterior, to the future of predictive narration when his position is anterior, or to the present of contemporaneous action;

(b) a tendency to use the generalizing first-person plural and/or whatever forms of neutral pronouns exist in the language ('one,' or the neutral 'you,' in English; 'on' in French; 'uno' in Spanish, etc.). The shift in pronoun immediately signals a shift in level, from the *diegetic* to the *extradiegetic*: the narrator no longer gives an account of events but establishes a discursive communication of the generalizing, abstract kind, with an equally extradiegetic interlocutor.

The two pieces of metaphoric narration that we have been examining for their effects on narrative tempo clearly belong to the narrative rather than to the gnomic form of discourse: both maintain a narrative tense (the past of the main narrative in the honey simile, the present of contemporaneous action in the sick-traveller sequence); both deal with events rather than with generalizations, and in both the dominant pronoun system is the third person. Metaphoric narration in Proust, however, does not always belong to the narrative discourse. Often, the filiation of many pieces of metaphoric narration is very difficult to determine. There are many passages abounding in metaphors and similes, whose syntactic frames clearly signal them as gnomic discourse; nonetheless, a narrative line is traced even though it constitutes an abstract or virtual narrative.

104 Metaphoric narration

In the 'drame du coucher' scene, for example, Marcel has just written a note to his mother and sent it to her with Françoise. What follows is a double simile: one comparing Marcel's deceptive joy to Swann's similar experiences with his mistresses, the other comparing the joy itself to a situation of deceit *narrated* at length in the form of a scene that even includes dialogue. The extended simile very nearly risks becoming a metadiegetic narrative without, however, ceasing to be part of the gnomic discourse that introduces it and indeed informs it throughout. I shall quote only a manageable piece of this unduly long simile:

> Et la joie avec laquelle je fis mon premier apprentissage quand Françoise revint me dire que ma lettre serait remise, Swann l'avait bien connue aussi, cette joie trompeuse que nous donne quelque ami, quelque parent de la femme que nous aimons, quand, arrivant à l'hôtel ou au théâtre où elle se trouve, pour quelque bal, redoute ou première où il va la retrouver, cet ami nous aperçoit errant dehors, attendant désespérément quelque occasion de communiquer avec elle. Il nous reconnaît, nous aborde familièrement, nous demande ce que nous faisons là. Et comme nous inventons que nous avons quelque chose d'urgent à dire à sa parente ou amie, il nous assure que rien n'est plus simple, nous fait entrer dans le vestibule et nous promet de nous l'envoyer avant cinq minutes. Que nous l'aimons – comme en ce moment j'aimais Françoise –, l'intermédiaire bien intentionné ... (1, 30–1).

As will be observed, the whole theatre-hotel sequence has exactly the same narrative structure and function as the sick-traveller sequence: it is metaphorically articulated (in the actual mode) with the main narrative by means of a simile structure, which is more or less explicitly marked, and by means of a series of conjunctive elements in both sequences acting as connectors of the two narrative isotopies; it has a paranarrative proleptic function since this virtual diegetic situation will be actualized in the main diegetic universe later on.[32] It also has a metaphoric diegetic duration of its own that exceeds that of diegetic time. As in the other instances of paranarrative duration, the theatre sequence contaminates the main one by magnifying the time of suspense in the waiting, thereby blowing up the intensity of the boy's suffering to its true subjective dimensions (apart from the interesting *reciprocal metaphor* developed later in 'Un amour de Swann' and in *La prisonnière*: mother = mistress = mother).

In structure and function, then, the two sequences are identical; yet one (the sick-traveller sequence) belongs to the narrative discourse, the other (the theatre sequence) to the gnomic discourse. In the theatre sequence the pronoun is no longer 'il' but 'nous,' a shift that automatically makes the sequence extradiegetic and in direct communication with an extradiegetic narratee. The shift is very clear in the following alternation: 'Que nous l'aimons – comme en ce moment j'aimais Françoise –, l'intermédiaire bien intentionné.' The pronoun 'nous' and the present tense set this utterance in the domain of gnomic discourse, in contrast to the parenthetical reversion to narrative discourse, signalled by the adverbial phrase 'en ce moment' and the imperfect 'aimais.'

Because of these formal differences one might be tempted to label the sick-traveller sequence as narrative and the theatre one as gnomic discourse. But in fact, the differences are not so clear-cut, for within this piece of gnomic discourse a whole narrative sequence unfolds, from which one can easily abstract a pattern of narrative functions; conversely, in the sick-traveller sequence, purely narrative at first sight, the tense of narration has been shifted from the imperfect of the main narrative to the present tense. Because events are narrated, one initially tends to consider this the present tense of contemporaneous action. Nevertheless, it would be difficult to say what this is *contemporaneous* to. Thus the very abstract character of the sequence and the shift of tense in itself make this sequence gravitate towards the domain of the gnomic discourse, since the 'events' narrated, being abstract, cannot be said to be 'contemporaneous' to anything. In any case, both sequences are extradiegetic, or, to be more precise, they constitute *metaphoric diegetic universes* that have no direct relationship to the diegetic universe of the main narrative, yet affect the duration of the latter paranarratively.

In summary, the effects of metaphoric narration on narrative tempo are manifold and complex. Long similes or threaded metaphors are, in their narrative content, extradiegetic; they exist only as *discourse*, therefore as pure discourse time with no counterpart in diegetic time. Consequently, metaphoric narration constitutes a pause, its status wavering between a narrative (or descriptive) and a digressive pause. Its global effect on narrative tempo is a sort of metaphoric *rallentando*. Simultaneously, owing to its *narrative* character, metaphoric narration establishes a sequence of narrative functions necessarily implying succession, therefore a temporal dimension, and consequently, a duration. This virtual paranarrative time, however, is not diegetic but metaphorical. Therefore, by its purely discursive existence – in other words by the very *textual space* it occupies – metaphoric narration as discourse time constitutes a *rallentando*; simultaneously, by its own narrative dimension, metaphoric narration projects a metaphoric diegetic universe with its own independent temporal dimension. Often, as in the honey threaded metaphor and the sick-traveller sequence, the metaphorical temporal dimension constitutes a kind of *accelerando* within the *rallentando* tempo of its discursive dimension. Thus, metaphoric narration, whether as *discourse time* or as *metaphoric diegetic time*, constitutes a temporal counterpoint that strongly affects the narrative tempo as a whole.

3   Frequency

Both narrative discourse and story have a capacity for repetition that outlines three basic kinds of patterns of narrative frequency. As in the other modes of temporal relations, these may be concordant or discordant. Concordant relations establish a one-to-one correspondence: an event occurring n times in the story is narrated the same number of times – the most usual form being the singular event narrated once. Genette calls this form of narrative frequency '*singulative narrative.*' Discordant relations of frequency establish *uneven* relations of repetition in both domains: when an event happens only once in the story but is narrated more than once, we get a '*repetitive narrative*'; by contrast, when similar events occurring more than once in the story are accounted for in one synthetic act of narration we speak of an '*iterative narrative.*' As Genette has observed,[33] in traditional forms of narrative the iterative is used for summaries, while repetitive narrative is usually restricted to anachronies whose function is to recall events already narrated (the repetitive analepsis), or to announce others (the repetitive prolepsis). Both the incidence and extension of such form of repetitive narrative, however, are usually very limited and in most cases subordinated to the main narrative, which tends to be singulative. Traditional narrative seems to favour the singulative narrative for scenes, the repetitive for anachronies, and the iterative for summaries, which may also be of the analeptic kind.

3.1 Metaphoric narration and iterative narrative

Genette's detailed and insightful analysis of iterative narrative has demonstrated its dominant role in Proust, for 'no novelistic work,

Metaphoric narration and temporal structures 107

apparently, has ever put the iterative to a use comparable – in textual scope, in thematic importance, in degree of technical elaboration – to Proust's use of it in the *Recherche du temps perdu*.'[34] This important emancipation of the iterative affects the temporal structures of narrative. In Proust 'l'ivresse de l'itératif' contaminates all other forms of temporal narrative, even the singulative; it assembles events in temporal syllepses, establishing internal rhythms that very often blur the chronology of his narrative. 'The central figure of the Proustian treatment of narrative temporality is, without a doubt, what I have called *syllepsis* ... [syllepses] bring about a thematic arrangement of events, disregarding their "real" chronological succession ... In a way reminiscence is an experienced form of temporal syllepsis. But metaphor is (in that sense) a syllepsis by analogy, which enables it, as we know, to *represent* reminiscence. One could therefore see in syllepsis what Spitzer would have called the Proustian stylistic *etymon*.'[35]

Two of the preceding remarks are precious for our purposes: the fact that metaphor may be considered as a syllepsis by analogy and the fact that iterative narrative itself is sylleptic by nature. Both the semantic and narrative homologues that Genette draws with the trope open up interesting vistas for metaphoric narration. Genette defines syllepsis loosely as 'the fact of taking together.'[36] But if syllepsis as a rhetorical figure is defined as the bringing together of *different meanings simultaneously active in the same syntactic structure*, the homologue is particularly apt for iterative narrative; it brings together various events – not identical though similar – under a single narrative and syntactic structure, just as metaphor brings together at least two different isotopies in the same structure of the linguistic manifestation. The conjunction of iterative narrative with metaphoric narration results in striking temporal effects in the *Recherche*. Genette has observed that 'the iterative syllepsis is not only an aspect of frequency: it also affects order (since by synthesizing "similar" events it abolishes their succession) and duration (since at the same time it eliminates their time intervals).'[37]

John P. Houston has said that Proust deliberately tries to break the temporal linearity of events – the iterative constituting the most powerful device to accomplish this.[38] Other 'stylistic devices,' as he calls them, are the temporal analogies that Proust superimposes on his narrative: 'in the analogy between the day, the season and the year, Proust has found the most condensed narrative form.'[39] If iterative narrative, by its sylleptic nature, abolishes succession and duration; in conjunction with metaphoric narration other forms of chronology and duration are virtually superimposed, thus giving the text its peculiar temporal organization. Take, for example, the narrative of the Intermediary Subject. Textually it is discontinuous (I, 3–9; 43–4; 186–7); its temporal localization in terms of the external chronology of the whole narrative remains extremely vague. Because of the iterative mode of narration it is impossible to determine the sequence of these oneiric and/or reflexive activities, nor is it possible to determine how long – weeks, months, or years – this state of affairs lasted. Nonetheless, despite the extraordinary indefiniteness and discontinuity, this narrative establishes a clear temporal progression from midnight to dawn, and hence a definite duration: one night of insomnia. *Sequence* and *duration*, however, are of a purely metaphorical nature, and depend on the sylleptic grouping of certain meditations around specific moments of the night, also sylleptically arranged in a pattern of chronological progression. They establish among themselves a *metaphorical progression*: 'Bientôt minuit' (I, 4); 'Quand réveillé la nuit' (I, 43); 'C'est ainsi que je restais souvent jusqu'au matin,' 'quand approchait le matin,' 'le doigt levé du jour' (I, 186–7).

The same kind of metaphorical temporality, on a vast scale, may be observed in the narrative of that paradigmatic Sunday at Combray, as well as in other narrative sequences, such as the promenades with Mme de Villeparisis, where the temporal treatment is exactly the same: the conjunction of the *iterative* and of the *metaphoric* results in a paradoxical abolition of diegetic sequential time, coupled with an-*other* temporality, of a clear metaphorical nature.

3.2 *Metaphoric narration and repetitive narrative*

Genette has remarked that the emancipation of the iterative from its traditional subservient role seriously affects the temporal aspects of order and duration. The same holds true – though this is a question he has not discussed – for repetitive narrative. As long as this latter form is subordinated to the singulative, its extension and degree of incidence are kept in check. But as soon as repetitive narrative becomes a full-fledged form in its own right, the aspects of temporal order and duration are also seriously affected. Repetition in itself extends the duration of the event well beyond its original diegetic proportions by making it linger in the reader's mind indefinitely. On the other hand, an event that is told again and again is strongly foregrounded, to the point of confusing the sense of *temporal sequence*, both as regards the

Metaphoric narration and temporal structures   109

repeated event in relation to others and as regards other events in relation to themselves. Repetitive narrative thus enhances the illusion of *temporal circularity*. A striking example of this temporal perturbation is the episode of the 'mille pattes' treated in this mode of repetitive narrative in Robbe-Grillet's *La jalousie*.

Nothing so radical ever happens in the *Recherche*, where repetitive narrative appears mostly in the form of *repetitive analepses*. While it is true, as Genette says,[40] that repetitive anachronies are more or less 'fugitive' realizations of repetitive narrative, the degree of recurrence of such anachronies in Proust turns them into more than just fugitive impressions of redundancy, the recurrence and extension far surpassing their subordinate role as mere recalls. In this chapter, 1.2 above, we saw how the repetitive analepsis may function as a constituent of metaphoric narration, thus bringing together thematic aspects that would otherwise remain separate or discontinuous in the diegesis. But often the repetitive analepsis multiplies its appearances for different purposes and with different effects. The last pages of *Le temps retrouvé* constitute a vast analeptic *reprise* of the whole of the *Recherche*, but particularly of *Du côté de chez Swann*, thus stressing the temporal circularity of this work that almost closes on itself just as it might tell the same story all over again.

The most insistent repetitive analepses are those that recall the privileged experiences of felicity involving analogical perception and reasoning. There is a tendency in Proustian criticism to associate those 'moments bienheureux' solely with the expériences of involuntary memory, but in fact, the abundant textual references to those experiences show that the ones in which involuntary memory is involved are only a subspecies of a more complex paradigm; and although each experience actualizes the paradigm with different variations, they are all patterned on the same configuration. Without attempting to be exhaustive, I shall try to list the most important of those privileged moments: the Petite Madeleine episode, which not only opens the series but is proposed as *the* paradigm for the rest (I, 44–8); the two hawthorn sequences (I, 112; 138–9); the delight at the sun's reflection on the water – 'Zut, zut' – (I, 155); the steeples of Martinville (I, 178–82); Vinteuil's sonata at Mme de Sainte-Euverte's (Swann) (I, 345–52); the water closet at the Champs Elysées (I, 492); the trees at Hudimesnil (I, 717–19); the 'miracle' of la Berma (II, 47–50); the noise recalling the central heating at Doncières (II, 346–7); the late realization of the grandmother's death (II, 755–9); Vinteuil's septet (III, 248–61); meditations on music and literature (III, 374–81); and finally, the last series of experiences of involuntary memory at the Guermantes's courtyard – Venice, Balbec, *François le Champi*, and so on (III, 866–85).

The paradigmatic elements that compose these experiences of bliss/sorrow are as follows: (a) the circumstances surrounding the events are against the habitual, or else the hero is in a depressed or indifferent state of mind, without expectations of any kind; (b) the external object, determined by chance not by choice, is an essential intermediary between the self and discovery; (c) the nature of the felicity or sorrow experienced is always sudden, inexplicable, and intense; (d) despite the intensity of the experience, the hero feels an urgent need to explain – the explanation always conceived in terms of 'deciphering' or 'translating'; (e) the attraction of the intermediary object is so strong that the hero is tempted to go out, towards the object, in order to find the explanation; (f) the outward movement is countered by the realization that the search can only proceed within: images of descent and depth always abound, the self is posited as the 'domaine inconnu' that must be explored, so that the deciphering of the world becomes equivalent to the deciphering of the self; (g) this activity involves an extraordinary intellectual-spiritual effort; (h) the last stage is the result of the experience and it varies: the experience may end in either success, whether partial or complete, or failure.

All the experiences listed above go through identical functional stages – some may be elided, others expanded, yet others abridged; only the last stage varies, the one that triggers metaphorization: the experience, passing through the same intermediary stages results in the resurrection of the past, in a spiritual equivalent of an aesthetic nature (verbal or otherwise), in a nascent original idea or in failure. It is very significant that the most recurrent of these analeptic forms of repetitive narrative are always abstracted and presented in the same list of four (III, 261; 374–5; 866–7; 878–9); the Petite Madeleine, the Martinville steeples, the Hudimesnil trees, and Vinteuil's music – all of them presented analogically as *equivalent* to one another. Only one, however, is strictly an experience of involuntary memory: the Petite Madeleine. From the long list I have given, more than half are in fact experiences of involuntary memory, yet Proust insists on these particular four as equivalent: music – 'ce retour à l'inanalysé' – is envisaged as a path of communication that humanity has abandoned, 'une possibilité qui n'a pas eu de suites' (III, 258); the steeples of Martinville propose a successful verbal equivalent of the experience; and the Hudimesnil trees represent failure – the undeciphered unknown. But since the four are repeatedly identified, and since all four are outlined on the same pattern, *with only the last stage in disjunctive position*, repetitive narrative makes these various episodes interact metaphorically with one another. Since the stages that make up the experience of the Petite Madeleine become paradigmatic for the configuration of the other experiences, *reminiscence* itself becomes a metaphor of cognition and creation – creation as re-creation, cognition as re-cognition:[41] 'des impressions obscures avaient ... sollicité ma pensée, à la façon de ces réminiscences, *mais qui cachaient non une sensation d'autrefois mais une vérité nouvelle*, une image précieuse que je cherchais à découvrir par *des efforts du même genre que ceux qu'on fait pour se rappeler quelque chose*, comme si nos plus belles idées étaient comme des airs de musique qui nous reviendraient sans que nous les eussions jamais entendus, et que nous nous efforcerions d'écouter, de *transcrire'* (III, 878) (italics mine).

Furthermore, the very paradigm of the Petite Madeleine is a metaphor of the process of metaphorization itself, transposed from the semantic to the spatio-temporal domain of the diegesis. As Ricardou remarks, 'far from being circumscribed to a local, expressive function, metaphor attains a decisive role of organization ... ordinal metaphor plays the role of the perfect machine for the subversion of representation in that its mechanism dissolves, whether conjointly or separately, the categories of time and space.'[42] The two different semantic fields that are connected by metaphorization find their *diegetic homologue* in the two different moments and places in the conjunction of which distance and succession are abolished in a metaphorical telescoping. The intermediary object or sensation that is identical in both (the conjunctive relation) is homologous to the semic intersection that extends its predication of identity to the totality of the two semantic fields. The identical intermediary object and/or sensation is the 'joint' that makes the metaphorical *articulation* possible. Just as the semantic distance between the two fields is abolished, so is time, as the narrator insists since the essence of time is succession, and succession is abolished in these privileged moments. In fact, the *illusion* of the intemporal, as we have seen, is the result of the conjunction of metaphoric narration with both the iterative and the repetitive forms of narrative; as succession and duration are thereby abolished, an impression of the simultaneous and of the instantaneous is created. Paradoxically, countering this effort to create a vision of the intemporal, the music analogue insists on the deployment of time and is posited as a metaphor of the self and of self-realization ('car on ne se réalise que successivement' III, 379).

une de ces impressions qui sont peut-être pourtant les seules purement musicales, inétendues, entièrement originales, irréductibles à tout autre ordre d'impressions. Une impression de ce genre, pendant un instant, est pour ainsi dire *sine materia* ... Mais les notes sont évanouies avant que ces sensations soient assez formées en nous pour ne pas être submergées par celles qu'éveillent déjà les notes suivantes ou même simultanées. Et cette impression continuerait à envelopper de sa liquidité et de son 'fondu' les motifs qui par instants en émergent, à peine discernables, pour plonger aussitôt et disparaître .... si la mémoire, comme un ouvrier qui travaille à établir des fondations durables au milieu des flots, en fabriquant pour nous des fac-similés de ces phrases fugitives, ne nous permettait de les comparer à celles qui leur succèdent et de les différencier. (I, 209)

Ainsi rien ne ressemblait plus qu'une belle phrase de Vinteuil à ce plaisir particulier que j'avais quelquefois éprouvé dans ma vie, par exemple devant les clochers de Martinville, certains arbres d'une route de Balbec ou plus simplement, au début de cet ouvrage, en buvant une certaine tasse de thé. Comme cette tasse de thé, tant de sensations de lumière, les rumeurs claires, les bruyantes couleurs que Vinteuil nous envoyait du monde où il composait promenaient devant mon imagination, avec insistance, mais trop rapidement pour qu'elle pût l'appréhender, quelque chose que je pourrais comparer à la soiérie embaumée d'un géranium ... les sensations vagues données par Vinteuil, venant non d'un souvenir, mais d'une impression (comme celle des clochers de Martinville), il aurait fallu trouver, de la fragrance de géranium de sa musique, non une explication matérielle, mais l'équivalent profond ... (III, 374–5)

The experience of felicity – 'ce retour à l'inanalysé' – abolishes time in the purity of an instant, but only effort and 'explication', and therefore, *temporal deployment*, may capture this 'fugitive' and transpose it into a spiritual equivalent. This is, as Deleuze would say, the 'supreme complication,' that 'original state which precedes any development, any deployment, any "explication": *complication*, which envelops the many in the One and affirms the unity of the multiple.'[43]

Thus, the paradigm of 'complication' that the Petite Madeleine episode proposes generates complex forms of metaphoric narration: due to a series of conjunctive and disjunctive relations, all these narrative sequences are metaphorically articulated on the virtual mode; at the same time, the sequences are metaphorically constructed on the pattern proposed by the first one in the sequence; finally, the

Metaphoric narration and temporal structures

paradigm itself (the Petite Madeleine sequence) constitutes a narrative homologue of the process of metaphorization itself. Such complex forms of metaphoric narration, which are already intense centres of metaphoric radiation, are further emphasized by *repetitive* narrative. In most cases, these repetitive analepses are taken over by the gnomic discourse as the material for extensive meditations and generalizations. Repetition and reflection turn this important form of metaphoric narration into powerful symbols: cognition as re-cognition, one of the most striking symbols in Proust. An eminently Platonic one, it is true, but the lack of novelty in the idea should not blind us to the originality and the vivid concreteness of the path that has taken us to it ('la même et pourtant autre, comme reviennent les choses dans la vie' [III, 259]). Thus, involuntary memory, important as it may be as a theme, is not at the centre of the *Recherche*; it is a powerful metaphor – elevated to a symbol – of something even larger than itself: creation and cognition as re-creation and re-cognition, resulting in self-realization.

6 Narrative modulations

In his 'Mode' chapter, Genette explores the relationship between story and discourse in terms of 'distance' and 'perspective.' The essential concept that encompasses and justifies this bipartition is that of the *filters or regulations that modulate the narrative information* – narrative information being Genette's alternative term to the highly misleading concept of 'representation' in literature.[1] There is no such thing as an inherent 'wholeness' in any narrative; a principle of *selection* is always at work, for nothing is ever narrated 'exhaustively' (the very notion is illusory) or indiscriminately. Every narrative is therefore, whatever its extension, the result of a selection – that is to say, of variable amounts – of information. But the very act of selection also implies a *restriction*. Selection and restriction are then the two basic filters, or *narrative modulations*, that Genette calls 'distance' and 'perspective.' 'Distance [is] the quantitative modulation ("how much?") of the narrative information – perspective ... [is] the qualitative modulation: "by which channel?"'[2]

1 Distance

Again and again,[3] Genette has denounced the fallacy of the concept of *mimesis* as applied to literature. As he has brilliantly demonstrated it in 'Frontières du récit,' the classical opposition between mimesis (representation or imitation) and diegesis (pure narration) is an illusion

Narrative modulations

because the only thing that language can 'imitate' perfectly is language itself, and even then it is no longer *imitation* but *reproduction* or *production* of verbal realities. Likewise, language cannot imitate non-verbal realities; it can only give a 'series of transpositions and equivalences.' Therefore, if 'the perfect imitation is no longer an imitation but the thing itself, [if] in the end the only imitation is the imperfect one, [then] *mimesis* is *diegesis*.'[4]

This very important conclusion, that mimesis is diegesis, is what gives Genette's notions of 'diégèse' (not 'diegesis' in the classical sense) and 'diégétique' their distinctive character: his variant term 'diégèse' is thus defined as the whole 'spatio-temporal universe designated by the narrative'[5] – the *whole* fictive universe, that is, everything: the mimetic and the diegetic included. The classical, mutually excluding opposition mimesis/diegesis, as such, is no longer pertinent in Genette's theory. For him there is no mimesis, only *degrees* of diegesis,[6] and therefore there is no such thing as 'representation,' only degrees of 'information': 'A narrative, like any other verbal act, can do nothing but *inform*, that is to say, transmit meanings.'[7]

The quantity of information provided creates the illusion in the reader of greater or less 'distance' (the spatial concept being used metaphorically only). The more details provided (of both descriptive and narrative kinds), the greater the illusion that the story is 'happening before our very eyes.' Another important factor is the number of marks that signal the presence of the narrator. The more discrete the narrative mediation, the greater the *illusion* that the story 'tells itself.' Conversely, the illusion of a greater distance is produced by the opposite proportional relation: a smaller amount of information coupled with a more marked presence of the narrator will give as a result a narrative that seems more distant, one that 'tells' more than it 'shows,' to use Henry James's famous distinction.

One important consequence of the concept of narrative modulations for our examination of the effects of metaphoric narration on narrative structure is that the diegetic universe, defined as the 'spatio-temporal universe designated by the narrative,' includes both the descriptive and the strictly narrative dimensions of fiction, which are closely related to its spatial and temporal dimensions. Metaphoric narration has this double status: by means of its transformations and the temporality necessarily implied in succession, it proposes a virtual narrative, hence, a *temporal* universe; but, due to the phenomenon of the associated image, it is also vividly descriptive, and therefore responsible for the projection of a spatial universe. This metaphoric

116 Metaphoric narration

spatio-temporal universe may interact in various ways with the universe of the main narrative – even to the extent of replacing it or constituting it, as we have seen in the 'chasseur arborescent' sequence (cf chapter 4) and in the metaphoric prolepsis of the sick traveller (cf chapter 5, 1.1). It is then possible to examine the effects of metaphoric narration on the 'representation,' or rather, on the *presentation* of the diegetic universe. Thus metaphoric narration may significantly contribute to *shape* the narrative by its own metaphoric modulations.

1.1 Metaphor in descriptions of diegetic space

So far I have emphasized the narrative – and therefore temporal – dimension of metaphoric narration; now the concept of narrative modulations, as the shaping of the diegetic content – including, therefore, the diegetic space – provides us with a good opportunity for analysing the purely *descriptive dimension* of metaphoric narration. Seymour Chatman's definition of story space will provide my starting point for examining this diegetic dimension more closely: 'How do verbal narratives induce mental images in story-space? One can think of at least three ways: the direct use of verbal qualifiers ("huge," "torpedo-shaped," "shaggy"); reference to existents whose parameters are "standardized," by definition, that is, carry their own qualifiers ("skyscraper," "1940 Chevrolet coupe," "silver-mink coat"); and the use of comparison with such standards ("a dog as big as a horse"). These are explicit, but images can also be implied by other images ("John could lift a 200-pound barbell with one hand" implies the size of John's biceps).'[8]

In the *Recherche*, diegetic space is created by constant 'reference to existents whose parameters are "standardized,"' as Chatman would say: steeples and churches, gardens and streets are named after similar objects in the real world. Combray and Balbec, devoid of extratextual reference,[9] are, nonetheless, 'filled' with churches, houses, landscapes and seascapes, hotels and beaches, named and described again and again, so that in turn *these very descriptions*, pure verbal creatures, become the referents of those names. Proust, however, does not restrict himself to naming and qualifying only by means of standardized qualifiers, and when he resorts to comparisons it is certainly not to comparisons with such standard parameters. The objects and places that constitute the diegetic space in the *Recherche* are forever subjected to profound transformations under the pressure of metaphorization. Even those nouns combined with definite articles and forming

Narrative modulations

'definite descriptions,' as Bertrand Russell would call them, or those lexemes with standardized parameters (church, beach, steeple) are radically 'de-standardized' by this pressure. If it is true that places are more stable than characters in Proust, this so-called stability, as will be seen, is only relative: the pressure of figurative language on diegetic space is truly subversive *and* creative.

Paradoxically, in a great number of instances, the main diegetic universe provides the foundation for, and orients the production of, metaphors that in turn radically transform the represented space from which they have sprung. These are the kinds of metaphors that Genette has called diegetic, because they are founded on metonymic relations of contiguity with their fictional environment. Genette has observed how the steeples of three churches, probably looking very much alike due not only to their similar shapes but also to the similarly rugged texture of their surfaces, are yet metaphorized one as a loaf of bread (I, 65), others as ears of wheat – 'épis de blé' (I, 146), and the last two as salmon (II, 1014–5); so that in spite of their 'original' similarity, we end up with three very different sets of diegetic objects.[10] The source of these differences, therefore, is not to be found in the objects themselves, but in the different contexts in which the steeples appear: the Sunday village context turns one into a domestic edible object, with religious connotations ('brioche'), while the agricultural and aquatic contexts produce vegetal and marine creatures respectively. Thus the very 'effect of the real' is distorted by this constant metaphorization of the same or similar objects; the effect is indeed one of metaphorical proliferation of objects superimposed onto the diegetic ones.

I shall try to show that this proliferation is not without consequence in terms of represented space. The metonymic foundations of metaphor, constituting what we might call the *denotative plane* of the description, are usually carefully laid down before metaphorization brings about those manifold transformations. In the ear-of-wheat steeple passage, for example, the agricultural context is well established before the simile appears. The illusion of the real is created by the description that precedes the simile, in which precise spatial deictics – 'sur la droite,' 'par-delà' – are used to enforce the referential illusion of the 'champs de blé: '*Sur la droite*, on apercevait *par-delà* les blés les deux clochers ciselés et rustiques de Saint-André-des-Champs, eux-mêmes effilés, écailleux, imbriqués d'alvéoles, guillochés, jaunissants et grumeleux, comme deux épis' (I, 146). Cf 'Quand, après la messe, on entrait dire à Théodore d'apporter une brioche plus grosse que d'habitude ... on avait devant soi le clocher qui, doré et cuit

118 Metaphoric narration

lui-même comme une plus grande brioche bénie, avec des écailles et des égouttements gommeux de soleil, piquait sa pointe aiguë dans le ciel bleu' (I, 65) (italics mine).

A series of qualifiers with 'relatively stable semantic properties,'[11] together with the spatial deictics, are responsible for that denotative plane in the representation of space in these passages: they constitute the diegetic contexts, the imaginary universe of discourse that fiction creates and to which the 'objects' will then refer. It is precisely on this *plane of fictive reference* that a reader like Genette is able to perceive similarities despite the metaphoric transformations of the three sets of steeples.

Qualifying phrases and adjectives – 'imbriqués d'alvéoles,' 'écailleux' or 'grumeleux' ('épis'); 'avec des écailles' ('brioche') – describe the material texture of the steeples and, at the same time, prepare for the fish metamorphosis later on (II, 1014–5). Others – 'jaunissants' ('épis'); 'avec ... des égouttements gommeux de soleil' ('brioche') – describe their colour. Both the texture and colour descriptions establish the *denotative* plane of diegetic space – a plane that is still fictive and not to be confused with extratextual reality. It is to this denotative plane that the metaphors will then refer. It must be noticed, however, that even these descriptions are already metaphoric in nature ('alvéoles,' 'écailles'), as though containing the seeds for the subsequent metaphors that radically transform the described object.

Thus the three sets of steeples, in their different contexts, look alike on the denotative plane of diegetic space, but on the metaphorical plane they look far more like the immediate diegetic environment and less like one another. This is one of the many effects of metaphor on diegetic space. On the denotative plane, descriptions in the *Recherche* always insist on the heterogeneous; on the metaphorical plane, by contrast, they very often tend to homogeneity, producing what Genette has called 'tableaux monochromes.'[12] 'Quand on se rapprochait et qu'on pouvait apercevoir le reste de la tour carrée et à demi détruite qui, moins haute, subsistait à côté de lui, on était frappé surtout du ton *rougeâtre* et *sombre* des pierres; et, par un *matin brumeaux d'automne*, on aurait dit, s'élevant au-dessus du *violet orageux* des vignobles, une ruine de *pourpre* presque de la *couleur de la vigne vierge*' (I, 63) (italics mine).

In the Proustian world, objects tend to be assimilated, in their shapes, colours, and textures, to other objects in their environment; they are equally assimilated to the prevailing light and time. The same steeple of Saint-Hilaire that looks purple on a misty autumn day, looks like a cushion at bedtime and like a loaf of bread at lunchtime. Thus the metonymic foundations of the Proustian metaphor turn out to be both spatial and temporal, making a homogeneous whole out of a spatio-temporal unit.

The diegetic assimilation is itself metaphoric of an exalted vision of a unified, homogeneous space. What Genette says about Mme Swann's salon could be said of most diegetic metaphors in the *Recherche*: 'around Mme Swann, all contrasts are effaced, all oppositions disappear, all partitions vanish in the euphoria of a continuous space.'[13] This exalted vision of space is the exclusive effect of metaphoric narration – and not just of isolated metaphors, diegetic or otherwise – which always plays a thematic counterpoint to the diegetic and rather *dysphoric* experiences of the hero in the realm of the discontinuous and the heterogeneous.

Paradoxically, the seeds of dissolution and dispersion are planted at the very heart of this 'euphorie d'un espace continu'; for if it is true that diegetic metaphor, by assimilating the object to its immediate environment makes it one with it, as the descriptions of the object are multiplied, as it is thereby assimilated to other equally 'immediate' environments, it ends up losing its identity. Overdetermined by spatial, temporal, and subjective parameters, the object ecstatically perceived as one with its environment is eventually dissolved in a multiplicity of ever changing and differing forms. Loaves of bread, black suns, purple ruins, and endless marks on the sky made by fingernails: all these proliferating metaphorical objects gradually cover the steeple of Saint-Hilaire that they initially attempted to describe, until its 'original' shape and identity are effaced in multiplicity.[14]

The same paradoxical effect is achieved by *non-diegetic metaphors*, particularly by threaded metaphors and extended similes. The mythical, marine world, so extensively superimposed onto the theatrical one in the 'baignoire' sequence (II, 40–4), all but obliterates the existence of the 'original' diegetic space – that is, the theatre. Metaphoric narration, by its extension and detail, often threatens to dissolve the main narrative due to the law inherent to language, as a temporal successive medium, which Ricardou has so aptly described: in reading, each successive sign hides the preceding one, pushes it to the background of the reader's mind, so that if a description multiplies its details beyond a certain limit, it will, paradoxically, end up destroying the very object it attempts to describe. This also explains why any digression – and metaphoric narration is after all a sort of digression from the diegetic world – pushed to extremes, tends to be perceived no longer as a digression but as *corps principal*.[15]

The notion of distance is therefore affected by the paradoxes of metaphoric narration: because of its vividness the illusion of proximity is very strong, yet the sense of proximity is definitely not of the mimetic kind. Because metaphoric narration superimposes another virtual diegetic universe on the main one, the superimposition may affect the reader as a concealment or as a *distancing* from the denotative plane of the description. In fact, it is the indirection of metaphoric narration that creates such a distancing effect. Finally, metaphor and analogies in general, as several narratologists have pointed out,[16] always signal the presence of the narrator. Thus the double status of metaphoric narration, as discourse and as metaphoric diegesis, may partially explain that special *nuance* of which Genette has spoken in relation to the Proustian paradox of maximal 'showing' coupled with maximal 'telling' – 'extreme mediation and at the same time complete immediacy.'[17] Yet that immediacy, often brought about by the intensity of the associated images in metaphorization, is far from being mimetic, far from creating an illusion of reality. If anything, metaphoric narration shows that intensity and immediacy are not necessarily identical with the mimetic, for metaphor gives the lie to that illusion by proposing a reorganized view of the world; nor is this kind of immediacy inimical to a strongly marked discursive presence, since metaphoric narration always signals the presence of the narrator.

2   Perspective: metaphoric narration and focalization

Perspective is the second *filter* in the regulation of narrative information, 'arising from the choice (or not) of a *restrictive* "point of view" (italics mine)[18]. Genette's theory of focalization constitutes a precise description of the kinds of narrative choices open to the narrator. *Restriction* is the basic concept that defines focalization.[19] 'By focalization I therefore mean a "field" restriction, that is in fact a selection of the narrative information.'[20] Since focalization is an essentially relational phenomenon (the specific relations of selection and restriction between *story* and *discourse*), in Genette's theory what is focalized is the narrative itself. The only agent capable of focalizing it is the narrator, though the focal point of that restriction *may be* – but not necessarily so – a character, in which case we speak of a narrative focalized *on* a given character.

There are three basic codes of focalization: zero focalization or nonfocalization, internal focalization, and external focalization.

(a) In *zero- or nonfocalization* the narrator imposes minimal restrictions upon himself: he goes in and out of his most diverse characters' minds *ad libitum*; his freedom to go in and out of places, from which characters are absent, is equally great. The focus ('foyer') of the narrative is constantly displaced from one fictional mind to the next, almost indiscriminately. This code of focalization corresponds to the traditional omniscient narrator, typical of much of nineteenth-century narrative, out of favour for a long time but coming back into its own in contemporary fiction (cf García Márquez' *Cien años de soledad*).

(b) In *internal focalization* the 'foyer' of the narrative coincides with one fictional mind;[21] that is to say, the narrator *restricts* his freedom in order to select only the narrative information that the cognitive and spatio-temporal limitations of a given character may allow. The narrative may be focalized on one character consistently (*fixed* internal focalization), as in Joyce's *A Portrait of the Artist as a Young Man*; it may also be focalized on a restricted number of characters, with alternating displacements of the 'foyer' (*variable* internal focalization), as in Flaubert's *Madame Bovary*, with both Charles and Emma as alternating focal characters. The last form of internal focalization is *multiple* internal focalization, in which the same series of events is narrated from different perspectives. Often the various focal characters are cast in the role of the narrator; this is typical of the epistolary novel, in which the narrative is alternately focalized on each of the epistolary correspondents.

(c) *External focalization*, despite the claims of certain narratologists to the contrary,[22] is also a restriction that the narrator imposes upon his narrative, except that here the restriction is not constituted by the limitations of fictional minds; quite the contrary, in external focalization the restriction is constituted by the very *inaccessibility* of fictional minds. 'In external focalization the focus ['foyer'] is located at a given point of the diegetic universe, chosen by the narrator, *outside the characters*, thereby excluding all possibility of information on the thoughts of no matter who.'[23]

As Genette observes,[24] three modes of focalization coexist in the *Recherche*: focalization on Marcel as a hero (internal), focalization on Marcel as narrator (also internal), and zero or nonfocalization, the narrator contradictorily adopting the omniscient role of his traditional counterpart, going in and out of other characters' minds – even into that of the dying Bergotte. This constitutes a striking violation of the code, forbidden by the very choice of first person narrative, which implies a pre-focalization.[25]

These focal displacements, particularly the ones between the

122 Metaphoric narration

experiencing and the narrating selves, are also reflected on metaphoric narration. In general the strongly metaphorical narrated perceptions are focalized on the hero, though often they are also focalized on the mature narrator, especially in the form of gnomic discourse, in which case one may adopt Genette's later views and call this pseudo-focalization on the narrator 'extradiegetic information.'[26] Genette has remarked on 'the highly subjective nature of Proustian descriptions, always bound to a perceptual activity of the hero's. Proustian descriptions are rigorously focalized: not only does their "duration" never exceed that of real contemplation, but their content never exceeds what is actually perceived by the contemplator.'[27] I might add that very often the metaphors used in those descriptions, focalized on the contemplator, betray his mood and idiosyncrasies. The following metaphorical description of M. de Palancy is a case in point: 'et cependant, derrière le sien [i.e. 'monocle'], M. de Palancy qui, avec sa grosse tête de carpe aux yeux ronds, se déplaçait lentement au mileu des fêtes en desserrant d'instant en instant ses mandibules comme pour chercher son orientation, avait l'air de transporter seulement avec lui un fragment accidentel, et peut-être purement symbolique, du vitrage de son aquarium ...' (I, 327).

Stephen Ullmann finds this particular metaphor unpleasant and far-fetched but he remarks that it is understandable as an expression of Swann's ironic mood at Mme de Sainte-Euverte's 'soirée.'[28] Indeed, if this image of the aristocrat is rather grotesque, it is mainly because the description is focalized on Swann; M. de Palancy himself would, no doubt, strongly disagree with such a representation.

Earlier in this chapter, in 1.1, we examined the transforming power of metaphoric narration in the presentation of diegetic space. Metaphoric narration may weave complex superimpositions that interact with the main diegetic universe, but often the weaving becomes so intricate that it may end up concealing and even supplanting the supposedly 'main' diegetic universe. At times, whole areas of that universe are metaphorically constituted, so that there remains no denotative plane, only a metaphoric existence (cf the 'chasseur arborescent,' the witchlike cashiers [I, 811], or the 'fishy' M. de Palancy himself). If it is true that an-*other* reality, which is the nature of the descriptive dimension of metaphoric narration, is responsible for the manifold transformations in diegetic space, *focalization* is responsible for their quality. If the aquarium metaphor sarcastically conjures the grotesque M. de Palancy, this is because it is focalized on Swann. If the steeple of Saint-Hilaire is transformed into a 'brioche' (I, 65), or the

Narrative modulations 123

horizon at Balbec looks like a salmon (I, 803), this is not only the result of a *neutral* metonymic contiguity with the diegetic environment but of focalization. The fact that these descriptions are focalized on Marcel suggests that the transformations are not just there, in diegetic contiguity, but are also the metaphorical creatures of a hungry Marcel.

Thus similar places may be differently described due to differences in the immediate diegetic environment and in time or light, but also – and very significantly – the transformations may be due to differences in perception. A beautiful example of this is Mme Swann's salon, described twice, at two different diegetic moments and focalized on two different characters: Swann and young Marcel. Let us examine first the description of her winter salon, mainly focalized on the experiencing hero and not on the mature narrator:

> Odette avait maintenant, dans son salon, au commencement de l'hiver, des chrysanthèmes énormes et d'une variété de couleurs comme Swann jadis n'eût pu en voir chez elle. Mon admiration pour eux ... venait sans doute de ce que, rose-pâles comme la soie Louis xv de ses fauteuils, blancs de neige comme sa robe de chambre en crêpe de Chine, ou d'un rouge métallique comme son samovar, *ils superposaient à celle du salon une décoration supplémentaire,* d'un coloris aussi riche, aussi raffiné, mais *vivante* et qui *ne durerait que quelques jours.* Mais j'étais touché par ce que ces chrysanthèmes avaient *moins d'éphémère que de relativement durable* par rapport à ces tons, aussi *roses* ou aussi *cuivrés, que le soleil couché* exalte si somptueusement dans la brume des fins d'après-midi de novembre et *qu'après les avoir aperçus avant que j'entrasse chez Mme Swann, s'éteignant dans le ciel, je retrouvais prolongés, transposés dans la palette enflammée des fleurs.* Comme des *feux* arrachés par un grand coloriste à l'instabilité de l'atmosphère et du soleil, afin qu'ils vinssent orner une demeure humaine, ils m'invitaient, ces chrysanthèmes, et malgré toute ma tristesse, à goûter avidement pendant cette heure du thé les plaisirs si *courts* de novembre dont ils faisaient *flamboyer* près de moi la splendeur intime et mystérieuse. (I, 595–6) (italics mine)

The passage is extraordinarily rich in metaphoric effects, deriving not so much from the explicit, verbal metaphors as from the metaphoric *relations* between the different elements of the description. The relations are of three kinds: *superimposition, incorporation,* and *transposition* – the one effect underlying them all is homogeneity and continuity in the presentation of diegetic space. In this 'tableau monochrome' – or, more precisely, 'tri-chrome' – the interplay of three colours (white,

124 Metaphoric narration

pale pink, and red), in carefully differentiated degrees of intensity, is doubly rooted in diegetic time and space: sunset at the beginning of winter, and Mme Swann's salon with the chrysanthemums prolonging the sunset. The chrysanthemums are at the centre of all three kinds of metaphoric relations:

(a) *Superimposition*. The flowers are the living, natural counterpart to the man-made decoration of the salon. In this superimposition, two other kinds of relations are at work simultaneously: one of *opposition* (natural/man-made), the other of *identity* (by means of the three corresponding similes, the chrysanthemums prolong the colours in the decoration of the salon and in Odette's 'robe de chambre'). The effect is of homogeneity and continuity (a conjunctive relation) in the midst of radical opposition (a disjunctive relation), and therefore a replica of the process of metaphorization itself.

(b) *Incorporation*. The same is true of the second kind of metaphorical relationship. Governed by the central spatial opposition, inside/outside, the pink and copper-coloured chrysanthemums effectively bring the sunset into Mme Swann's salon, thus establishing conjunctive relations between the sunset and the flowers in the midst of the disjunctive relations marked by the spatial opposition.

(c) *Transposition*. As the sunset is metaphorically incorporated into the salon, it is simultaneously transposed into a work of art, by means of the art metaphor, 'la palette enflammée,' which marks the transition from the sunset-flower to the sunset-painting. The art metaphor is then developed by the simile 'comme des feux arrachés par un grand coloriste.' Thus, the flowers themselves constitute 'a centre of aesthetic radiation,' as Genette has called this phenomenon:[29] all the metaphors and similes are generated around them, transforming them, now into an ephemeral setting sun, now into a more permanent work of art. The chrysanthemums remain cohesive objects that do not lose their diegetic identity as flowers, yet are capable of simultaneously encompassing and radiating vastly different metaphoric transformations.

The flowers are also at the centre of the extraordinary *temporal gradations* that inform the whole passage with their particular dynamism. These temporal gradations are made to coincide with the three metaphorical relations examined: the colour superimposition is relatively static (though the flowers are already described as a more *ephemeral* form of decoration); the incorporation of the sunset, as we shall see, is described in strongly dynamic terms; while in the final transposition there is a beautiful synthesis of both: the static and the dynamic coexisting in a creative tension – 'des feux arrachés ... à l'instabilité de l'atmosphère et du soleil.' Let us examine these effects more closely.

Unlike the relatively static quality of the relation of superimposition, there is a remarkable dynamism in the metaphorical prolongation of the sunset, generated by subtle temporal modulations: oppositions such as before/after, ephemeral/permanent, are *relativized*, almost made *reversible*, by the fusion of diegetic space. The chrysanthemums are first described as ephemeral ('ne durerait que quelques jours'). In relation to the sunset, however, they are declared to have something 'moins d'éphémère que de relativement durable.' A greater sense of permanence is then suggested by the sudden art metaphor – 'la palette enflammée des fleurs.' The contemplation of the sunset is also carefully located in time, in a 'before' and an 'after' made unstable due to the pressure of metaphorization. In diegetic time, the contemplation of the sunset occurs *outside*, *before* Marcel arrives at Mme Swann's. Such diegetic precisions imply the following *spatio-temporal equivalences/oppositions*: outside = before = light (the pink and red 'tons'); inside = after = darkness ('s'éteignant dans le ciel'). The metaphorical incorporation of the sunset *reverses* those diegetic equivalences: the fiery chrysanthemums *inside* bring time back, making the sunset last longer. As so often in Proust, space becomes a metaphor for time: 'inside' has now become both 'before' and 'after'; the passage of time is abolished: the metaphor fixes the ephemeral sunset in a timeless image.

'L'euphorie d'un espace continu,' time grasped and transposed into a work of art, the ephemeral made to endure, even if only relatively so. This ecstatic vision of Mme Swann and her salon seems to be the projection of young Marcel's imagination rather than just a more or less impartial description produced by the narrator in his own voice. It is thus focalized on Marcel as experiencing hero, in full consonance with his exalted opinion of the Swanns at the time.

In fact, the whole process of idealization of Mme Swann – initiated in the last part of *Du côté de chez Swann* (I, 417–24) – continues in the descriptions of her winter and spring salons, reaches a climactic point as she is herself metaphorically transformed into a flower, and finally ends in the apotheosized salute made by the Prince de Sagan at the end of 'Autour de Mme Swann' (I, 592–641). Nowhere in the whole of the *Recherche*, before or after this section, is Odette presented in such flattering terms. Mme Swann in the zenith of her glory becomes a flower, 'la plus belle fleur et qui ne s'ouvrirait qu'à midi'; an artist, 'créateur qui a accompli son oeuvre et ne se soucie du reste' (I, 636); her toilette, a work of art comparable to that of a musician, 'comme ces parties d'orchestre auxquelles le compositeur a donné tous ses soins,' comparable even to a cathedral, 'comme ces sculptures gothiques d'une cathédrale .... aussi parfaites que les bas-reliefs du grand porche'; her elegance and knowledge of her art are paid homage to by the others, 'comme à une sagesse supérieure dont elle eût été la grande prêtresse' (1, 638). Flower, artist, priestess, goddess, queen ('As 'twere all life's epitome!'). The extraordinarily high semantic overdetermination and redundancy with which Mme Swann is described almost turn her into a mythical creature. And the narrative modulation that achieves these incredible effects is a strongly *consonant focalization* on the adolescent Marcel. This *formal* modulation corresponds to the recurrent *thematic* motif of the self colouring reality even as reality is perceived: 'j'acceptais d'avance comme une révélation l'apparition de leur toilette, de leur attelage, de mille détails au sein desquels *je mettais ma croyance comme une âme intérieure qui donnait la cohésion d'un chef-d'oeuvre* à cet ensemble éphémère et mouvant' (1, 418) (italics mine).

Nevertheless, as the process of idealization is intensified, at the very height of Mme Swann's glory, the narrator begins to sound a few dissonant notes – one of them being the metaphoric (and ironic) allusions to her 'virginity' (cf chapter 5, 1.2). At its climax, Mme Swann's almost mythical stature is subtly deflated by a cluster of metaphors appearing in succession. Her admirers are suddenly metaphorized as lifeless pieces in a clock mechanism – 'Il déclenchait seulement, comme un mouvement d'horlogerie, la gesticulation de petits personnages salueurs.' The prince's salute is like one in a 'tableau ancien,' rendering the whole scene allegorical of the ritual salute to 'la Femme,' but it is alternatively described as a salute in a *circus* or a *theatre*; while 'la Femme' is immediately deflated down to a disreputable woman 'que sa mère ou sa soeur ne pourraient pas fréquenter' (1, 640). The dissonant notes of the farcical and the vulgar, though subtly demythicizing the idealized woman, actually emphasize, by sheer contrast, the strongly focalized quality of this picture of Odette. It is interesting to notice that this deflation of the idealized woman is accompanied by a corresponding reversion of names: from Mme Swann back to Odette.

Now, the description of her salon in 'Un amour de Swann' offers a series of similarities and differences that are worth going into in order to describe the different effects of meaning deriving from two descriptions of two very similar places, focalized on two different characters:

L'isolement et le vide de ces courtes rues ... la neige qui était restée dans le jardin et aux arbres, le négligé de la saison, le voisinage de la nature, donnaient quelque chose de plus mystérieux à la chaleur, aux fleurs qu'il avait trouvées en entrant.

... une caisse rectangulaire où fleurissaient comme dans une serre une rangée de ces *gros chrysanthèmes* encore rares à cette époque ... Swann ... avait eu plaisir, cette fois, à voir la pénombre de la pièce *zébrée* de *rose, d'orangé et de blanc* par les *rayons odorants de ces astres éphémères* qui s'allument dans les jours gris. Odette l'avait reçu en robe de chambre de soie rose, le cou et les bras nus. Elle l'avait fait asseoir près d'elle dans un des nombreux retraits mystérieux qui étaient ménagés dans les enfoncements du salon, protégés par d'immenses palmiers contenus dans des cache-pot de Chine, ou par des paravents auxquels étaient fixés des photographies, des noeuds de rubans et des éventails ... quand le valet de chambre était venu apporter successivement les nombreuses lampes qui, presque toutes enfermées dans des potiches chinoises, brûlaient isolées ou par couples, toutes sur des meubles différents comme sur des autels et qui dans le crépuscule déjà presque nocturne de cette fin d'après-midi d'hiver *avaient fait reparaître un coucher de soleil plus durable, plus rose et plus humain* ... (I, 219–21) (italics mine)

As will be noticed, many diegetic elements and determinations in this passage are identical to the corresponding ones in the passage from 'Autour de Mme Swann':[30] big chrysanthemums, the same three colours (white, pink, and red), Odette's 'robe de chambre' of the same colour as one set of flowers; the chrysanthemums in both passages compared to the sun; in both the sunset brought inside after it has been 'extinguished' outside. Both passages have the same temporal determinations (shortly after sunset on a winter evening); the ephemeral quality of the flowers is highlighted. Finally, both Marcel and Swann have come from outside, where it is cold and getting dark, indoors where it is warm and the sunset seems prolonged.

Yet the overall effect is completely different in the two passages. In this one, unlike the one from 'Autour de Mme Swann,' metaphorical *relations* among these diegetic elements have not been drawn as an *organizing* principle, so that the reader does not perceive an effect of cohesion and unity in the presentation of diegetic space. In the passage focalized on Swann the metaphorical effects of meaning are isolated and restricted to actual verbal metaphors. In fact, there are even more verbal metaphors here than in the description focalized on Marcel – 'zébrée,' 'rayons odorants' (a synaesthesic metaphor), 'astres éphé-

128 Metaphoric narration

mères,' 'allument' – against the meagre 'palette enflammée des fleurs' and 'feux arrachés' (itself belonging to a simile). Significantly, however, there are far more similes in the description focalized on Marcel. The effect of homogeneity there contrasts sharply with that of heterogeneity in the one focalized on Swann. Formally, this is due mainly to the different principles of organization underlying each descriptive passage: a principle of *analogy*, generating metaphorical effects of meaning even in the absence of verbal metaphors, is at work in Marcel's; while a principle of *juxtaposition* and *disjunction*, despite the numerous isolated verbal metaphors, is at work in Swann's. In the latter, Odette's 'robe de chambre' is also of the same colour as one set of flowers, but the relation is never developed; the effect of the sunset brought in from outside is split between the chrysanthemums – as 'astres éphémères' – and the Chinese lamps, thus making the metaphorical incorporation *discontinuous*. The effect of both metaphors remains local, without any relationship being drawn between the two. Nor is the inside/outside opposition/fusion activated in this passage as the organizing principle. The fact that Swann comes from outside remains a local notation, of the purely realistic or mimetic kind, one in the list of items that make up the description of the streets around Odette's house. The elements are all there but simply *juxtaposed* and/or *listed*, with only a few isolated metaphoric concentrations here and there in the verbal texture of the description but without creating any cumulative effects. The principle that dominates this description, then, despite the relatively numerous *verbal* metaphors, is that of the *catalogue*: the items are just listed, ordered on logical and spatial principles,[31] but with no attempt at the superimposition of any other networks of *metaphorical relations*.

By contrast, in the description of Mme Swann's winter salon, the one focalized on Marcel, all elements are ruled by relations of a metaphorical nature – fusion and continuity at the heart of radical opposition such as inside/outside, natural/man-made, ephemeral/permanent. In turn, all these metaphorical relations are orchestrated in such a way as to impress the reader with the sense of *gradation* and *progression*. By means of a carefully graded redundancy, there is a clear semantic intensification in the three colours, corresponding metaphorically to the similar gradations inherent in the colours themselves: from white to deep red. The white – dominant in the long description of Mme Swann's 'robe de chambre' that precedes the chrysanthemums description – disappears after the three similes *superimposing* the flowers onto the decoration; the pink survives beyond these three well into the sunset

Narrative modulations

incorporation ('aussi roses'), but disappears after this simile; while the red continues to multiply and grow in intensity in the art metaphor *transposition* ('enflammée,' 'feux,' 'flamboyer'). The gradual intensification also corresponds to the progression from the static to the dynamic and to the synthesis of both that the art metaphor achieves.

All these formal differences between the two descriptions have an important thematic correspondent: the difference in *vision*. As we have seen, the diegetic components of both salons are, in many respects, identical; yet because one description is focalized on Swann and the other on Marcel, the descriptive effects are radically different: in Swann's it is the purely sensuous vision of objects perceived in relative isolation and discontinuity; in Marcel's, the ecstatic vision of time and space unified.

The difference in the effects is largely brought about by the strong presence of *metaphoric narration* in Marcel's vision and its relative absence in Swann's. For we must remember that the *isolated* metaphor, at the level of the manifestation in language, *is the weakest – because most virtual – form of metaphoric narration*. It is in threaded metaphor and in the extended simile, as well as in the organizing principle of the process itself, that metaphoric narration becomes fully actualized.

According to Michel Leguern,[32] the simile is a very rational structure that keeps both semantic fields in their appropriate place and therefore entails no semantic incompatibility. For this reason, he argues, the simile lacks the 'power of persuasion,' the appeal to the sensitivity and imagination that the 'true' metaphorical identification has.[33] This may be true of the isolated metaphor as against the isolated simile in poetry, but when metaphorization is at work in a narrative text, the 'power of persuasion' of metaphor operates quite differently. In a narrative text, effects of meaning are generated *in time* – that is, the time of reading. Therefore, redundancy in the more extended forms of metaphorization creates *cumulative* effects of meaning that are perceived by the reader as more strongly metaphorical than the effects produced by the isolated metaphor, however vivid it may be. That is why the metaphoric effects of meaning are more intense in the passage focalized on Marcel, despite the relative absence of *verbal* metaphor.

One last observation to be made regarding metaphorization in a narrative text is that the metaphoric *description*, by multiplying its isotopic connections, inevitably becomes *metaphoric narration*, due to the series of transformations implied. This feature of metaphorization emphasizes even more the narrative function of description, particularly in Proustian narrative.

2.1 *Metaphoric narration and ambiguity in focalization*

Metaphor is a privileged instrument for *duplicity*; its very existence as a 'figure du discours' inevitably betrays the speaker – in this case, the narrator – behind it, but its content may sometimes create the illusion that it is well rooted in the diegetic universe; we have seen this in the so-called 'diegetic metaphors.' The *constructed degrees* of meaning trace back the path of its production to the narrator who is the ultimate source of the metaphor, while its *given degrees* may be borrowed from the immediate diegetic environment, thereby emphasizing the illusion of the diegetic filiation of metaphor; that is, the illusion of metaphor's being the direct result of the environment or being directly produced by fictional characters who in most cases have not actually said, or even thought, in those terms.

This duplicity gives rise to an interesting problem in perspective. Sometimes, it is precisely the diegetic content of metaphor that is responsible for the ambiguity. I have argued, for example, that the two descriptions of Odette's salon are so different because they are focalized on two different characters at two different times of their lives. But it could also be argued that the descriptions are different because the salons are diegetically different, that the discontinuity and heterogeneity of the salon in 'Un amour de Swann' reflect, metaphorically, similar qualities in Odette herself. Thus, in 'Un amour,' the description of her body is equivalent to that of her salon: 'quant à son corps qui était admirablement fait, il était *difficile d'en apercevoir la continuité ... tant le corsage ... donnait à la femme l'air d'être composée de pièces différentes mal emmanchées les unes dans les autres* (I, 197) (italics mine).

The argument seems quite plausible, perhaps even more so than the one that attributes those qualities to focalization. Moreover, even if focalization were solely responsible for these effects, we would still have to account for the problem of the *identity* of so many diegetic components in both salons – which the text so slyly seems to forget – and the similar isolated metaphors to which their combination gives rise. The narrator's inadvertence or oblivion? Perhaps. In the passage from 'Autour de Mme Swann' he says that 'maintenant' Odette had enormous chrysanthemums, as if she had never had them before, when we know she had.

The argument might be followed consequently on the same lines to interpret Mme Swann's winter salon: that the description is not idealized, that it is Odette herself who has favourably changed – the different effect resulting from a diegetic change in her rather than from a difference in focalization. After all, the narrator in his own voice has described that diegetic change in the same terms of continuity as against discontinuity, thereby also establishing a line of continuity in the *narrative voice*: this is the same narrator who described Odette in 'Un amour de Swann'; the terms he uses here are almost the same as the earlier ones; he seems to remember his own earlier description almost in a kind of narratorial analepsis.

> Les coussins, le 'strapontin' ... avaient disparu, ainsi que ces corsages à basques qui, dépassant la jupe et raidis par des baleines, avaient ajouté si longtemps à Odette un ventre postiche et lui avaient donné l'air *d'être composée de pièces disparates* qu'aucune individualité ne reliait. La verticale des 'effilés' et la courbe des ruches avaient cédé la place à l'inflexion d'un corps qui faisait palpiter la soie comme la sirène bat l'onde ... maintenant qu'il s'était dégagé, comme une forme organisée et vivante, du long chaos et de l'enveloppement nébuleux des modes détrônées. Mais Mme Swann ... *avait su garder un vestige de certaines d'entre elles, au mileiu même de celles qui les avaient remplacées* ... Comme dans un beau style qui superpose des formes différentes et que fortifie une tradition cachée ...
> (I, 618–19) (italics mine)

The *narratorial* filiation of this account of Odette's change is undeniable. Therefore one could interpret all those effects of continuity, of superimposition, and of the fusion of spaces in the description of her salon as a metaphorical reflection of Odette's own artistic qualities. 'Comme dans un beau style qui *superpose* des formes différentes': thus Mme Swann, the artist, seems to possess the same stylistic attributes in her own person as the ones that have gone into the making of the description of her salon. She could be therefore 'read' as the diegetic counterpart of the artist, including the verbal artist, and therefore a counterpart of the narrator or Proust himself, since her achievements in the art of dressing are like those proclaimed by Marcel as the supreme qualities of style: the superimposition of different forms, the intangible but perceptible presence of the past in the concrete forms of the present, giving it 'le soubassement, la consistance d'une riche orchestration' (II, 396). Plausible. But what about the dissonant needles the deflate Odette so mercilessly?

The point could be argued indefinitely. Much later, in *La prisonnière*, Marcel says that the two most elegant women he knows are Mme Swann and Mme de Guermantes, and that of the two the duchess is the more elegant. That is what he *says*, but the fact is that Mme de Guermantes's toilettes *are described in exactly the same terms as Mme Swann's – without the idealization*: 'je trouvais la duchesse ennuagée dans la brume d'une robe en crêpe de Chine gris ... je me laissais envahir par l'atmosphère qu'il dégageait, comme la fin de certaines après-midi ouatée en gris perle par un brouillard vaporeux; si, au contraire, cette robe de chambre était chinoise avec des flammes jaunes et rouges, je la regardais comme un couchant qui s'allume ...' (III, 33).

As will be noticed, the tendency to associate beautiful clothes with the outside world – the season, the time of day, the weather – may no longer be attributed solely to the unifying imagination of an adolescent Marcel. This seems to be a consistent and constant trait in the mature narrator. What is missing from the description of Mme de Guermantes's robes is the careful orchestration and gradation in the effects of meaning produced, the sustained effort in creating the illusion of ecstasy. It is this sustained effort and its achievements that make Mme Swann infinitely more beautiful and elegant than Mme de Guermantes, despite the narrator's avowed preferences; *textually* the idealized Mme Swann remains longer in the reader's imagination as the 'priestess' of elegance, as the accomplished artist in the 'beau style' of dressing.

The ambiguity, I believe, is fruitfully unresolved; in fact, it is the *recurrence* of certain metaphors that renders their filiation ambiguous. Metaphors that may at first sight seem clearly attributable to one character's vision may, *due to redundancy*, turn out to be a trait in the narrator or a specific vehicle chosen for expressing or developing a given theme. A case in point is that aquarium metaphor that gives life to the grotesque M. de Palancy (I, 327, cf p 122 above). Examined in terms of the *local* context, we tend to attribute the metaphor solely to Swann because it corresponds quite well with his ironic mood of the moment and his consistently ironic speeches elsewhere. But the very same metaphor, with appropriate variations, crops up in many other places.[34] This recurring metaphor is interesting because it questions the initial impression of focalized metaphoric narration; it also puts into question Genette's theory that metaphor in Proust is *always* founded on metonymical relations of contiguity with the diegetic environment. In the case of M. de Palancy (as in the case of the honey metaphor, for that matter), there is no diegetic motivation whatsoever.

When we find the aquarium metaphors elsewhere, they seem diegetically founded because they occur in the marine environment of Balbec. The conjunction of light and large windows, with the sea forever in the background, produces a clearly motivated metaphor: the dining-room

> devenait comme un immense et merveilleux aquarium devant la paroi de verre duquel la population ouvrière de Balbec, les pêcheurs et aussi les familles de petits bourgeois, invisibles dans l'ombre, s'écrasaient au vitrage pour apercevoir, lentement balancée dans des remous d'or, la vie luxueuse de ces gens, aussi extraordinaire pour les pauvres que celle de poissons et de mollusques étranges (une grande question sociale, de savoir si la paroi de verre protégera toujours le festin des bêtes merveilleuses et si les gens obscurs qui regardent avidement dans la nuit ne viendront pas les ceuillir dans leur aquarium et les manger). (I, 681)

It is to be noted, incidentally, that this metaphor, in its local context, is clearly focalized on the workers watching outside, while its multiple connections in the parenthetical prolongation of the metaphor evince an interesting shift in perspective: inside the parentheses, as inside the dining-room–aquarium, it is the narrator, and no longer the workers, who meditates on the limits of such precarious social demarcations.

All the narrative and descriptive elements that compose this threaded metaphor may be said to be prompted by the immediate diegetic environment: the water and fish in this metaphoric aquarium are from the neighbouring sea; the glass windows, establishing clear inside/outside demarcations, are furnished by the hotel environment; the light is the immediate result of the diegetic time of day (dinner time). The same elements appear in the Rivebelle aquarium and women-fish metaphors (I, 813). Again the seaside resort provides enough diegetic motivation. A few diegetic elements have changed: in the women-fish metaphor, the light comes from the sun, and it is earlier in the day; in the Rivebelle aquarium metaphor, later in the evening, the perspective – as compared to the one in Balbec – has changed; the aquarium is now outside and seen from the dining-room, 'comme les végétations d'un pâle et vert aquarium géant à la lumière surnaturelle' (I, 813).

At two other points in the *Recherche*, the same basic metaphor reappears but in contexts that are alien to the seaside resort and therefore have no diegetic motivation whatsoever. One is, as we have seen, the fishlike M. de Palancy (I, 327); the other occurs at the 'matinée' at Mme de Villeparisis in *Le côté de Guermantes*. Robert de Saint-Loup has just left the reunion to seek a reconciliation with Rachel. This starts a train of thoughts in the narrator, who reflects on the eternal ignorance

134 Metaphoric narration

of the lover and his inability to communicate with those who *do* know his beloved: 'D'un côté, l'amoureux se dit: "C'est un ange" ... Cependant, de l'autre côté de *la cloison de verre* à travers laquelle ces conversations *ne passeront pas plus que celles qu'échangent les promeneurs devant un aquarium*, le public dit: "Vous ne la connaissez pas? je vous en félicite, elle a volé, ruiné je ne sais pas combien de gens"' (II, 282) (italics mine). Not only is this metaphor independent of its immediate diegetic environment, its context is not even diegetic but gnomic. Yet its *thematic* relations are similar to those in the other aquarium metaphors: estrangement and non-communication.

Furthermore, the fictional situation that gave rise to the aquarium metaphor in I, 681, when replicated later in Balbec, gives rise to an entirely different metaphor. This time, unmotivated by the diegetic environment, it develops on the same *thematic* lines of non-communication and estrangement: '*l'essaim des pauvres* et des curieux attirés par le flamboiement *qu'ils ne pouvaient atteindre pendait, en noires grappes morfondues* par la bise, aux parois lumineuses et glissantes de la *ruche de verre*' (I, 806) (italics mine).

The same diegetic elements are present: the seaside resort hotel, dinner time, glass, light, an inside/outside demarcation, people outside watching the insiders. In the earlier metaphor the result was an aquarium – justified by a diegetic contiguity – here it is a honeycomb that nothing but *thematic* relations justify. What has changed is the perspective, but not the significant relationship of estrangement between the ones outside and the ones inside. In the earlier metaphor, the perspective was from the outside, from the workers who marvelled at these idle rich creatures as one marvels at strange gaudy fish; now it is the guests inside whose perspective orients not only the metaphoric production but the *tonal* value of this description: the rich see the poor as a disgusting swarm, mere insects attracted by the light of their comfort. Here one recognizes a Proustian constant in his apprehension of otherness: incomprehension or inability to communicate with the other is very often expressed in metaphors with animals or stars as the given degrees, whose contexts always orient constructed degrees in which those themes of incomprehension, non-communication, and/or estrangement are apparent.

Thus metaphoric narration, often owing to its diegetic vehicle, may create the illusion of focalized narration, may even effectively function as such in the local context, but as soon as there is redundancy in the diegetic content of the metaphors, the *narratorial* filiation is betrayed; the resulting zone of ambiguity blurs the otherwise clear-cut frontiers between the narrator and his characters and between the gnomic and narrative discourses. It is interesting to notice that critics like Jean-Pierre Richard or Inge K. Crossman, who examine, though with completely different methods, the diegetic and thematic content of Proust's figurative language, never make a distinction between metaphor belonging to the narrative discourse and that belonging to the gnomic discourse. That they can draw their illustrations from either, indiscriminately, in order to examine the continuity or consistency of a given thematic line, shows to what extent the dividing line between the two has been deliberately effaced by metaphoric narration.[35] This ambiguity has interesting effects on narrative voice.

7 Narrative voice

This aspect of the narrative reality involves the examination of the various determinations that define the narrator, no longer in terms of his *discursive* activities of selection and arrangement of the narrative material, but in terms of his *involvement* in the created fictional world and of his *identity* as narrative agent and mediator. These determinations are: temporal, relational, and functional.[1]

(a) *Temporal*. By the ineluctable constriction to choose a grammatical tense, the narrator must fix his temporal position *vis-à-vis* the fictional world he narrates: the past tense if his position is *ulterior*, the future if it is *anterior* (predictive narration), or the present tense of contemporaneous action if his position is *simultaneous* or *intercalated*.

This temporal determination is irrelevant in our study of metaphoric narration, unless we want to see in those shifts to the gnomic present (paradoxically containing an abstract narrative – the theatre-salon simile for example, cf chapter 5, 2.1) a significant shift in the narrator's temporal position; as though metaphoric narration, due to its 'other-diegeticity,' entailed a shift in temporal position as well. Nonetheless, that degree of virtuality in the narrative line may also be conveyed by the same tense of the main narrative (the 'baignoire' sequence); or there may be a convergence of the gnomic and the narrative discourses to give birth to metaphoric narration, like the long narrative of the insect and the flower, taken up now by the gnomic discourse as a meditation on botany, now by the narrative discourse as the description of the corresponding diegetic plant and insect in Mme de Guermantes's courtyard, both lines converging in the *diegetically motivated* metaphoric narration of Charlus and Jupien's homosexual encounter (II, 601–7). Whether such shifts or temporal mixtures in metaphoric narration are relevant to vocal determinations would have to be subjected to a more careful examination and consideration than the limitations of this study allow for.

(b) *Relational*. The status of the narrator is defined by a twofold relation: (i) narration and story; (ii) narration and narrative discourse.

(i) The relationship between the act of narration and its narrative content defines the narrator's degree of personal involvement in the story he tells. In *homodiegetic*, or first-person narratives, fictional character and narrator are one and the same, though displaying two distinct functions, the diegetic and the vocal, which should never be confused. If the homodiegetic narrator is the same 'person' as the hero, the narration is *autodiegetic*; if the narrator is one of the characters involved in the story but tells somebody else's, then the homodiegetic nature of the narrator is qualified as *testimonial* – he is not the hero but a witness. In *heterodiegetic*, or third-person narratives, the narrator does not participate in the related events.

(ii) The relationship drawn between the act of narration and narrative discourse defines the narrator's position in terms of *narrative level*: if the act of narration is produced within the frame of an already established narrative, then the narrator is *intradiegetic* – he is already a character before undertaking the act of narration. If the narrator assumes the primary act of narration, then he is an *extradiegetic* narrator.

(c) *Functions of the narrator*. Following Jakobson's description of the functions of language,[2] Genette offers these narrative homologues: (i) In terms of the story itself, the narrator has a strictly *narrative function*. (ii) In terms of the organization of the narrative text, the narrator exerts a *directing function* ('fonction de régie'); he marks 'its articulations, connections, interrelationships, in short, its internal organization.'[3] (iii) In terms of the relationship between the narrator and the narratee, the narrator performs a *function of communication* that subsumes both the 'phatic' and 'conative' functions in Jakobson's system.

The narrator's orientation towards himself is behind the last two functions, the *testimonial* and the *ideological*. In *Nouveau discours*,[4] Genette proposes to rename the ideological function after Susan Suleiman's *interpreting function*, because it marks, as she says, 'any interpretative comment formulated by the narrator, about the character, the context or the events.'[5]

138 Metaphoric narration

Genette has recently questioned these functions. He says that only the first is strictly narrative (and therefore identical to the whole of 'Discours du récit'), and that the other four are *extranarrative*.[6] Nevertheless, if according to his own theory, the narrative reality is made of three aspects, inextricably related – discourse, story, and narration – those other four functions cannot be called extranarrative, for each of them is related to one aspect or another. The functions of communication and of interpretation, for example, are usually performed by the gnomic discourse, which makes them, it is true, *extradiegetic* but not *extranarrative*, since the gnomic discourse is part and parcel of the aspect of *enunciation* in a narrative text.

Concerning the role of metaphor in the functions of the narrator, I shall only suggest a few openings for future examination.

In Proust, perhaps the most marked functions that heavily rely on the use of metaphors are those of *communication* and of *interpretation*. Analogies, by themselves, have an inherent function of communication, since even the most discrete comparisons, as Prince has remarked,[7] constitute signals to the narratee, thus virtually shaping the kind of reader to whom the text is addressed. In Proust, this inherent function of communication is further emphasized by his constant use of the pronouns *nous, vous, on,* which openly invite the reader to identify himself with the narrative (cf the discussion of the theatre simile in chapter 5, 2.1). Accordingly, countless similes are cast in this particular pronominal form, thus establishing an extradiegetic link between the narratee and the narrative that forcefully involves the reader personally – 'Car ils ne seraient pas, selon moi, mes lecteurs, mais les propres lecteurs d'eux-mêmes, mon livre n'étant qu'une sorte de ces verres grossissants ... mon livre, grâce auquel je leur fournirais le moyen de lire en eux-mêmes' (III, 1033).

The *interpreting function* of the narrator is also very conspicuous in the *Recherche*. Most of the abundant narrative sequences articulated metaphorically with others are usually *doubled* by a commentary from the narrator who makes the analogical connection explicitly. Very often the textual construction of the sequences alone would be enough to trigger metaphorization. A case in point is the opening of *La prisonnière*. Both structural narrative functions (i.e. 'being in bed,' ' "reading" what is going on in the street by means of a clear activity of interpretation and deciphering,' etc.) and the proliferation of metaphors drawn from the cultural-semantic field of liturgy, are evident nexus in the metaphorical articulation of this sequence with that of Léonie's Sundays in 'Combray.' These links act as connectors of isotopies and as a sort of semic intersection, the conjunctive relations upon which the interplay of disjunctive elements trigger metaphorization (*disjunctive*, diegetic elements such as: Combray/Paris, Léonie/ Marcel, 'decoding the activities in the street by means of *sight* (Léonie)/by means of *hearing* (Marcel),' etc.). The metaphoric articulation of these areas of the narrative, textually and diegetically discontinuous, is triggered by the peculiar organization of both texts, but it is reinforced – or even authorized, so to speak – by the narrator's making the analogy himself later on in his narrative (III, 78-9). Ricardou strongly objects to this Proustian practice, arguing that the comment diminishes the effectiveness of the 'metaphoric ordination' (i.e. what I have called metaphoric narration).[8] Nevertheless – for *de gustibus non est disputandum* – this particular practice is consistent with Proust's effort to efface frontiers between domains, to encompass *all*, even at the price of contradiction. We shall see, for example, how the narrative discourse and the gnomic interpenetrate and contaminate each other (cf p 145ff below). Genette's analyses of the structure of the *Recherche* show, again and again, paradoxes in every aspect: the use of mutually excluding codes of focalization,[9] the paradoxical extremes of maximal narratorial 'interference' and maximal 'mimetic' illusion coexisting in the same text,[10] and the paradox of the intemporal instant coupled with its infinite deployment in Proust's handling of narrative time.[11] In the same fashion analogical thinking pervades all: the verbal texture, the organization of the text, the narrative discourse, the diegetic content – it is, in short, elevated to an ideological position ruling even the narrator's descriptions and analyses of politics and war. Thus, metaphorization serves all purposes: a vehicle for narrative both at the level of events and at the level of description, a principle of organization, and a powerful instrument for interpretation: a lens to read the world and the self.

Let us now examine the effects of metaphoric narration on some vocal determinations: first, the role of metaphoric narration in the *thematic* relationship between metadiegetic and main narratives, and then the ambiguity in the vocal origins of certain pieces of metaphoric narration.

1 Metaphoric narration and narrative level

So far we have referred to the diegetic universe as a fictional construct of any narrative. Nonetheless, there are many narrative texts that are made up of more than one diegetic universe (the story within the story).

140 Metaphoric narration

The passage from one to the other entails a shift in narrative level and, often, a change of narrators. The story told within the frame of an already established fictional world will be designated as a metadiegetic narrative. It depends on the main narrative not only in terms of its structure but also in terms of its narrative meaning. Metadiegetic narration, says Genette,[12] establishes different types of meaningful relations with the main narrative. The first is a relation of *causality*: the metadiegetic narrative has an *explanatory* function. The second is *thematic*: relationships of *contrast* or of *analogy*. The third type 'involves no explicit relationship between the two story levels: it is the act of narration in itself that fulfills a function in the diegesis, independently of the metadiegetic content – a function of distraction, for example, and/or of obstruction.'[13]

From the vocal functions outlined above, it is clear that if metaphoric narration appears at the metadiegetic level, it will tend to establish a thematic relationship of analogy and of contrast with the main narrative.

The case of 'Un amour de Swann' is an interesting one in terms of narrative level. Due to the vast scale of the architecture of the *Recherche*, its analeptic function is not quite clear in a first reading. Likewise, the very dimensions of this vast analepsis make it appear, at first sight, as an independent novel or long short story. This apparent self-sufficiency leads to a number of interesting ambiguous effects and false perspectives in the narrative situation of 'Un amour.' As an independent narrative it could be classed as an extradiegetic, heterodiegetic narrative; that is, a third-person narrative in which the narrator does not participate in the narrated events. Seen from the perspective of the whole of the *Recherche*, however, 'Un amour,' long as it is, constitutes the narrative act of a homodiegetic narrator who already figures as a character: the Intermediary Subject. His diegetic activities, though low-keyed, are various: 'trying to sleep,' 'waking up intermittently,' 'enjoying the silence and darkness of his room,' 'dreaming,' and among these: *remembering*. This anamnesic delight is declared to be identical with the act of narration that produces not only 'Un amour' but the whole of the *Recherche* – itself a vast analepsis when seen from this peculiar perspective.[14]

The position of the Intermediary Subject *vis-à-vis* 'Un amour' is very much like that of the homodiegetic narrator of 'Sarrasine.' Balzac's story of that name is produced by an extra-homodiegetic narrator; that is, we are initially confronted by a first-person narrative in which the narrator is the same person as his hero but his *act of narration* remains *outside* the narrated world. But when that same narrator tells the story of Sarrasine, the sculptor, he has already had a diegetic function: he is the narrator-character who observes and wants to seduce his partner, and among his various strategies of seduction is this particular act of narration. At the moment in which he begins to tell his partner the story of Sarrasine, he becomes an intra-heterodiegetic narrator (he has so far narrated in the first person, but from this point his narrative will be in the third person). This is very much the same status of the narrator in 'Un amour': the extra-homodiegetic 'I' of the *Recherche* becomes an intra-heterodiegetic narrator telling Swann's story, not his own. Nonetheless, at various points, this pseudo-heterodiegetic narrator reverts to his homodiegetic status by drawing explicit analogies between Swann and himself. The strong impression of 'heterodiegeticity' is such that the intermittent reappearances of the narrator's 'I' are distinctly received as intrusions – at least in a first reading; nevertheless, they are deliberate reminders of the analeptic nature of this narrative. All the homodiegetic intrusions draw analogies between the narrator and Swann, thus constituting intimations of the essentially metaphorical nature of this text.

Now, the whole metadiegetic narrative of 'Un amour' *interacts metaphorically* with the last three chapters of *Sodome et Gomorrhe* (particularly from the soirée at La Raspelière [II, 866–1131]) and with most of *La prisonnière*. The two levels in the narrative draw a series of conjunctive and disjunctive relations that, read together, generate metaphoric effects of meaning. In both texts – 'Un amour' and *Sodome* – the Verdurins are responsible for the centripetal and the centrifugal movements that inform the narratives at a given point. Other *recurring* diegetic and thematic elements are Vinteuil's music as an experience of bliss and revelation; both women, Odette and Albertine, as 'êtres de fuite,' both suspected of homosexuality; the same experiences of boredom and jealousy that affect Swann and Marcel. In fact, the similarities are so numerous and so close, that the two narratives might be simply read as obsessively *redundant*. There are, however, important differences constituting the *disjunctive* relations that trigger metaphoric narration and give these two narratives in conjunction a meaning that is radically other than just redundancy. I have already made reference to the differences in spiritual evolution entailed by the confrontation of the two Vinteuil sequences in disjunctive relation.[15] Other differences *on the basis of similarity* are also narratively significant.

The movement in 'Un amour' goes from the centripetal to the

centrifugal. In the first part, all the meetings of the lovers take place at the Verdurins, where they 'communicate.' As soon as Swann is 'excommunicated' from the Verdurins, the centrifugal movement begins; henceforward his jealous persecution will be projected onto the diegetic space. As he pursues the unattainable, impenetrable Odette, outside, there is a parallel spiritual progression (or regression?) and intensification of his jealousy, with each discovery perceived as more sordid and painful than the last: from the all-too individual Forcheville, through hints of countless anonymous men in brothels, to the suspicion of homosexuality. Homosexuality, as the last stage in this progression, constitutes the nadir of Swann's jealousy.

In the relationship of Marcel and Albertine we notice a *reversal* in the movement. In the first phase of their relationship, Albertine is a free agent and must be pursued; in the second she is Marcel's prisoner. Significantly Albertine becomes Marcel's prisoner *after* 'elle avait renoncé à l'idée d'aller faire une croisière' (III, 10). Odette's frequent 'croisières' (I, 374), by contrast, constitute the farthest point in spatial dispersion, the greatest distance between the pursuer and the pursued. In *La prisonnière* the distance is reduced to zero by Albertine's 'voluntary' surrender of herself and of her projected cruise. But physically imprisoned or in flight, the beloved remains spiritually inaccessible – spiritual inaccessibility, in itself, constituting one of the many *conjunctive* relations in the metaphorical articulation of these narratives.

Swann's crowning discovery, homosexuality, is only the point of departure for Marcel. In *La prisonnière*, the concept of love is pushed further into the dark zone of homosexuality. Swann is bored with Odette until he finds that she is attractive and desirable to others (I, 271) – the inevitable triangularity of desire; as Girard would say, 'Proustian desire is *always* a borrowed desire.'[16] Here *love is identical with jealousy*, as though jealousy were the only possible form of love in the Proustian world. Swann's jealousy, and therefore his love, is intensified by his successive discoveries. But it is not until the whole story is 'repeated' in Marcel and Albertine that we realize the full significance of homosexuality: Marcel is bored with Albertine, ready to break with her, when he discovers – or thinks he does – Albertine's homosexuality. *Then* he falls in love. The intricacies of the love = jealousy = desire identity in Proust's work are lit up by the other's desire. The beloved's involvement with an-*other*, as we saw in Swann, renders her lovable because then she becomes unattainable and immersed in the realm of the *other*. With the repetition of this pattern – 'being bored

Narrative voice 143

with the beloved until jealous of another' – homosexuality *in disjunction* becomes metaphorically significant: homosexuality as the extreme form of otherness (and therefore of desire?).[17] And here the dark regions of the *Recherche* begin, a darkness deepened by the second important metaphoric relation established between the metadiegetic and the main narrative: Charlus-Morel (in counterpoint to Swann-Odette and Marcel-Albertine).

We have seen how a double movement, centripetal and centrifugal, informs the whole of 'Un amour,' with the Verdurins at the centre of this double movement. We have seen how this movement is *reversed* in Marcel and Albertine, but in this latter relationship the Verdurins play a very secondary role. Not so with Charlus and Morel. Exactly the same pattern of 'Un amour' is replicated: a first, relatively idyllic stage in the relationship between Charlus and Morel has the Verdurins' salon as its point of convergence, its privileged space of communication. But like Swann before him, and for similar reasons, Charlus is cruelly 'excommunicated'; the Verdurins turn Morel against him, just as they once turned Odette against Swann. As in 'Un amour,' the whole theme of 'la femme entretenue' is replayed here, including the same kind of blindness on the lover's part. Again, it is the disjunctive element that triggers metaphorization: Morel, in the exact position of 'la femme entretenue,' inevitably and by *metaphorical extension* identifies Charlus with Swann and Marcel (and consequently Morel with Odette and Albertine). That Swann's love story should be 'repeated' but *split* between two couples, a homosexual and a heterosexual one, greatly emphasizes the *metaphorical identification* of the three couples.

If Swann is the avowed 'prefiguration' or avatar of Marcel, Charlus is his dark *alter ego*: at the frontiers between the same and the other.[18] How deliberate are all these metaphorical parallels? This question is difficult to answer, though the narrator says, cryptically, in the midst of his botanic-homosexual meditations, that he had 'déjà tiré de la ruse apparente des fleurs une conséquence sur toute une partie inconsciente de l'oeuvre littéraire' (II, 603). This unconscious part seems to be in keeping with the subtle valorization of homosexuality (and despite the more consistent and vociferous devalorization) as the dark, arbitrary, yet necessary side of creation (III, 261–4): for without the devoted efforts of Mlle Vinteuil's friend, no septet and therefore no wholeness in the perception of the musician's universe; without the baron's efforts and without Morel's interpretative art, no renown, therefore no circulation, no dissemination of the work of art, which, according to Marcel, is the only true communication between individuals – 'Grâce à l'art, au lieu de voir un seul monde, le nôtre, nous le voyons se multiplier ...' (III, 895–6).

As we have seen, the dimensions of this particular metaphorical interaction are truly vast, but even on this scale the same principles of metaphoric narration at the level of the organization of the text are observable. Because of its extension, 'Un amour,' whose function is essentially *analeptic*, is transformed into a metadiegetic narrative, extension itself becoming a phenomenon of narrative level. The whole narrative text, like the more manageable sequences that we have analysed, is metaphorically articulated with two other very long and complex texts (the Charlus-Morel and the Marcel-Albertine narratives). Since the three are textually discontinuous, the mode of articulation is *virtual*: through the mediation of retrospective reading, a number of diegetic and thematic elements interacting conjunctively and disjunctively bring about metaphoric narration. The elements are of various kinds: (a) a series of *narrative functions* abstracted from the specific events ('being bored with the beloved until discovering her attraction to others,' 'being "kept" by the lover,' 'the beloved turned against the lover by an agent that initially seems favourable to the relationship,' etc.), in which there is always *redundancy*. Nevertheless, *based on that common ground of redundancy*, a number of *disjunctive* elements are made to play against it, thus triggering metaphorization (Swann falls in love with Odette when he discovers that she is attractive to *men*; Marcel with Albertine when he discovers she is attractive to *women*; Odette and Morel in the position of 'la femme entretenue,' etc.); (b) specific diegetic elements repeated, verbatim, in disjunctive functions (the particular 'cruise' motif, diegetically actualized and multiplied in Odette, sacrificed in the case of Albertine); (c) the explicit analogies made by the narrator's gnomic discourse.

It might be argued that if the narrator himself makes the analogies, then the metaphorical mode of articulation should be actual, not virtual. First of all, there is the undeniable textual discontinuity, which in itself activates the retrospective reading at the basis of the virtual mode of articulation. Secondly, although the narrator constantly makes these analogies, he never goes into the details of *how* one situation interacts metaphorically with another. It is as though, conscious of the vast scale of his design and of the role of oblivion in reading as in life,[19] the narrator felt the need to call his reader's attention to the analogies, thereby calling his attention to the role of analogy itself in the construction of the *Recherche*. The narrator only *triggers* the act of retrospective reading without engaging himself in a

Narrative voice

detailed interpretation or analysis of the elements that relate conjunctively and disjunctively. He may do so later in *Le temps retrouvé* when he does embark on a long analytical meditation about his whole life, which is no other than the diegetic universe of the *Recherche*.

One last observation to be made about metaphoric narration and narrative level is that when the metaphorical articulation of two narrative sequences or texts entails a change in narrative level, the metadiegetic narrative tends to have a thematic function of simultaneous analogy and contrast. This is due to the particular simultaneity of disjunctive and conjunctive relations, so characteristic of the process of metaphorization itself.

2   Metaphoric narration and vocal ambiguity

Marcel Muller has called attention to a very important 'hypostasis' of the 'I': the Intermediary Subject. So ambiguous is his position that he might be easily interpreted either as an 'aging *Hero*' or as the '*Narrator*' himself in the recent past.[20] Strictly speaking, however, the narrator cannot be this insomniac avatar, since this latter constitutes the narrative content of an *act of narration* that already embodies him and can only be produced by someone whose temporal position is different (he refers to that recent self in the past). Nevertheless, the ambiguity lies in that *reminiscence itself* is constantly envisaged as an act of narration. Thus, it is the metaphoric fusion of these two that makes the Intermediary Subject eligible for either position, diegetic or vocal. Genette, also aware of this ambivalence, calls this narrative situation 'pseudo-diegetic.'[21]

Other sources of ambiguity are in the constant merging of the act of narration-as-reminiscence and the hero in the act of reminiscing; or in the long meditations that the narrator engages in precisely during the narrative of the hero's moments of reflection. At Mme de Sainte-Euverte's, for example, the narrator accounts for Swann's intense activities of reasoning, interpretation and the search for equivalents in metaphors that may faithfully account for his auditory impressions and feelings. The gnomic discourse of the narrator tends to merge with the narrative of Swann's own reflections and generalizations. The following meditation has in it all the marks of gnomic discourse: the analytical language, the gnomic present, and the neutral 'nous': 'de nous montrer quelle richesse, quelle variété, cache à notre insu cette grande nuit impénétrée et décourageante de notre âme que nous prenons pour du vide et pour du néant' (I, 350).

146 Metaphoric narration

Nevertheless, this metaphor of the soul's impenetrable night closes the very long sentence that started with 'Il savait,' which in its intricate but syntactically coherent meandering subtly makes the shift from 'il' to 'nous,' from the past to the present – as though it were Swann himself who made these generalizations. In the syntactic structure of the whole sentence, this piece of gnomic discourse is effectively integrated with the narrative of Swann's thought, thus suggesting that it is Swann who thinks all this. But because of the strongly gnomic tone of these meditations, we are also made to assume that the narrator shares these opinions. The merging of the gnomic and narrative discourses is even more explicitly marked later:

> Peut-être est-ce le néant qui est le vrai et tout notre rêve est-il inexistant, mais alors nous sentons qu'il faudra que ces phrases musicales, ces notions qui existent par rapport à lui, ne soient rien non plus. Nous périrons, mais nous avons pour otages ces *captives divines* qui suivront notre chance. Et la mort avec elles a quelque chose de moins amer, de moins inglorieux, peut-être de moins probable.
> Swann n'avait *donc* pas tort de *croire que la phrase de la sonate existât réellement*. (I, 350–1) (italics mine)

Within the context of the gnomic discourse that produces it, the metaphor that transforms musical phrases into more or less anthropomorphic creatures – 'captives divines' – is first attributed to the narrator alone (due to the narratorial character of gnomic discourse), but the narrator, in turn, clearly attributes it to Swann – 'Swann n'avait donc pas tort de croire que la phrase de la sonate existât réellement.' Furthermore, the emphatic 'donc' stresses the continuity of the imaginative form of reasoning initiated in the previous paragraph. The metaphor and the 'donc' are therefore the explicit links in the merging of both narrative and gnomic discourses.

In the rest of the *Recherche* there are countless examples of metaphoric narration, playing on the same motifs, used in both the narrative and the gnomic discourses. One of these recurring motifs is the complex cluster of metaphors about weaving, velvetlike textures and orchestration. The recurrence of these metaphors develops the theme of the pluridimensionality and simultaneity of real life. One of the *digressive pauses* that more fully develops this theme is part of an analeptic sequence that goes back to Doncières: 'Nous ne profitons guère de notre vie, nous laisson inachevées dans les crépuscules d'été ou les nuits précoces d'hiver les heures où il nous avait semblé qu'eût pu pourtant être enfermé un peu de paix ou de plaisir. Mais ces heures ne sont pas absolument perdues. *Quand chantent à leur tour de nouveaux moments de plaisir qui passeraient de même, aussi grêles et linéaires, elles viennent leur apporter le soubassement, la consistance d'une riche orchestration'* (II, 396) (italics mine).

The reader will have noticed all the marks that signal this piece of metaphoric narration, vivid as it is, as gnomic discourse. A brief version of the same kind of threaded metaphor appears in another reminiscence of Doncières – 'impressions richement tissées les unes dans les autres qui les *orchestraient'* (II, 346). The grammatical tense is enough to betray the narrative filiation of this variation. Other variations on the same theme have a more ambiguous filiation:

> Et la diversité des points de ma vie par où avait passé le fil de celle de chacun de ces personnages avait fini par mêler ceux qui semblaient le plus éloignés, comme si la vie ne possédait qu'un nombre limité de fils pour exécuter les dessins le plus différents. (III, 972)

> ... je voyais que la vie n'avait pas cessé de tisser autour de lui [i.e. 'objet matériel'] des fils différents qui finissaient par le feutrer de ce beau velours inimitable des années, pareil à celui qui dans les vieux parcs enveloppe une simple conduite d'eau d'un fourreau d'émeraude.[22] (III, 973)

In the first passage above, the narrative filiation of that piece of metaphoric narration is clear, until 'comme si la vie ne possédait.' The imperfect here is no longer univocally the tense of narration but also that of the conditional, which could just as easily be interpreted as a generalization on the part of a digressing narrator, rather than on the part of the experiencing self reflecting and reminiscing. The same is true of the second passage: the narrative gravitates towards the gnomic discourse from that clear signal to the narratee – '*ce* beau velours' – and the simile that follows, where the gnomic discourse fully takes over.

Thus metaphoric narration, in equal degrees of vividness, playing variations on the same thematic lines and sometimes even establishing the same semantic connections, proves to be sufficiently flexible to make constant shifts from the narrative to the gnomic discourse, thereby blurring the frontiers between both.

According to Genette, up until the final revelation the narrator's discourse and the hero's 'had been juxtaposed, interwoven, but, except for two or three exceptions,[23] never completely merged: the

148 Metaphoric narration

voice of error and tribulation could not be identified with the voice of understanding and wisdom ... On the contrary, starting with the *final revelation* ... the two voices can blend and merge, or spell each other in a single speech, since henceforth the hero's *I thought* can be written *I understood, I observed* ... that is, coincide with the narrator's *I know.*'[24]

Although I agree that there is a definite *intensification* in the merging of the two discourses after the 'final revelation,' I do not concur with the view that there had been no fusion before. The exceptions that Genette isolates – the specific meditations on the art of Elstir, Wagner, and Vinteuil – are far too few and too specific, thus making them appear as truly exceptional. But in fact, as we have just seen, there are countless instances occurring before the final revelation, in which meditations on a number of other topics are recounted not as the opinions of the narrator at the time of narrating but of the hero meditating on these issues at the time of experience.

The question of the merging of 'discourses' calls for an important qualification at this point. When we speak of a merging of 'voices,' the term itself is metaphorical and certainly not restricted to speech alone. It also encompasses 'vision of the world.' As Muller observes,[25] the hero of the *Recherche* has *no* voice; just as for a long time he has no name (the fact that he is given one so late is in itself significant). He has no other voice than that borrowed from the narrator.[26] When the narrating self is in *consonance* with the experiencing self,[27] the former's discourse becomes the equivalent of the latter. One can therefore speak of the merging not of discourses but of visions.

The narrator may explicitly sound the triumphant note of self-discovery, he may *say* that finally 'I thought' may now coincide with 'I know,' but in fact the merging of voices has become a textual reality long before that final revelation. As in so many other instances, the avowed opinion of the narrator does not always correspond to the textual reality. We have seen how he declares that Mme de Guermantes's toilettes are more elegant and beautiful than Mme Swann's, when in fact the textual reality and the dimension of idealization (i.e. focalization on young Marcel) make Mme Swann's superior, and Mme de Guermantes's a mere copy. The narrator says that Odette had never had such enormous chrysanthemums, when in fact the very same kind of flowers and colours are already present in 'Un amour.' Elstir's pictorial metaphors are a revelation for Marcel, yet the narrative teems with precisely that kind of reciprocal metaphors long before this particular revelation. Many other instances could be cited of this disparity between the overt declarations and the textual reality. Likewise, the fusion of the two 'voices,' intensified after the final revelation, is present all along as a formal fusion corresponding to the thematic development of 'essence' as unification in the midst of difference (or difference at the heart of sameness).

Let us analyse another of the many instances of this fusion. The passage I have chosen is particularly interesting because of the interplay of three thinking minds – the hero's, the narrator's, and Brichot's – and because it also constitutes one of the many thematic variations on the velvet-weaving-orchestrating motif.

> *je compris* Brichot quand il me dit en souriant: 'Tenez, voyez-vous ce fond de salon, cela du moins peut à la rigueur vous donner l'idée de la rue Montalivet, il y a vingt-cinq ans, *grande mortalis aevi spatium*.' A son sourire, dédié au salon défunt qu'il revoyait, *je compris* que ce que Brichot, *peut-être sans s'en rendre compte*, préférait dans l'ancien salon, plus que les grandes fenêtres, plus que la gaie jeunesse des Patrons et de leurs fidèles, c'était cette partie irréelle (que *je dégageais moi-même* de quelques similitudes entre la Raspelière et le quai Conti) de laquelle, dans un salon comme en toutes choses, la partie extérieure, actuelle, contrôlable pour tout le monde, n'est que le prolongement, cette partie qui s'est détachée du monde extérieur pour se réfugier dans notre âme, à qui elle donne une plus-value, où elle s'est assimilée à sa substance habituelle, s'y muant ... en cet albâtre translucide de nos souvenirs, duquel nous sommes incapables de montrer la couleur qu'il n'y a que nous qui voyons ... Et *sans doute* par là le salon de la rue Montalivet faisait, pour Brichot, tort à la demeure actuelle des Verdurin. Mais, d'autre part, il ajoutait à celle-ci, pour les yeux du professeur, une beauté qu'elle ne pouvait avoir pour un nouveau venu. Ceux de ses anciens meubles qui avaient été replacés ici, un même arrangement parfois conservé, et que *moi-même je retrouvais* de la Raspelière, intégraient dans le salon actuel des parties de l'ancien qui par moments l'évoquaient jusqu'à l'hallucination et ensuite semblaient presque irréelles d'évoquer, au sein de la réalité ambiante, des fragments d'un monde détruit qu'on croyait voir ailleurs. Canapé surgi du rêve entre les fauteuils nouveaux et bien réels ... tous ces objets enfin qu'on ne saurait isoler des autres, mais qui pour Brichot, vieil habitué des fêtes des Verdurin, avaient *cette patine, ce veluté des choses* auxquelles, leur donnant une sorte de *profondeur, vient* s'ajouter leur double spirituel;[28] tout cela, éparpillé, *faisait chanter* devant lui comme autant de touches sonores qui éveillaient dans son coeur des ressemblances aimées, des réminiscences confuses ... (III, 284–6) (italics mine)

The dissonant note is clearly heard in the account of Brichot's feelings – 'peut-être sans s'en rendre compte,' 'sans doute.' If, strictly speaking, we can say that there are three distinct minds here, in terms of a *Weltanschauung*, however, there are only two 'voices': that of inchoate feelings and that of lucid interpretation carried along very specific lines of thought. The analysis of Brichot's feelings is clearly made by Marcel, not as narrator, but as *experiencing self*: this is what he thought *at the time* – 'je compris,' 'que je dégageais moi-même,' 'moi-même je retrouvais.' But this is also what the narrator *continues to think* – '*cette* partie irréelle ... cette partie qui *s'est* détachée du monde extérieur.' The merging of the hero's and the narrator's 'voices' along the same lines of thought is achieved by the weaving in and out of the narrative and gnomic discourses, which ends up embroidering a piece of metaphoric narration whose pattern and figure, as we have seen, are constant in the *Recherche* (velvetlike textures, weaving, and orchestrating).

The whole complex meditation-narration-description is woven in this manner: a brief narrative piece nourishes a generalization: 'ce que Brichot ... *préférait* dans l'ancien salon ... *c'etait* cete partie irréelle ... *cette* partie qui *s'est détachée* du monde extérieur pour se réfugier dans *notre* âme ... s'y muant ... en *cet* albâtre translucide de *nos* souvenirs duquel *nous sommes* incapables de montrer la couleur' ; 'tous ces objets ... qui pour Brichot ... *avaient cette* patine, ce velouté des choses auxquelles ... *vient* s'ajouter leur double spirituel.' Thus, not only in structure and texture is the merging of the two 'voices' perfect, the thematic fusion brought about by metaphor is equally striking: metaphoric narration is made to span both narrative and gnomic discourses, as the abridged quotations above illustrate.

Furthermore, the central motif of this piece of metaphoric narration links it to many others, the motif appearing now as part of the narrative, now as part of the gnomic discourse. In terms of the gnomic discourse, the vivid descriptive images and the narrative lines generated by metaphoric narration change its quality from the purely abstract to the concrete; in terms of narrative discourse, these pieces of metaphoric narration very often tend towards the general, therefore towards gnomic discourse. If, at the level of the manifestation in language, the migrant velvet-weaving-orchestrating motif is an agent of contamination of the narrative and the gnomic discourses, at the level of the organization of the text, metaphoric narration also tends to blur these frontiers. The account of Brichot's feelings could be seen as a metaphoric narrative correspondent to the description of Odette's

Narrative voice 151

clothes, which in turn may be read as a descriptive illustration of a gnomic utterance. Let me explain more fully.

The beauty of the Verdurin salon as perceived, inchoately by Brichot, lucidly by Marcel, is that the *absent* salon continues to make its presence felt in the new one; *the presence of absence* is thus the 'weaving' and 'orchestrating' of reality, 'ce velouté des choses.' The pattern is so striking that we may affirm that Marcel's perception of the salon corresponds exactly to the description of Odette's clothes as a work of art and to his meditations on the work of art in general: 'le "dépassant" en dents de scie de sa chemisette avait l'air du revers entrevu de *quelque gilet absent*, pareil à l'un de ceux qu'elle avait portés quelques années plus tôt ...' (I, 619) (italics mine).

Odette's clothes then furnish an illustration for the narrator's gnomic discourse that equates them with a beautiful style: 'Comme dans un beau style qui superpose des *formes différentes* et que fortifie une *tradition cachée*, dans la toilette de Mme Swann, ces souvenirs incertains de gilets ... faisaient *circuler sous la forme concrète la ressemblance inachevée d'autres plus anciennes* qu'on n'aurait pu y trouver effectivement réalisées par la couturière ou la modiste, mais *auxquelles on pensait sans cesse* ...' (I, 619) (italics mine).

The perception of the absent incorporated in the concrete, of the past in the present, is the perception of 'essence,' the 'absolute and ultimate Difference,' as Deleuze would say, for 'essence is not only individual, it *individualizes*.'[29] The *recurrence* of the motif we have been examining is truly unifying. Velvet, weaving, or orchestrating, as complex metaphors for essence, appear in connection with the narrative-description of the most disparate, heterogenous objects or events: (a) the Verdurin salon in question is thus individualized; (b) Odette's clothes have an '*individualité* vestimentaire, particulière à cette femme, et qui donnait à ses mises *les plus différentes un même air de famille*' (I, 619); (c) the work of art, be it that of a Vinteuil, an Elstir, or a Dostoievsky, has 'réfracté à travers des *milieux divers une même beauté* qu'ils apportent au monde' (III, 375); (d) even reminiscence and love have this *essential* quality – 'comme s'il en était de notre vie ainsi que d'un musée où *tous les portraits d'un même temps ont un air de famille*, une *même tonalité*' (I, 20); 'notre amour ... est une portion de notre âme, *plus durable* que les *moi divers* qui meurent successivement en nous' (III, 897) (italics mine).

The perception of a person's essence seems to depend on the consciousness of those absent selves in the present body (cf Mlle de Saint-Loup, III, 1035ff). Of Albertine the narrator says: 'Je la voyais aux

152   Metaphoric narration

différentes années de ma vie, occupant par rapport à moi des *positions différentes* qui me faisaient sentir la beauté des espaces interférés ... il y avait eu *enrichissement, solidification et accroissement de volume* dans la figure jadis simplement profilée sur la mer' (III, 69) (italics mine).

All this clearly shows that the same theme, often expressed with the same cluster of metaphors, recurs throughout the *Recherche*: it is present in narrative sequences, in descriptive pieces, in the gnomic discourse of the narrator, in the narrated meditations of the hero. It is indeed a unifying motif, not least because it also blurs the frontiers between narrative discourse and narration. Often one wonders whether the gnomic discourse is born from the narrative or the narrative is just an excuse for the unfolding of the gnomic discourse. More than one reader has asked himself whether the *Recherche* is an unduly long essay with extensive narrative illustrations or a long narrative with countless 'essayistic' digressions, with *Le temps retrouvé* perhaps tilting the balance in favour of the former.

Summing up, there are several deliberate *vocal ambiguities*: the act of narration itself is metaphorized as reminiscence; the narrator's telling the hero's own reminiscences gives way to gnomic discourse also in the form of reminiscence; the narrator accounts for the hero's meditations in the very language of gnomic discourse. All these deliberate vocal ambiguities are reinforced by metaphoric narration, contaminating the general with the particular, the concrete with the abstract. Thus, metaphoric narration may give the abstract a fictional dimension and the narrative a dimension of the general.

Conclusion

In order to sum up the role of metaphor in narrative discourse, three among its various peculiarities must be highlighted: its semantic density, its spatio-temporal dimension, and its organizational power.

Metaphor as a bi- or pluri-isotopic phenomenon produces complex effects of meaning derived from the confrontation of different semantic fields – new meanings that cannot be ascribed to one or the other but result from that unique interaction. Since the decoding metaphor is always oriented by the main, non-metaphoric context, the semantic interaction will be dominated by the field that constitutes the main or primary isotopy, thus forcing *similar* semantic units in the other field(s) to interact conjunctively in order to construct a semic intersection that will produce a *rationally satisfying* meaning.

Often the conjunctive relations responsible for the intelligibility of the metaphoric utterance tend to assimilate the more abstract and general semes, or units of meaning, whereas the more concrete semantic features in each field resist assimilation and therefore can only relate disjunctively. Nonetheless, due to the semantic expansion forced by metaphor, the decoding of which extends 'to the *union* of the two terms a property that is, in fact, true only of the intersection.'[1] The concrete, different semantic features are also assimilated, but by contamination. This paradoxical *assimilation in disjunction* triggers an associated image that escapes from the 'control of rational intelligence.'[2] Two important features of the associated image may be isolated:

154 Metaphoric narration

(a) the fact that the image is 'associated' points to this paradoxical form of assimilation that the metaphoric predication of identity forces upon dissimilar semantic features;

(b) the fact that it is an 'image' suggests a process of 'iconization' at work in those semantic features relating disjunctively. In fact, it is the iconic nature of those semantic features that is responsible for the imagelike quality so characteristic of metaphor. Greimas has defined the phenomenon of *iconization* in language as 'the last stage in the figurativization of discourse, in which two phases may be observed: *figuration* as such, accounting for the conversion of themes into figures, and *iconization*, investing already constituted figures with particularizing features which may be susceptible of producing the referential illusion.'[3]

Thus the associated image, triggered by the most concrete (i.e. iconized) features in disjunction, could be described as a particular effect of meaning akin to the visual – without being necessarily or strictly visual – and producing something like a 'referential illusion,' twice as illusory since nothing in extratextual reality corresponds to the 'image' projected by metaphor. Yet, as Ricoeur has suggested, it may well be that 'the reference to everyday life must be abolished so that some other kind of reference to other dimensions of reality are released.'[4] But the associated image is not wholly irrational; it is strongly tainted by the rationally satisfying meaning that the semic intersection has constructed, and therefore the *image* actively participates in the production of metaphoric meaning. That is why the originality of metaphor is not to be located only in the metaphoric meaning but also in the associated image, for

> A metaphoric referent corresponds to the metaphoric meaning, just as an impossible literal reference corresponds to an impossible literal meaning.
>
> ... How could the proximity in meaning not be, at the same time, a proximity in the things themselves? Isn't it from this proximity that new ways of seeing may spring up? It is therefore the category mistake that opens up the path to the new vision.
>
> ... [yet] the previous classification, tied to the previous use of words, is resistant, thus creating a sort of stereoscopic vision in which the new state of affairs is only perceived through the density of the state of affairs that has been dislocated by the category mistake.
>
> Such is the scheme of the split reference. It consists, essentially, in making correspond a metaphorization of the reference to the metaphorization of meaning.[5]

Conclusion 155

The associated image is thus *semantically pertinent* and not merely a decorative by-product of metaphorization. As we saw in Conrad's *Heart of Darkness* (see chapter 3, 2.1.3), the stones = bones metaphorical interaction projects an associated image that, though well rooted in the diegetic environment of Conrad's narrative, is far from having a purely denotative or referential function. The stones = bones image, by semantic contamination, is made to embody the new meaning born from the metaphoric interaction: *growth as death and corruption*; the apparent order of civilization (the streets of Brussels) as a cover for ruthless exploitation and death (the abandoned bones). And yet they do not cease to be what they are: the cobble-stone streets of a European metropolis; abandoned bones in Africa. Thus metaphor forces a 'stereoscopic' perception of the narrative reality, thereby enriching it.

This stereoscopic vision triggered by metaphor – and particularly by the associated image – is an essential component of what I have called metaphoric narration: a paranarrative phenomenon that affects narrative in various ways. Since the diegetic universe is temporally and spatially determined, it is clear that the associated image, proposing a sort of metaphoric referential illusion, will constitute a *virtual* space, which, in confrontation with the main diegetic one, may cause important perturbations in the reader's perception of the spatial co-ordinate of narrative:

(a) metaphor may give diegetic space semantic density by adding new, original meanings to a given description of space, as in the Conrad sequence under consideration, or the description of Mme Swann's winter salon (see chapter 6, 2);

(b) the virtuality of metaphoric space may be actualized and superimposed onto the main diegetic space, even to the extreme of replacing it. This is what happens in the 'baignoire' sequence in Proust, where the main diegetic space, the theatre, is almost obliterated as the metaphoric marine world of nereids and tritons gradually takes over (see chapter 3, 1).

Now, if the *associated image* is responsible for the *spatial* dimension of metaphor, the *semantic transformations* that occur in metaphor, particularly at the transphrastic or discursive level, are responsible for its *temporal* dimension and the semantic peculiarities resulting from it. In fact, Ricoeur's observation that in metaphor the literal reference and meaning are impossible brings up an interesting distinction between the purely verbal and the narrative forms of metaphorization: the 'impossible' literal (i.e. non-metaphoric) reference and meaning are only impossible for the former, not for the latter. This simultaneity, *and* pertinence, of the metaphoric and the non-metaphoric is one of the specific features of metaphoric narration, especially in its mode of virtual articulation of sequences: due to the time shift involved, the first sequence is perceived as non-metaphoric in a linear, syntagmatic reading, but when the second sequence triggers a metaphoric interaction with the first, through the paradigmatic activity of back-reading, the new, metaphoric meaning is generated *without cancelling the previous non-metaphoric one*. This curious semantic coexistence is only possible in metaphoric narration, only possible in fact when metaphor becomes a temporal (therefore potentially narrative) phenomenon (see chapter 2, and chapter 3, 2.1.2).

Now, these spatial and temporal determinations, inherent to the process of metaphorization are central to my concept of metaphoric narration: a virtual narrative produced by relations and operations that are essentially identical to those in metaphorization.

At the level of the *manifestation in language*, threaded metaphor may (a) superimpose its spatial and temporal coordinates onto the main narrative (the 'baignoire' sequence); (b) cover the diegetic object with its own 'image' (a church steeple as bread, ear of wheat, or salmon); (c) metaphorically constitute a narrative object (the fishlike M de Palancy, the 'chasseur arborescent').

At the level of the *organization of the text*, and regardless of whether metaphor is present in the verbal texture or not, the *process* of metaphorization may be observed (a) in the way certain narrative sequences interact with one another (i.e. metaphoric *articulation* of narrative sequences); (b) in the various modes of construction of narrative sequences.

These different forms of metaphoric organization of a text generate new meanings that are not to be located on the surface texture of the narrative sequence or in the sequences as such, in isolation, but in the very process of metaphorization, be it as narrative program or as narrative interaction. In fact, all these new meanings constitute a *virtual or paranarrative dimension*.

This paranarrative dimension constitutes a counterpoint affecting the main narrative in various ways: when the interaction or narrative articulation is *actual*, that is, brought about by textual proximity and/or syntactic links, another diegetic dimension is projected paranarratively in which the spatio-temporal counterpoint is emphasized (see chapter 3, 2.1.1, the Lezamian simile, and chapter 5, 1.1, the sick-traveller sequence); when the articulation is *virtual*, that is, brought about by semantic or diegetic similarities, and by similarities in construction programmed to relate conjunctively and thereby to be

Conclusion

articulated metaphorically by means of back-reading, what is emphasized is the *addition* of new meanings (see Odette's metaphoric 'virginity' and the way she is metaphorically contaminated by Mlle Vinteuil's homosexuality in chapter 5, 1.2). In this case the temporal dimension of metaphoric narration maintains and preserves both the metaphoric and the non-metaphoric meanings.

At the level of the organization of the text, metaphoric narration may also be brought about by various *modes of construction* of narrative sequences:

(a) a sequence may be composed on the *model provided by another* (this mode of construction is one of the important factors that trigger the virtual articulation of sequences);

(b) the very *process* of metaphorization may be used as the underlying narrative program of a given sequence (for example, all the experiences of bliss in Proust; chapter 5, 3.2);

(c) a *lexicalized metaphor* may constitute the underlying narrative program ('el llamado de la sangre' in García Márquez's *Cien años de soledad*; see chapter 3, 2.2.1).

In these various modes of construction, what is stressed is the unique *organizational power of metaphor*; one could even, by analogy, call these modes of construction a sort of metaphoric 'deep structure' of narrative sequences.

From the foregoing remarks, and from the many instances of metaphoric narration analysed in this study, it is clear that each of the different modes of metaphoric narration, though involving the three aspects under consideration – a semantic density, a paranarrative spatio-temporal dimension, and an organizational power – tends to bring forth one over the other two aspects: the *virtual* mode of metaphoric articulation, for example, stresses accretion of meaning, while the *actual* mode highlights metaphoric space and/or time as paranarrative counterpoints – the same being true of threaded metaphor. This does not mean, however, that the temporal dimension is absent from the virtual mode of articulation, since it is precisely the time shift that allows the *accretion* – rather than the mere *substitution* – of meaning; nor does it mean that important semantic transformations are not at work in the spatio-temporal confrontation brought about by threaded metaphor or by the actual mode of articulation. It is just a matter of which aspect becomes *dominant* in these forms of narrative metaphorization. The same could be said of the various modes of metaphoric *construction*: its purely organizational role as narrative program is emphasized, but this also results in particular effects of meaning and in the production of unique metaphoric space-time narrative objects.

Because metaphoric narration is a virtual paranarrative dimension, its 'absent presence,' so to speak, modifies both narrative structure and content: due to its temporal dimension, metaphoric narration constitutes an important perturbation of the temporal structures of narrative (especially in its order and duration); due to the pseudo-spatial effects of the associated image, metaphoric narration proposes new forms of distance and immediacy; due to its discursive peculiarities and to its organizational power, metaphoric narration may become a privileged instrument for focalized (or pseudo-focalized) descriptions and perceptions (its special metaphorical effects as the projection of a given fictional mind's idiosyncratic peculiarities); and, lastly, the discursive nature of metaphoric narration betrays the organizing conscience behind the created fictional world: a narrator and *his* vocal idiosyncrasies. All these structural perturbations result in a host of different meanings for which the metaphoric dimension of narrative alone may be responsible.

Thus metaphoric narration in all its modes of functioning may be fruitfully explored in certain narrative texts. But, as I have demonstrated it, this paranarrative dimension of metaphor must be described as *process*, for metaphorization may be at work *narratively* not only at the level of the manifestation in language but also, and more significantly, in the very organization of a text. In other words, metaphorization is clearly observable and describable in both the verbal texture and the ways in which narrative sequences are constructed and interact with each other. Certain texts, in which metaphoric narration is present, will favour either or both levels of narrative metaphorization (that is why Proust was chosen for extensive analysis throughout this study, but particularly in part 2, since the *Recherche* favours metaphorization at both levels).

Although metaphoric narration constitutes a paranarrative, therefore *virtual*, dimension, its different components may yet be described and analysed in order to map out structural perturbations and semantic transformations, and in order to discover the underlying programs that may be responsible for the particular shape and meaning of a given narrative. A careful analysis of the metaphoric dimension in certain narratives may thus account for the peculiarly rich and complex effects of meaning that such narrative texts may produce.

Appendix:
The operational concepts

Since the purpose of the present work has been to explore the potential metaphoric dimension in narrative, well beyond the local verbal manifestation of metaphor as a trope, I have felt the need to resort to operational concepts that may transcend the level of the manifestation in language so as to examine metaphorization as a semiotic and semantic phenomenon capable of organizing the meaning of certain narrative texts. For this to be accomplished, a series of operations must be performed on a given text in order to reach an *infralinguistic* level of meaning. One thing to be noted is that, whereas the level of the manifestation in language is something *given*, subject to direct observation, the infralinguistic level is a *constructed* dimension, an abstraction depending on the analytical and operational tools used. As regards metaphor, its potential narrative dimension is to be *constructed*, for it is not directly observable on the verbal texture of isolated metaphors, but generated by forms of decoding that may best be analysed both at the *infralinguistic* and at the *transphrastic* levels; in other words, by resorting to semantic concepts that may go *below* the word, so to speak, and *beyond* the phrase or sentence.

In order to achieve this goal, my semantic analysis has often proceeded on the basis of a structural model – particularly that of a *semic analysis* and the establishment of *semantic isotopies* – proposed by Greimas as early as 1966 in *Sémantique structurale*, and considerably developed and refined later by the Liège Group (Group μ) in its

Rhétorique générale (1970) and *Rhétorique de la poésie* (1977), and by Rastier in his *Sémantique interprétative* (1987). As in phonology, from which the model is homologically built, the structural analysis of meaning attains an infralinguistic level of *decomposition*: the meaning of a given unit of discourse may be semantically decomposed in smaller and smaller units that are no longer observable on the manifested level of language. Thus semic analysis takes on the form of a componential analysis:

> Whether on the plane of the signifier (phonic or graphic) or on the plane of the signified (meaning), the manifested chain may be considered as a hierarchy of planes where discrete units are 'articulated ...'
>
> Decomposition proceeds, on each of these planes, down to an atomic or indivisible level. On the plane of the signifier we shall thus arrive at the distinctive features, on the plane of the signified, the level of semes. It is to be noted that in all cases the last stage of decomposition reached is infralinguistic: neither distinctive features nor semes have an explicit, independent existence in language. The units of meaning, as they are manifested in discourse, begin at a level immediately above the infralinguistic.[1]

These infralinguistic units of meaning that make up or *compose* (hence the possibility of a *componential* analysis) the *signified* – that is to say, the meaning of a word – are called *semes*, or *semantic features*, which, from the phonological perspective, would correspond to the *phemes* or *distinctive features* of the *signifier*. Semes, however, are not atomic autonomous elements, as the previous quotation might suggest, but *terms in a differential relation*. As Rastier observes, 'semes are defined by relations between sememes, both on the paradigmatic and on the syntagmatic planes.'[2] This means that a semic or componential analysis is not performed *in vacuo*, as an abstraction, taking the whole system of language as its reference, but *in loco*, proposing context as a universe of discourse and its sole referent. Nonetheless, even in context, 'the sememe is still paradigmatically related to others, since its inherent semes are defined in relation to a class of sememes, though the other members of the class are not ordinarily present in the context.'[3] That is why a semic analysis must always proceed both on the paradigmatic and on the syntagmatic planes, even if the semes to be isolated as relevant are only so in reference to a given context.

This said, we may now define a *sememe* as one of the many possible meanings of a word: what we know as the particular meaning of a word in a specific context. The sememe is then *a structured set of semes*

Appendix

appearing in context. A word, or lexeme, as it appears in dictionaries, is the synthesis of its many possible contextual meanings, and its existence is purely paradigmatic, whereas a sememe actualizes only *one* meaning, its existence is always *syntagmatic* and, therefore, always in context.

Now, if semes are the semantic components of a sememe this is only as a *relational* phenomenon, not as substance. They are points of intersection resulting in the establishment of meaningful relations. Because they are *constructs,* the names given to semes are arbitrary in that they do not 'paraphrase' the meaning of a word but propose an abstract concept with an arbitrary name (cf the pair *verticality/ horizontality*). Since there is, however, no exhaustive inventory of semic categories, semes, as *minimal* units of meaning, tend to be relativized and *contextualized: minimal only in relation to the context in which they appear.*

The sememe is not just a cluster of semes but a network of *hierarchically* related semes, of which two kinds may be isolated: (a) the *generic semes* (Pottier, Rastier), also called *classemes* (Greimas) or *semantic markers* (Katz and Fodor), which the sememe shares with others in a given utterance; they are units of meaning of great generality and abstraction; (b) the *specific semes* (Pottier, Rastier), also called *nuclear semes* and *semic figures* (Greimas), or *semantic distinguishers* (Katz and Fodor), which *particularize* the meaning of the sememe, thus giving it its specificity.

The differential relations between sememes on the *paradigmatic* plane result in the isolation of units of meaning that determine the inclusion of the sememe in a *class* of sememes. It is precisely the generic semes that are responsible for the inclusion of a given unit of meaning in a class. According to Pottier, a generic seme *'brings together* two closely related sememes, by referring them to a more general class, whereas a specific seme ... *brings into opposition* two closely related sememes, by means of *an individual feature.'*[4] If the generic semes make sememes share a 'field' of meaning with others, the specific semes *differentiate* one sememe from another, giving it its meaning, its uniqueness, its identity as such, despite its belonging to a more general class. Hence the name: *specific* or *nuclear* semes.

Generic semes are defined, according to their level of generality, as *micro-generic, meso-generic,* and *macro-generic* semes. When performing a semic analysis, the analyst may choose to work *only* on the level of generality that may be pertinent to the given context. So, for example, in the semic analysis of the word *spoon,* the context may call for emphasis on the micro-generic semes, those that are of weakest generality, in order to record its belonging to a taxeme (/cutlery/), or else the context may require the activation of a broader, more abstract class ('spoon' as belonging to the /alimentation/ domain), or, finally, the context may activate semic categories of such generality as /inanimate/. In all cases, the context is responsible for the activation or de-activation of semes that may then be classified according to their degree of generality: the *taxeme* (micro-generic semes), the *domain* (meso-generic semes), or the *dimension* (macro-generic semes). These three classes of increasing generality describe in greater detail what has been loosely called *lexical* or *semantic field*.

Coseriu defines a lexical field as 'a paradigmatic structure made up of lexical units ("lexemes") sharing a common zone of meaning and establishing an immediate opposition one to the other ...'[5] In fact there seems to be a sort of conceptual overlapping between the notion of 'lexical field' and that of 'semantic field,' since both designate a structured *set of words* related by a common zone of *meaning*, well beyond simple synonymy, or morphological kinship. A semantic field is, then, like the lexical field, a set of lexical units related to each other by meaning, sharing a thematic zone of different degrees of generality.[6] In fact, the *generic semes*, responsible for the inclusion of a sememe in a class, are the ones that account for the shared 'common zone of meaning.'

It is important to insist that the common thematic zone varies in the level of generality. That is why Rastier has felt the need for a more precise description of this notion of the shared meaning or thematic zone; his concepts of taxeme, domain and dimension define the different degrees of abstraction that characterize the shared area of meaning pertinent to the analysis and thoroughly dependent on context: the *taxeme* constitutes the lowest level of generality to which *micro-generic* semes are indexed; the *domain*, a zone of greater abstraction to which *meso-generic* semes are affixed; and, finally, those semic categories of the greatest generality, such as /animate/ or /human/, are referred to the *dimension*.

Now sememes appearing in context tend to relate to each other through the iteration of some of their semes, in order to produce a semantically coherent text or utterance. Since the generic semes are responsible for the inclusion of a sememe in a class, their iteration is essential in order to constitute that class; that is why Greimas calls generic semes *classemes*. But even the recurrence of *specific* semes already points to a class of feeble or minimal generality, the taxeme.

Thus, generally speaking, a semantically coherent text reveals, through a semic analysis, a significant iteration of semes, whether generic or specific. The semantic recurrence orients the decoding of the text and results in a univocal or coherent reading. This recurrence of semes, responsible for the coherence of meaning, is Greimas's concept of *isotopy*, of central importance to our definition of metaphor. Initially defined as a cluster of recurring generic semes, or classemes, assuring the coherence of a text,[7] the concept has been expanded by Rastier to cover the *iteration of any linguistic unit*: 'An elementary isotopy will then be constituted by at least two units of the linguistic manifestation. An isotopy may be established in a linguistic sequence which may be smaller than, equal to, or greater than a sentence. An isotopy may appear at any level of the text; one may give simple examples: at the phonological level: assonance, alliteration, rhyme; at the syntactical level: agreement by mark redundancy; at the semantic level: definitional equivalence, narrative triplication ... Hence the possibility of a stylistics of isotopy.'[8]

But, as the members of the Liège group (or Group μ) have observed,[9] Greimas's definition, which was originally restricted to *content-isotopies* (classematic), is expanded by Rastier to include *expression-isotopies* (prosodic, phonemic, syntactic). Nevertheless, one must distinguish between them carefully for, if classematic recurrence, at the basis of the content-isotopy, is *necessary* in order to render a message homogeneous and coherent, the expression-isotopies, by contrast, appear as additional structures (such as rhythm and prosody), in themselves rhetorical phenomena.

One general observation to be made is that, with Rastier's expansion, isotopy as an operational concept is now applied on two fundamental levels: the manifested and the infralinguistic. In Greimas's original concept, an isotopic text implies an underlying homogeneous base of an infralinguistic nature, supporting the variety of the linguistic manifestation: 'the isotopy of a text is the permanence of a hierarchized classematic base which, due to the opening of paradigms constituted by the classematic categories, allows for the variations of the units of the manifestation, variations which, far from destroying the isotopy, do nothing but confirm it.'[10]

With Rastier, an isotopy may be established also at the *sememic*, therefore manifested, level.[11] So that one may speak of sememic isotopies, drawn from the same lexical field, capable of organizing different readings of the same text (cf Rastier's readings of Mallarmé's 'Salut,' based on sememic isotopies).[12]

Now, coming back to the infralinguistic units of meaning, the classification of semes as generic and specific responds to the dialectic of the general and the particular that shapes meaning. But sememes may also be classified qualitatively as *inherent* or *afferent*. Inherent semes 'depend on the functional system of language; while afferent semes are the product of other types of codification: socialized, even idiolectal, norms.'[13] So, for example, /sex/ and /feminine/ are inherent semes in 'woman,' while /weakness/ is an afferent seme. 'An inherent seme entails a relationship between sememes within the same taxeme, whereas an afferent seme draws a relation between two semes, the second of which does not belong to the strict set of definitions of the first.'[14] Rastier's semantic definition of inherent and afferent semes is a refinement of the corresponding notions of *denotative* and *connotative* forms of meaning. What is interesting is that his definition and the constant emphasis on context make these two forms of meaning relative: semes that are defined as inherent in a given context may become afferent in another.

These are, mainly, the basic operational concepts that I have used as analytic instruments to probe into the process of metaphorization in order to discover and describe its narrative dimension; they have also allowed me to build up a model of metaphoric narration as a potential paranarrative dimension in certain narrative texts. What is to be stressed in both is the *constructed* nature of all these dimensions of meaning, which only a theory of meaning that works on the infralinguistic level can make possible. I only hope that the 'readings' of Proust's *Recherche* and of the many other texts that I have used as illustrations are sufficiently illuminating to justify, or at least compensate for, the heavy weight of the theoretical apparatus.

Notes

Introduction

1 'Toute contiguïté peut être conçue comme une série causale.' Jakobson, *Huit questions*, 66
   Unless otherwise specified the English translations for the critical and theoretical passages quoted are mine. In order to maintain a sort of conceptual continuity in the argument I give the English version in the body of the text and provide the original French text in note form, so that the reader may verify the accuracy with which concepts have been rendered. For the handling of quotations from narrative texts, see the last paragraph of note 6 to the Introduction.
2 Cf Jakobson, *Essais de linguistique générale*, 62, 66; 'Linguistics and Poetics,' in *Style in Language*, 374–5; *Huit questions*, 63–4.
3 'Il est des poèmes à texture métonymique et des récits en prose émaillés de métaphores (la prose de Biély en est un exemple manifeste), mais une parenté à coup sûr plus étroite et plus fondamentale unit le vers à la métaphore et la prose à la métonymie. C'est sur l'association par similarité que reposent les vers; leur effet est impérativement conditionné par la similarité rhythmique, et ce parallélisme des rythmes s'impose plus fortement s'il est accompagné d'une similitude (ou d'un contraste) entre les images. La prose ignore un tel dessein de frapper l'attention par l'articulation en segments d'une similitude voulue. C'est l'association par contiguïté qui donne à la prose narrative son impulsion fondamentale; le récit passe d'un objet à l'autre, par voisinage, en suivant des parcours d'ordre causal ou spatio-temporel, le passage

de la partie au tout et du tout à la partie n'étant qu'un cas particulier de ce processus.' Jakobson, *Huit questions*, 63–4

4 'La structure, constituée par un énoncé de faire régissant un énoncé d'état [i.e. *transformation*], est appelée programme narratif ... elle sera considérée comme l'unité élémentaire opératoire de la syntaxe narrative.' Greimas, *Sémiotique. Dictionnaire raisonné de la théorie du langage*, 'syntaxe narrative de surface'

5 Agatha Christie, *The Hollow*, 66–7

6 José Lezama Lima, *Paradiso*, 196–8

'As he cut his beet, he lost the whole thing, and while he was attempting to recover it, the untimely pricked red ball began to bleed. Demetrio trapped it for a third time, but it broke and slid away: half was stuck to the fork and half, with a new malign insistence, laid its wound once more upon the delicate cloth, which soaked up the red liquid with slow avidity. As the ancestral cream color of the tablecloth mingled with the beet's monsignorate, three isles of bleeding showed up among the rosettes. But those three stains actually gave the relief of splendor to the meal. In the light, in the resistant patience of craftsmanship, in the omens, in the way the threads absorbed the vegetable blood, the three stains opened up in somber expectancy.

'Alberto took the shells of his two prawns, using them to cover the two stains, which thereupon disappeared under a saddle of delicate red. "Cemi, give me one of your prawns, because we've been the first to enjoy their meat, and we can cover the other half stain." With Cemi's prawn now in his hand, he comically pretended that the tasty morsel was flying, like a dragon setting fire to the clouds, until it fell into the mutilated red nest formed by the half-moon of beets ...

'While the dessert was being served, Doña Augusta signaled Baldovina to bring the fruit bowl, colorful with apples, pears, tangerines, and grapes. A glass stand supported the scalloped plate and the colors of the fruit could be seen through varied, intertwined stripes, with the predominance of violet and orange reduced by the refraction. The fruit bowl had been set in the center of the table, over one of the beet stains. Alberto picked up one of the prawn shells and stood it up, as if it were going to climb up the glass stand until it could sink its claws into a soft piece of fruit. The fruit bowl, like a sea plant being rubbed by a fish, sparkled in a cascade of colors, as the prawn stretched out, content in its new environment, stretching out toward the curved sky of the fruit-painted plate.' José Lezama Lima, *Paradiso*, trans. Gregory Rabassa, 182–3

Quotations from *narrative* texts are given in the original language throughout. English versions are provided only for texts in Spanish, since most readers of Proust are proficient in French. I have used the 1954 Pléiade edition of *A la recherche du temps perdu*. A reference to the volume and page of the *Recherche* follows each quoted passage, e.g. (II, 450).

7 '... la poésie est centrée sur le signe alors que la prose, pragmatique, l'est, au premier chef, sur le référent.' Jakobson, *Essais*, 66
8 Lezama Lima, 211. Subsequent references to *Paradiso* in the body of the text are to the Spanish edition.
   'But he could only remember the warmth of the hand that had taken the prawn out of his so that it could hug the crystal base of the fruit bowl. He seemed to see the prawn once more, leaping merrily in the cascade of iridescence unleashed by the tray of fruit. The fruit bowl again let loose a cascade of light, but now the prawn advanced, refracting the fruitful colors toward a coral cemetery.' *Paradiso*, trans. Rabassa, 196
9 Jean Ricardou, *Problèmes du Nouveau Roman* and *Nouveaux problèmes du roman*. For a summary of Ricardou's theoretical model see chapter 3, n 10 below.

PART ONE: METAPHORIC NARRATION

1 In general a working definition is offered when the analysis calls for it, but for a more detailed description and discussion of the most important operational concepts see the appendix.
2 Cf Eisenstein's concept of montage as collision: 'from the collision of two given factors *arises* a concept,' *Film Form*, 37. Eisenstein's description and effective use of montage involve a *semiotic mechanism* identical to that of verbal metaphor.
3 ... les figures de rhétorique dépassent, semble-t-il, la problématique des seules langues naturelles: le fait que le cinéma, par exemple connaisse métaphores et métonymies, montre au moins que, dans le cadre du parcours génératif du discours, les figures relèvent du "tronc commun" sémiotique, antérieurement donc à toute manifestation dans une substance particulière de l'expression.' Greimas, *Sémiotique*, 'figure'

1 Metaphor within the boundaries of the sentence

1 For a more detailed definition and discussion of the concept of 'semantic field,' see appendix, p 161. For 'conceptual and referential modes of decomposition,' see pp 15–16. Corresponding entries in the glossary define these concepts in greater detail.
2 See appendix, 160ff.
3 'De caractère opératoire, le concept d'isotopie a désigné d'abord l'itérativité, le long d'une chaîne syntagmatique, de classèmes qui assurent au discours-énoncé son homogénéité. D'après cette acception, il est clair que le syntagme réunissant au moins deux figures sémiques peut être considéré comme le contexte minimal permettant d'établir une isotopie.' Greimas, *Sémiotique*, 'isotopie'
4 Allotopy is the property of non-isotopy of a text.

168 Notes to pages 12–13

5 '... nous pouvons proposer une nouvelle définition de l'isotopie: on dira qu'elle est *la propriété des ensembles limités d'unités de signification comportant une récurrence identifiable de sèmes identiques et une absence de sèmes exclusifs en position syntaxique de détermination.*' Group μ, *Rhétorique de la poésie*, 41
6 Michel Leguern, *Sémantique de la métaphore et de la métonymie*, 16ff
7 Group μ, *Rhétorique de la poésie*, 46ff
8 This would correspond to Max Black's terminology (the 'focus' of the metaphoric utterance – i.e. the *allotopic* lexeme(s)), while the rest of the utterance, what he calls 'frame,' is what I have been calling the *isotopic* lexemes. Cf Max Black, *Models and Metaphors*, 28.
9 The rhetorical operation defined in these terms corresponds closely to Jean Cohen's concept of the perception and reduction of the 'semantic impertinence' in *Structure du langage poétique* (Flammarion 1966). In a later text he says that 'Any figure, in fact, involves a process of decoding in two stages: the first is the perception of the anomaly, the second its correction by an exploration of the paradigmatic field where relations of similarity, contiguity, etc., are tightly woven. These relations will lead to the discovery of a meaning that may give the utterance a semantically acceptable meaning. If such an interpretation is impossible, the utterance will be discarded as absurd.' ['Toute figure, en fait, comporte un processus de décodage en deux temps, dont le premier est la perception de l'anomalie, et le second sa correction, par exploration du champ paradigmatique où se nouent les rapports de ressemblance, de contiguïté, etc, grâce auxquels sera découvert un signifié susceptible de fournir à l'énoncé une interprétation sémantique acceptable. Si cette interprétation est impossible, l'énoncé sera renvoyé à l'absurde.'] Jean Cohen, 'Théorie de la figure,' 22

The concepts of *semantic impertinence* and its necessary *reduction* implicitly and inevitably carry a negative value working to the detriment of metaphoric meaning, especially in the case of poetic metaphor, where the 'acceptability' of meaning, even once the utterance has been successfully decoded, always remains highly questionable. When metaphorization is transposed to the narrative domain, as we shall see, there is an important time shift that makes metaphoric meaning an addition and an enrichment, rather than a substitution and/or reduction of the semantic impertinence. In certain forms of metaphoric narration both the given and the constructed meanings are maintained and are semantically 'acceptable.' Therefore, the concept of semantic impertinence is 'impertinent' for metaphoric narration; that of 'revaluation' proposed by Group μ is a more useful tool in the examination of the process. Furthermore, Cohen's argument presupposes the complementary yet still highly problematic concept of the zero degree of language, which would, theoretically, determine the appropriate-

Notes to pages 14–17

ness and the acceptability of meaning, thus re-establishing the old dichotomy between 'sens propre' and 'sens figuré,' with its consequent hierarchization and valorization. Retaining, nonetheless, the concept of metaphor as an operation involving two distinct moments in its decoding, I have chosen to follow the path explored by the Liège Group (Group μ) in its *Rhétorique de la poésie*, in which analysis proceeds at the infralinguistic level, redefining the operation of reduction in terms of a semic revaluation of the given degree of metaphor.

10 'Le trope constitue, comme toute figure, une modification du niveau de redondance calculable du code, perçue grâce à une impertinence distributionnelle. Cette impertinence est réduite grâce à la présence d'un invariant induit par le contexte, en un phénomène de *feedforward* ou de *feed-back*. Cet invariant est, dans le cas de la métaphore, que nous prendrons pour exemple, l'intersection des sèmes du degré donné de la figure, et de la classe de ses degrés construits ... Il est fourni par les classèmes, ou sèmes récurrents ... Nous insistons sur le fait que l'opération rhétorique définit non pas la figure elle-même, mais la *relation* entre degrés donné et construits, relation qui ouvre ce que Genette nommait "l'espace du langage."' Group μ, *Rhétorique de la poésie*, 47

11 See appendix, 159ff.

12 '... c'est la manipulation des arrangements de sèmes qui produira les figures.' Group μ, *Rhétorique générale*, 94

13 Ibid., 94ff

14 'La relation métonymique est donc une relation entre objets, c'est-à-dire entre réalités extra-linguistiques; elle est fondée sur un rapport qu'existe dans la référence, dans le monde extérieur, indépendamment des structures linguistiques qui peuvent servir à l'exprimer.' Leguern, *Sémantique*, 25

15 What Max Black says about metaphor may also apply to Yeats's *metonymy*: 'It would be more illuminating in some ... cases to say that the metaphor *creates the similarity* than to say that it formulates some similarity antecedently existing.' *Models*, 37. Black's observations are in keeping with what the members of Group μ call the construction of a semic intersection. The intersection does not exist as such; it is a *conceptual construct*, which is, in turn, determined by the context, always local and unique, of the figurative utterance.

16 It would be interesting, at this point, to draw a parallel between Greimas and I.A. Richards. For the latter, context also implies iteration; context is 'a name for a whole cluster of events that recur together.' *The Philosophy of Rhetoric*, 34

For Richards, words have meaning only because they are presented as an 'abridgement of context.' This is what he calls the 'delegated efficacy' of words: 'what the word means is the missing parts of the contexts from which it draws its delegated efficacy' (ibid., 35). In these terms, Richards's 'delegated efficacy' of words corresponds closely to Greimas's concept of 'lexeme' as a virtuality of different possible discursive trajectories that are only realized, punctually, by the 'sememe' (sememe = nuclear figure + classematic base) in a given utterance. What Richards's analyses fail to distinguish, however, and which is a vital aspect of meaning, is the *invariant* component of a lexeme, the nuclear semes, which remain unaffected by the different contextual realizations and from which the lexeme derives its identity as such. The semantic invariant also explains, though negatively, certain semantic phenomena such as *homonymy*, for example: in homonymy, although an identical morphological cover in the shape of an identical word or lexeme is shared, there is no invariant. That is to say, the same word designates at least two totally different meanings, as in the case of the French 'baignoire' (bath-tub and ground-floor box); whereas the different meanings of a *sememe* retain a basic semantic *identity*, as in the case of 'stain,' which shares the semes /colour/ and /matter/ despite different contextual meanings, be it 'contamination' or 'glass painting.' This invariant nuclear figure can be elucidated only by a semic analysis, therefore at the infralinguistic level; whereas Richards's analysis proceeds on the purely referential plane: 'context' is defined in terms of 'events' that recur together.

17 Cf Greimas, *Sémiotique*, 'métaphore.'
18 '... si cette partie commune est nécessaire comme base probante pour fonder l'identité prétendue, la partie non commune n'est pas moins indispensable pour créer l'originalité de l'image et déclencher le mécanisme de réduction. La métaphore extrapole, elle se base sur une identité réelle manifestée par l'intersection de deux termes pour affirmer l'identité des termes entiers. Elle étend à la *réunion* des deux termes une propriété qui n'appartient qu'à leur intersection.' Group μ, *Rhétorique générale*, 107
19 Black, *Models*, 27
20 Ibid., 28
21 Ibid., 41
22 For these complex iconic and abstract dimensions of metaphoric meaning see Greimas, *Sémiotique*, 'iconisation' and 'figure.' See also Ricoeur, *La métaphore vive*, 142–262.
23 One may object that the recurrence of such a general category as /abstraction/ is not pertinent or significant in the establishment of an isotopy, but it *is* when the context opposes /abstraction/ to /concreteness/. For example, it is precisely the perturbation of the level of generality that is responsible for the particular effect of meaning of such rhetorical figures as Pope's sylleptic /Whether the nymph shall ... / Or *stain* her honour or her new brocade/; Eliot's simile /*Streets* that follow like a tedious argument/ Of insidious intent/; or Yeats's /Arise and bid me *strike a match*/ And strike another till time catch/. Furthermore, as the members of the Liège Group observe, '... the

Notes to pages 22–7   171

   positive condition of isotopy presupposes an invariance in the level of
   generality.' ['... la condition positive de l'isotopie prévoit également
   la constance du niveau de généralité.'] *Rhétorique de la poésie*, 40
24 Other semes such as /deprivation/ have become peripheral and are
   apparent only in the obsolete meanings of the word: ('To deprive of
   colours [obs.]'; 'of the Sun etc.: to deprive of their lustre [obs.]'; 'to
   obscure the lustre of lit. and fig. [obs.]'; 'to lose colour or lustre
   [obs.].') *Oxford English Dictionary*
25 T.A. van Dijk, *Some Aspects of Text Grammars*, 250, 257
26 Ibid., 251
27 This double movement is what has made Group μ conceive metaphor
   as a combination of two synecdoches, one of which must be particularizing, the other generalizing, in order to reach the same level of
   generality. *Rhétorique générale*, 102–4
28 'Saisi dans le parcours génératif global, le niveau figuratif du discours
   apparaît comme une instance caractérisée par de nouveaux investissements – des installations des figures du contenu – se surajoutant au
   niveau abstrait. Dans cette optique, on cherchera à interpréter certaines *figures de rhétorique* – telle la métaphore – comme une relation
   structurale particulière qui recouvre la distance entre le niveau abstrait et le niveau figuratif du discours.' Greimas, *Sémiotique*, 'figure'
29 'C'est là le caractère spécifique de la métaphore: en obligeant à abstraire
   au niveau de la communication logique un certain nombre d'éléments de signification, elle permet de mettre en relief les éléments
   maintenus; par l'introduction d'un terme étranger à l'isotopie du
   contexte, elle produit, à un autre niveau que celui de l'information
   pure, l'évocation d'une image associée que perçoit l'imagination et
   qui exerce son retentissement sur la sensibilité sans le contrôle de l'intelligence logique, car il est de la nature de l'image introduite par la
   métaphore de lui échapper.' Leguern, *Sémantique*, 22
30 'Traitée comme schème, l'image présente une dimension verbale; avant
   d'être le lieu des percepts fanés, elle est celui des significations nais-
   santes. De même donc que le schème est la matrice de la catégorie,
   l'icône est celle de la nouvelle pertinence sémantique qui naît du
   démantèlement des aires sémantiques sous le choc de la contradiction
   ... le moment iconique comporte un aspect verbal, en tant qu'il constitue la saisie de l'identique dans les différences et en dépit des différences, mais sur un mode préconceptuel.' Ricoeur, *La métaphore vive*,
   253

2 Metaphor as a discursive phenomenon

1 'La métaphore est alors un événement sémantique qui se produit au
  point d'intersection entre plusieurs champs sémantiques. Cette construction est le moyen par lequel tous les mots pris ensemble reçoivent
  sens. Alors, et alors seulement, la *torsion* métaphorique est à la fois

172   Notes to pages 28–31

un événement *et* une signification, un événement signifiant, une signification émergente créée par le langage ...

'Dans l'énoncé métaphorique ... l'action contextuelle crée une nouvelle signification qui a bien le statut de l'événement, puisqu'elle existe seulement dans ce contexte-ci. Mais, en même temps, on peut l'identifier comme la même, puisque sa construction peut être répétée; ainsi, l'innovation d'une signification émergente peut être tenue pour une création linguistique ... Seules les métaphores authentiques, c'est-à-dire les métaphores vives, sont en même temps événement et sens.' Ricoeur, *La métaphore vive*, 127

2 'La métaphore développe son pourvoir de réorganizer la vision des choses lorsque c'est un "règne" entier qui est transposé: par exemple les sons dans l'ordre visuel; parler de la sonorité d'une peinture, ce n'est plus faire émigrer un prédicat isolé, mais assurer l'incursion d'un règne entier sur un territoire étranger ... l'organisation effectuée dans le royaume étranger se trouve *guidée par* l'emploi du réseau entier dans le royaume d'origine.' Ibid., 297

3 'On appelle *connecteur* ... *d'isotopies* une unité du niveau discursif, qui introduit une seule ou plusieurs lectures différentes ... Dans le cas de la pluri-isotopie, c'est le caractère polysémémique de l'unité discursive jouant le rôle de connecteur, qui rend possible la superposition d'isotopies différentes.

Du point de vue typologique, on pourra distinguer, entre autres, les *connecteurs métaphoriques* qui assurent le passage d'une isotopie abstraite (ou thématique) à une isotopie figurative, la relation qui les unit étant orientée (ce qui se dit sur la seconde isotopie étant interprétable sur la première, et non inversement).' Greimas, *Sémiotique*, 'connecteur d'isotopies'

4 'Ce qu'on appelle métaphore filée est en fait une série de métaphores reliées les unes aux autres par la syntaxe – elles font partie de la même phrase ou d'une même structure narrative ou descriptive – et par le sens: chacune exprime un aspect particulier d'un tout, chose ou concept, que représente la première métaphore de la série.' Michael Riffaterre, 'La métaphore filée,' 47

5 Philippe Dubois, 'La métaphore filée,' 209ff

6 '... il suffit qu'un énoncé, cohérent sur une isotopie [1] (où s'indexent les unités de discours selon la chaîne syntagmatique ABCDEF) voie tout à coup, sous l'effet d'une métaphore [M], son isotopie [1] connectée à une seconde isotopie [2], pour qu'aussitôt une ré-activation du texte survienne qui tende à inscrire un maximum d'unités discursives de [1] sur [2], donc à produire le plus grand nombre possible d'unités polysémiques pouvant fonctionner (être lues) sur [1] aussi bien que sur [2], c'est-à-dire à produire de nouvelles métaphores dérivées (M', M'', M''').' Ibid., 206

7 Since Aristotle, the extraordinary complexity of the process of meta-

phorization has often been compared to that of poetry itself (cf Ricoeur, *La métaphore vive*, 289ff, who sees in metaphor a miniature poem). Its fascinating complexity accounts for the current 'metaphorocentrism.' (Cf Genette, 'La rhétorique restrainte,' in *Figures III*.) But it also explains why so many poets have given metaphor a central place in their poetic theory (Shelley or Lezama Lima, for example): the complex mechanisms of metaphor seem to be homologous to that of poetry. Metaphorization, especially at the discursive level, actually performs what Jakobson describes as the poetic function of language: metaphor also *'projects the principle of equivalence from the axis of selection into the axis of combination'* (Jakobson, 'Linguistics,' 358). The paradigmatic aspect of metaphor is particularly emphasized by the phenomenon of 'back-reading' ('rétrolecture'), which discursive metaphor forces upon the text.

8 'If, in the course of a syntagmatic analysis ... certain elements are provisionally suspended because they do not seem, at first, to find their place in the organization of the text under examination, *back-reading* ... due, particularly, to the effect of subsequent connectors of isotopies, allows us to reconsider ... those elements that had been momentarily left aside: that "going back" must be considered as one of the possible forms of reading (understood, in the semiotic sense, as a simultaneous syntactic and semantic construction of the discourse-utterance).' ['Si, au cours de l'analyse syntagmatique ... certains éléments sont provisoirement mis entre parenthèses parce que ne semblant pas trouver d'emblée leur place dans l'organisation du discours examiné, la *rétrolecture* ... grâce, en particulier, aux connecteurs d'isotopies subséquents, peut permettre de prendre en considération ... les éléments un moment délaissés: ce "retour en arrière" est donc à reconnaître comme une des formes possibles de la lecture (entendue, au sens sémiotique, comme la construction, à la fois syntaxique et sémantique, de l'énoncé-discours).'] Greimas, *Sémiotique*, 'rétrolecture'

9 For a detailed analysis of this sequence from the perspective of metaphoric narration, see chapter 3, 1.

10 'Partant de la reconnaissance de la bi-isotopie, il parcourt tout le texte sur la nouvelle isotopie dans le but d'y indexer le plus grand nombre possible d'unités discursives, lesquelles se constituent ainsi en nouvelles unités rhétoriques.' Dubois, 'La métaphore filée,' 207

3 The narrative dimension of metaphor

1 Cf Jakobson, *Essais*, 48–9, 61–3
2 The term *actor* is here used in the Greimasian sense, as a discursive entity that subsumes *actantial roles*, an entity that has nothing to do with psychological or ontological existence. Hence 'actor' is not neces-

sarily human or even animate, but a subject that can be defined only in terms of the object to which it relates, and in terms of *a doing* (*un faire*), i.e. an actantial role (cf Greimas, *Sémiotique*, 'acteur,' 'actant,' 'rôle').

3 I am certainly aware of Inge K. Crossman's book whose title is so similar to mine: *Metaphoric Narration: The Structure and Function of Metaphor in 'A la recherche du temps perdu.'* Crossman's book, however, does not deal at all with the strictly *narrative* dimension of metaphor. She has chosen a group of metaphors that are thematically homogeneous and syntactically heterogeneous; her analyses are restricted to *verbal* metaphor, with analytical methods that rely heavily on Christine Brooke-Rose's *A Grammar of Metaphor*. Once Crossman's thematic choice has been made (i.e. time), she classifies the various metaphors according to different grammatical categories ('noun metaphors in genitive link,' for example), and according to extension (from 'single' metaphors and what she calls the 'brief conceit' to 'continued metaphors' and 'accumulated metaphors'). Thus, despite the title, the narrative dimension of metaphor, *per se*, is never discussed.

4 This is, in fact, the main definition of 'articulation' given in the *Oxford English Dictionary*.

5 Cf pp 40–3 for the *actual*, pp 44–7 for the *virtual*, and pp 47–50 for the *mixed* modes of metaphoric articulation.

6 'L'enfilade des signes détermine une perspective singulière où chacune des particularités décrites s'interpose entre la précédente et le lecteur, et donc, d'une certaine manière, la cache. Ce processus d'enfouissement que suscite l'ordre successif des signes explique notamment pourquoi une description, si elle se risque à en multiplier les caractères, finit par dissoudre l'objet qu'elle prétendait construire. Il permet aussi de comprendre ce phénomène par lequel, même présentée comme telle, toute digression, si elle se prolonge amplement, tend à devenir *corps principal*.' Ricardou, *Problèmes*, 31

7 Sainte-Beuve, *Pensées de Joseph Delorme*, xi. Quoted in Riffaterre, 'La métaphore filée,' 47

8 Eco defines that cultural 'encyclopaedia' of the reader as a series of intertextual 'frames.' In turn, a frame is defined as a structured set of interrelated data and informations describing a given cultural situation. 'In that sense, *a frame is always a virtual text or a condensed story*.' ['In tal senso una sceneggiatura è sempre un testo virtuale o una storia condensata.'] *Lector in Fabula*, 80. See also 81–4, 128–41.

It will be noticed that this concept of 'frame' is not too different from that of lexical or semantic field. The latter is also defined as a structured set of terms interrelated by a common zone of meaning. The main difference would lie in the scope: a lexic or semantic field is defined by relationships drawn *within the system of language*; whereas a 'frame,' or an 'encyclopaedic' description of a term, goes out of the system,

Notes to page 40   175

in order to include all sorts of social and cultural codifications that establish the kinship among objects and/or situations related to a given term. In a semantic field the interrelated sememes would rely mainly on their *inherent* semes, while those interrelated in a frame would also include *afferent* semes.

9 'Il se peut que la référence au réel quotidien doive être abolie pour que soit libérée une autre sorte de référence à d'autres dimensions de la réalité.' Ricoeur, *La métaphore vive*, 187

10 In the analysis of metaphoric articulation I adhere, to a certain extent, to the very suggestive work that Ricardou has done in the field of metaphor in narrative discourse: *Problèmes du Nouveau Roman* and *Nouveaux problèmes du roman*. Since I have adapted and modified his ideas according to the model presented here, I shall sum up Ricardou's original thinking:

There are three kinds of metaphor, which he calls expressive, structural (or ordinal), and configural. Ricardou considers metaphor as an *exoticness* that brings together two spaces: the here, i.e. the compared (le comparé), and the elsewhere, i.e. the comparing element (le comparant). In *expressive* metaphor the effect is always local and implies a pre-established notion that metaphor is supposed to 'express'; expressive metaphor, therefore, subordinates the elsewhere to the here and discards it as soon as the rhetorical translation has been operated (*Problèmes*, 134). Ricardou defines *structural* or *ordinal* metaphor (he uses these two terms indiscriminately) as the literalization of the trope (ibid., 13); more often, and most insistently, as a specific device whereby the text is constructed and functions: ordinal metaphor joins two narrative 'cells' ('cellules') by means of a number of common elements (*Nouveaux problèmes*, 98). Ordinal metaphor has an organizing role in the arrangement of the cells.

Ordinal metaphor may be *actual* or *virtual*. It is actual 'when it acts on the plane of writing and, consequently, on that of reading, if it occurs in the same order. But metaphor is said to be virtual when it works only on the plane of reading, since two entities [ensembles] are brought together which writing has deliberately separated in the body of the text. In the first case the proximity is *actual*: the separate events are explicitly brought together by the text. What we have here is *time in short circuit* [*temps court-circuité*]. In the second case, the proximity is *virtual*: by distributing here and there certain passages that bear similarity to one another, the text programmes the virtuality of the connections which reading actualizes as it passes from one to the other. What we have here is a *text in short-circuit* [*texte court-circuité*]. In other words: *actual* ordinal metaphor short-circuits the time of *fiction*; whereas virtual ordinal metaphor short-circuits the time of *narration*.' Ibid., 124

Configural metaphor, as its name suggests, is defined by the configuration of a cell according to the scheme or pattern presented by another cell: 'it is the whole or part of the organization of each cell that bears similarity to the other' (ibid., 98). Configural metaphor may be *external* when the scheme of one cell serves to construct a different cell; it is *internal* when 'part of the cell is elaborated from the scheme of the same cell' (ibid., 49).

11 Lezama Lima, *Paradiso*, 7
'Baldovina was desperate, dishevelled, [*she looked like a lady of the Queen's wardrobe, with an infant in her arms, moving back, room after room, in the burning castle, thus obeying the orders from her fleeing master and mistress*]. She needed help now: each time she drew back the mosquito netting, she saw the body lying there and the welts on it more prominent. To assuage her terrified urge to run away, she pretended to search for the servant couple at the other end of the house.' *Paradiso*, 3

Unfortunately, Rabassa's translation altogether omits the long simile under consideration, which I have now translated (the words in italics).

12 'C'est avant tout au niveau de l'écriture ... que le rapprochement a lieu; l'arbitraire est réduit au niveau textuel de l'écriture affranchie des lois de la dénotation. Ce qui veut dire que la connotation et les champs isotopiques se chargent de la production de liens nouveaux ("structure, une autre," Mallarmé).' Jean-Michel Adam, *Linguistique et discours littéraire*, 178

13 James Joyce, *Ulysses* 43. Subsequent page references will be given between parentheses after the quoted passage.

14 In the 'Nestor' episode, 31

15 Joseph Conrad, *Heart of Darkness*, 9–10

16 For a detailed description of narrative isotopies see chapter 3, 2.1.4.

17 Matthew 23:27

18 See the glossary for the definitions of terms in Genette's narrative theory.

19 Marcel Muller, *Les voix narratives*, 59ff

20 Barthes has defined a narrative *function* as the minimal narrative unit or segment of the story that stands in correlation to another. See his 'Introduction à l'analyse structurale des récits,' in *Poétique du récit*, 16. Strictly speaking, both 'functions' and 'indexes' are *functions*, since they appear as terms in a correlation, but following Barthes's own practice, I shall reserve the term *function* to denote *kernels* (strong functions) and *catalysts* (weak functions) as responsible for the syntagmatic deployment of a narrative, while the term *index* will be reserved for thematic collections of semes and actorial qualifications. In this synthesis, I am also following Barthes's own implicit assimilation of the semic code and what he had earlier classified as indexes (*S/Z*, 25–6, 98–100, 196–7).

The usefulness of these Barthean concepts is such that I do not mind incurring in the often confusing and contradictory polysemic value of the term *function*, an ambiguity that unfortunately I cannot avoid. I therefore use the term in two different senses: (a) the instrumental notion of function as the 'role' played by something; (b) the more specific Barthean sense – which he, in turn, derives from Hjelmslev – of function as the term in a correlation. When using 'function' in this latter sense I prefix it with the adjective *narrative* in order to distinguish it from the former. See also the corresponding entries in the glossary.

21 Ibid., 26, 196

Following Barthes, I have described the recurrence of semes as productive of thematic fields. Greimas, too, conceives a theme essentially as the 'dissemination of values, already actualized by narrative semantics, along narrative programmes and processes.' *Sémiotique*, 'thème,' 'thématisation.' The very notion of *dissemination*, however, implies some sort of recurrence. Therefore, we may also speak of thematic isotopy as the dissemination of meanings of connotation sharing similar semantic fields.

22 Redundancy, as Susan Suleiman has remarked, is a necessary 'surplus of information,' an essential means to preserve information, which is not restricted to the limits of the sentence but operates at the level of the text as well.

The estabishment of an isotopy, as we have seen, depends on the redundancy of semic categories. At the discursive level, metaphorization multiplies the redundant elements since it generates a *pluri-isotopic* text.

Even in verbal metaphor redundancy is essential in the construction of the semic intersection – the semantic similarities between the two fields necessarily entailing a semic redundancy. At the discursive level and especially in threaded metaphor, redundancy is observable not only at the infralinguistic level of semic categories, but even at the level of the manifestation, often in the repetition of similar sememes belonging to the same semantic field. Metaphoric narration assimilates this characteristic of the process at the discursive level: for two narrative sequences to interact metaphorically redundancy is essential, whether on the purely semantic level, on the sememic level, or at the level of narrative functions or thematic elements.

For a more detailed discussion of the role of redundancy in narrative see Suleiman, *Le roman à thèse*, 185–237.

23 Gabriel García Márquez, *Cien años de soledad*, 118

'As soon as José Arcadio closed the bedroom door, the crack of a shot sounded loudly all over the house. A streak of blood went out under the door, crossed the living-room, went out into the street, proceeded in a straight line along the uneven sidewalks, went down stairs and up window-sills, it went along Turks Street, turned right on the corner, left on another; made a right angle in front of the Buendías' house and went under the locked door, across the formal living-room, very close to the walls for fear of staining the carpets; it proceeded through the other room, avoided the dining-room table by tracing a wide curve; it advanced along the begonia corridor and went unseen under the chair on which Amaranta, who was teaching arithmetic to Aureliano José, was sitting; it got into the corn-loft and appeared in the kitchen where Ursula was about to break thirty six eggs to bake bread.

– Oh Blessed Virgin! – cried Ursula

She followed the streak of blood in the opposite direction.' (my translation)

24 Ricardou, *Problèmes*, 136
25 For a more detailed discussion and analysis of this phenomenon in Proust, see part 2, especially chapters 6 and 7.
26 Lezama Lima, *Paradiso*, 174
27 'Las imágenes como interposiciones naciendo de la distancia entre las cosas. La distancia entre las personas y las cosas crea otra dimensión, una especie de ente del no ser, la imagen, que logra la visión o unidad de esas interposiciones. Pues es innegable que entre la jarra y la varilla de marfil, existe una red de imágenes, participadas por el poeta cuando las concibe dentro de una *coordenada de irradiaciones*.'
Lezama Lima, 'Las imágenes posibles,' in *Obras completas*, 2: 180
28 Lezama Lima, *Paradiso*, 173–5
'Rialta did not wish to break the circle formed by her children, completely absorbed in their game. She sat up on the floor beside them, penetrating the silence that was intent on the rising and the falling of the ball. The square formed by Rialta and her three children changed into a circle. The children shifted slightly to let their mother in. She was anxious to reach their island that was held up by the circle with flickering edges and a vertical line determined by the moving points of the ball propelled toward a small imaginary sky, falling momentarily down to the tiles that seemed to be liquid plates as the fixed looks that were the sum of the square transformed them into waves traveling toward infinity.

'Violante had reached seven ... Rialta began to throw the ball and her earlier concern helped the rise of the ball coincide with the semicircle of her hand as it picked up the jacks. The looks of the four absorbed people came together at the center of the circle. The total concentration of will on the rhythm of the ball bouncing on the tiles had the effect of isolating the tiles, of giving them a liquid reflection, as if they were contracting to capture an image ...

'The rim of the circle was hardening until it began to look like incandescent metal. Suddenly, in a flash, the cloud broke up to make way for a new vision. On the tiles imprisoned by the circle the full tunic of the Colonel appeared, a darkish yellow that grew lighter, the buttons on the four pockets brighter than copper' ... *Paradiso*, trans. Rabassa, 160–1

29 Unlike the two Vinteuil sequences in Proust where specific events are practically repeated (Vinteuil's music heard in a mundane reunion, the ensuing experience of bliss, etc.), what is replicated in Cortázar is the *arrangement* of narrative functions *abstracted* from events that are individually very different in both sequences. Because the arrangement of narrative functions is the same, the conjunctive relations drawn between the two sequences are *constructed*, since the similarity in pattern must be abstracted from the individual, concrete events. The disjunctive relations, by contrast, are already *given* in the radical differences between the concrete events of each sequence, a difference in diegetic universe. The diegetic status of the two sequences is then radically different: the oneiric sequence has a metadiegetic status, that is, it is a story projecting a completely different fictional universe, apparently with no possible contact, except as a dream, with the main narrative. As a metadiegetic narrative, the dream sequence depends on the main narrative – at least as long as the moment of reversal has not come; it also presents a radically different diegetic universe, therefore constituting a breach in the diegetic isotopy of the main narrative.

30 For a definition of these terms in Barthes see above, n 20, and the corresponding entries in the glossary.

31 Julio Cortázar, 'La noche boca arriba,' *Final del juego*, 162, 166
'... as if the sky had been set on fire in the horizon, he saw torches moving, very close, among the branches.'
'... a dream in which he had run along the strange avenues of a wonder city, with green and red lights burning without flame or smoke.'
The English translations of the quoted passage from Cortázar, here and elsewhere, are mine.

32 It goes without saying that this story could be fruitfully analysed in terms of Freud's concepts of condensation and displacement, as two essential aspects of the dream-work. But, in turn, as has often been observed, Freud's description of condensation and displacement closely parallels the mechanisms of metaphor and metonymy respectively.

33 'Metadiegetic' since the dream sequence constitutes a different 'story,' a distinct diegetic universe, with distinct spatial and temporal coordinates and actors relating in particular ways that are only possible in that universe.

34 'Since he was sleeping on his back, he was not surprised to recognize himself again in that position.'

35 '... now he knew that he would not wake up, that he was awake, that

the marvellous dream had been the other, absurd as all dreams, a dream in which he had run along the strange avenues of a wonder city, with green and red lights burning without flame or smoke, with a huge metal insect buzzing between his legs ...'
36 Greimas, *Sémiotique*, 'connecteur d'isotopies.' For the original French version of this text see chapter 2, n 3.
37 Cf Dubois, 'La métaphore filée,' 204. For a more detailed presentation of Dubois's ideas see chapter 2.

4 Metaphor and metaphoric narration

1 At this point I need to differentiate the *linguistic* from the *circumstantial* context. The former constitutes the immediate linguistic set of interrelated terms belonging to the same semiotic system, whereas the latter implies the coexistence of more than one semiotic system. Recent textual theories call the linguistic *co-text*, and the circumstantial *context*. I make the distinction only as long as it is useful or necessary; elsewhere I resort to the more common term *context*. See, among others, van Dijk, *Some Aspects of Text Grammars* and *Text and Context*, and Eco, *Lector in Fabula*.
2 Eco's concept of 'frame' is discussed in *Lector in fabula*, 80–4, 128–41. See also chapter 3, n 8.
3 In pre-Hispanic cultures there still exist ritual dances dedicated to deer hunting ('la danza del venado'), in which the dancers wear symbolic deer heads as headpieces.
4 Cf John P. Houston, 'Les structures temporelles dans *A la recherche du temps perdu*,' in *Recherche de Proust*, and Gérard Genette, 'Fréquence,' in 'Discours du récit'.

PART TWO: METAPHORIC NARRATION AND NARRATIVE STRUCTURE

1 'Toute oeuvre littéraire forme un système. Dans la sémantique de ce système, les rapports entre les mots du texte l'emportent sur les rapports que ces mots entretiennent avec les choses, ou même, s'y substituent entièrement.' Riffaterre, 'Système d'un genre descriptif,' 15
  On the important question of the referential illusion see Roland Barthes, 'L'effet de réel'; Gérard Genette, 'Frontières du récit,' in *Figures II*; Phillippe Hamon, 'Qu'est-ce qu'une description?'; 'Un discours contraint,' in *Littérature et réalité*; and *Introduction à l'analyse du descriptif*; Michael Riffaterre, 'Système d'un genre descriptif' and 'L'illusion référentielle' in *Littérature et réalité*; Jean Weisberg, *L'espace romanesque*.
2 Gérard Genette, 'Discours du récit' in *Figures III*. The English translation for 'Discours du récit' is, *with some modifications*, Jane E. Lewin's *Narrative Discourse: An Essay in Method*.

3 These correspond closely to Genette's tripartition 'Time,' 'Mood' ['Mode'], and 'Voice' in 1972. Because the concept of 'mood' in English is not the exact equivalent of 'mode,' I have decided to call this middle section 'Narrative Modulations,' instead of Lewin's 'Mood.' In this I have followed Genette's revisions regarding his concept of 'mode' as quantitative and qualitative modulations. See Genette, *Nouveau discours*, 29.
4 For an excellent summary of Genette's narrative theory see Shlomith Rimmon, 'A Comprehensive Theory of Narrative: Genette's *Figures III* and the Structuralist Study of Fiction.'
5 Genette, 'Discours,' 72
6 Ibid., 280
7 I have chosen to retranslate some of the quotations from Genette's text, due to the great number of imprecisions and to the confusing terminology in Lewin's version. Her translation of this specific passage illustrates the confusion. I reproduce Genette's French, then Lewin's English:

'Histoire et narration n'existent donc pour nous que par le truchement du récit. Mais réciproquement le récit, le discours narratif ne peut être tel qu'en tant qu'il raconte une histoire, faute de quoi il ne serait pas narratif (comme, disons, *L'Ethique* de Spinoza), et en tant qu'il est proféré par quelqu'un, faute de quoi (comme par exemple une collection de documents archéologiques) il ne serait pas en lui-même un discours. Comme narratif, il vit de son rapport à l'histoire qu'il raconte; comme discours, il vit de son rapport à la narration qui le profère.' Genette, 'Discours,' 74

'Story and narrating thus exist *for me* only by means of the intermediary of the narrative. But reciprocally the narrative (the *narrated discourse*) can only be such to the extent that it tells a story, without which it would not be narrative (like, let us say, Spinoza's *Ethics*), and to the extent that it is uttered by someone, without which (like, for example, a collection of archaeological documents) it would not in itself be a discourse. As narrative, it lives by its relationship to the story that it recounts; as discourse, it lives by its relationship to the *narrating* that utters it.' (italics mine) Lewin, 29

Several problems in Lewin's translation may be isolated. In the first place, it is evident – if only for obvious conceptual reasons – that the aspects of story and narration derive their existence from the mediation of discourse, and that this is not restricted to Genette's perception as an individual ('story and narrating thus exist *for me*'), but constitutes a general narrative phenomenon, equally valid for any reader.

Another serious problem is Lewin's term 'narrated discourse.' Again and again, Genette defines 'récit' as 'discours narratif,' or uses one in apposition to the other (cf Genette, 'Discours,' 72ff). This latter practice is apparent in the passage in question. There is no justification for

182 Notes to pages 81–3

bracketing the apposition; it weakens the syntactic link of identity with 'récit.' Even less justifiable is the translation of 'discours narratif' as *narrated discourse*, a completely different concept, one closer to Dorrit Cohn's 'narrated monologue' than to Genette's 'discours narratif.'

Finally, the word *narration* exists in English with the same meaning as that denoted by the French term that Genette uses. The *Oxford English Dictionary* lists this meaning as the very first: '1. The *action* of relating or recounting, or the fact of being recounted.' A secondary meaning makes 'narration' denote content rather than the act of production: '2. that which is narrated or recounted; a story, narrative account.' This ambiguity, however, parallels that of 'récit' in French; hence the need of defining terms more or less univocally. So, if Genette's concept of 'narration' exists in English, even with the same term, *narration*, one wonders why the awkward and rather cumbersome *narrating* has been chosen.

An even worse confusion in terminology occurs in the 'narrative of words' section of 'Mood,' where the incredibly misleading *reported speech* (Lewin, 172) is given as the equivalent of 'discours rapporté' (Genette, 'Discours,' 192). Anyone familiar with old manuals of English grammar knows that 'reported' or 'indirect' speech is the opposite of 'quoted' or 'direct' speech. Therefore, 'reported speech' is the equivalent rather of 'style indirect libre' and not of 'discours rapporté' ('quoted or direct speech').

For these reasons, in all subsequent *direct* quotations from Genette's 'Discours du récit,' I modify Lewin's translation when and if I think it necessary.

8 '... des trois niveaux distingués à l'instant, celui du discours narratif est le seul qui s'offre directement à l'analyse textuelle, qui est elle-même le seul instrument d'étude dont nous disposions dans le champ du récit littéraire, et spécialement du récit de fiction.' Genette, 'Discours,' 73; Lewin, 27

5 Metaphoric narration and the temporal structures of narrative

1 On the question of these temporal determinations, see Christian Metz, *Essais sur la signification au cinéma*; T. Todorov, *Qu'est-ce que le structuralisme? Poétique* 2, 49ff; Jean Ricardou, *Problèmes*, 161–70; Seymour Chatman, *Story and Discourse: Narrative Structure in Fiction and Film*; and Gerald Prince, *Narratology. The Form and Function of Narrative*. See also, both for a philosophical perspective and for an extensive summary of the structuralist and semiotic treatment of time in narrative, Paul Ricoeur's monumental work *Temps et récit*, vols. 1–3.

2 Another form of time that may be determinant in a narrative is time as a theme. This is particularly true of Proust's text. Since this aspect of his work has been so extensively and intensively studied, I do not deal

with it directly, except when my examination of the effects of metaphoric narration on the temporal structures of narrative may bear tangentially on the theme.

Besides the great number of critical works dealing with the *Recherche* in general, a number of studies examine specifically the theme of time. I refer the reader to just a few that seem interesting to me. I do not in any way claim my selection is exhaustive or even representative: Germaine Brée, *Du temps perdu au temps retrouvé*; Inge K. Crossman, *Metaphoric Narration*; John P. Houston, 'Les structures temporelles'; Georges Poulet, 'Proust,' *Etudes sur le temps humain*, 1; Roger Shattuck, *Proust's Binoculars*.

3 Genette, 'Discours,' 123
4 Ibid., 90–115
5 I do not go into the details of their reach and amplitude or of the distinction between *homodiegetic* anachronies (those that follow the main diegetic line of action) and *heterodiegetic* anachronies (those that follow a different line). For the purposes of this study, only the distinction between different *anachronic functions* is relevant.
6 Ibid., 95
7 '... *amorce*, simples pierres d'attente sans anticipation, même allusive, qui ne trouveront leur signification que plus tard et qui relèvent de l'art tout classique de la "préparation" ... A la différence de l'annonce, l'amorce n'est donc en principe, à sa place dans le texte, qu'un "germe insignifiant," et même imperceptible, dont la valeur de germe ne sera reconnue que plus tard, et de façon rétrospective.' Genette, 'Discours,' 112–13

Lewin translates 'annonces' as *advance notices* (a term that I keep), and 'amorces' as *advance mentions* (Lewin, 75–6). However, the difference between the English terms chosen is too tenuous to account for the stronger difference in French, between the explicit and direct 'annonces' and the implicit and indirect 'amorces,' which in turn signifies metaphorically. For the word *amorce* means 'beginning,' 'bait' and 'allurement' or 'enticement.' An amorce, therefore, entices the reader to read on, begins – without seeming to do so – to recount a state of affairs that will be developed later on in the narrative. I have chosen *hints* as a word that renders the metaphorical meaning of Genette's 'amorces.'
8 In *Les voix narratives*, Marcel Muller carefully distinguishes the different 'voices' heard in the *Recherche*: the Writer, the Narrator, the Intermediary Subject, and the Hero. His distinctions are based on stylistic peculiarities and on the various temporal points of reference.

'The Hero does not allow his voice to be heard. That which Picon hears ("a self ... that we recognize by his tone of voice") is not the Hero's but the Narrator's voice, which the latter borrows from the Writer.' ['Le Héros ne laisse pas entendre sa voix. Celle qu'entend Picon ("un moi ... que nous reconnaissons à son timbre de voix") est celle, non du Héro, mais du Narrateur, lequel l'emprunte à l'Ecrivain.'] Ibid., 16

'We are then concerned with an *I* who remembers a past *self* who, in turn, remembers an even older *self*. We shall call Intermediary Subject the hypostase of a moment which we could , to our taste, refer to a previous form of the Narrator, or else, to the aged Hero.' ['Nous avons donc affaire à un *je*, qui se souvient d'un *je*, lequel se remémore à son tour un *je* plus ancien encore. Nous appellerons Sujet Intermédiaire l'hypostase d'un moment qu'on pourrait à son gré rapporter à une forme antérieure du Narrateur, ou, au contraire, à celle d'un Héros vieilli.'] Ibid., 19

In fact, the status of the Intermediary Subject as that self, half-way between the narrator as the actual source of narration and Marcel as experiencing hero, is the one responsible for the zone of ambiguity in the narrative situation.

9 Cf a similar interaction in Cortázar's 'La noche boca arriba,' in which the waking sequence plays on the positive connotations, while the dream sequence multiplies the negative ones on the basis of conjunctive relations established among the various narrative and linguistic elements in both sequences (see chapter 3, 2.2.3).

10 Group μ, *Rhétorique générale*, 107. See chapter 1, n 18, for the text in French.

11 See also I, 798, 804.

The earliest actualization of this metaphoric diegetic universe is in the 'drame du coucher' sequence, in which the horror of spending the night alone is vividly evoked (I, 9–10, 28). The outcome of the sequence is not a lonely night, however, but one shared with the mother.

There are also many allusions to illness that prevents Marcel from leaving his room in the opening pages of *La prisonnière* (III, 9ff); the emphasis, however, is on waking up and on the early hours of the morning, rather than on the long nights of insomnia. Finally there are the various elliptical allusions to the 'maison de santé.' (III, 723, 751, 854)

12 Genette uses the term *paralipsis* in its etymological sense of 'passing by omission,' 'to leave on one side, pass by,' rather than in the sense of the traditional rhetorical figure 'in which the speaker emphasizes something by affecting to pass it by, without notice, usually by such phrases as "not to mention," "to say nothing of"' (OED). In narrative theory, therefore, paralipsis 'as a narrative trope is contrasted to ellipsis the way *put it aside* is contrasted to *leave it where it is*.' ['la paralipse en tant que figure narrative s'oppose à l'ellipse comme *laisser de côté* s'oppose à *laisser sur place*.'] Genette, 'Discours,' 93; Lewin, 52. Paralipsis as opposed to ellipsis is not just an omission but a *lateral* omission. Cf Genette, 'Discours,' 211; Lewin, 195.

13 Another interesting paranarrative prolepsis is to be found in the extended theatre simile describing Marcel's relationship with his mother (I, 28–31). The universe of this piece of metaphoric narration features desperate lovers hopelessly waiting at the entrance of theatres or salons for a favourable word from the beloved; actors and actresses who must on no account be disturbed; well-meaning friends who fail at their self-appointed mission as go-betweens, and so on. Here are all the diegetic elements, virtual and disembodied at this point (the beloved is either an actress or a 'femme du monde,' a theatre or a salon is the place that invisibly bars the entrance to the lover; the intermediary is either a porter or a well-meaning friend). All these virtual, indeterminate diegetic elements will become variously incarnated later: Robert de Saint-Loup as that well-meaning go-between who fails in his mission in arranging a *rendezvous* with his aunt Oriane (II, 100–4); Swann, irremediably 'excommunicated' from the Verdurin salon, must wait and roam the streets of Paris in order to see Odette; Odette herself as the perfect synthesis of 'femme du monde' and actress, the 'demi-mondaine' with a dubious acting past (cf 'Miss Sacripant') – after all, Marcel's initial perception of her is as an indistinguishable mixture of actress and cocotte; Robert desperately trying to be reconciled to Rachel, sending endless messages, messengers, and gifts, getting nothing but cool contempt in return; Charlus pathetically sending envoys to bring about a reconciliation with Morel, to no avail ...
14 The sea metaphors are so inherent to Albertine's mystery that, in Marcel's imagination, the disappearance of the one entails the disappearance of the other: 'Parce que le vent de la mer ne gonflait plus ses vêtements, parce que, surtout, je lui avais coupé les ailes, elle avait cessé d'être une Victoire, elle était une pesante esclave dont j'aurais voulu me débarrasser.' (III, 371)
15 'Time is therefore like a fourth dimension which, in combination with the other three, *completes* space, frames and brings together its opposite fragments, encloses in the same continuity a wholeness that would otherwise remain irremediably dispersed. Seen through time, space is freed, transcended.' ['Le temps est donc comme une quartrième dimension qui en se combinant avec les trois autres, *achève* l'espace, rapproche et rentoile ses fragments opposites, enferme en une même continuité une totalité qui autrement resterait toujours irrémédiablement dispersée. Vu à travers le temps l'espace se trouve délivré, transcendé.'] Poulet, 'Proust,' 436

'... however mythical, the individuality of places is actually far more emphasized in Proust than that of beings.' ['... si mythique soit-elle, l'individualité des lieux est en fait beaucoup plus marquée, chez Proust, que celle des êtres.'] Genette, 'Proust et le langage indirect,' in *Figures II*, 234

'... the Proustian being is as insensitive to the individuality of moments as he is, contradictorily, spontaneously sensitive to that of place ... opposition between the "singularity" of his spatial sensitivity and the *iterativeness* of his temporal sensitivity ... individuality of place, indeterminate, almost erratic ("sometimes") recurrence of the moment.' ['... l'être proustien est aussi peu sensible à l'individualité des moments qu'il est au contraire, spontanément, à celle des lieux ... opposition entre le "singularisme" de sa sensibilité spatiale et *l'itératisme* de sa sensibilité temporelle .... individualité du lieu, récursivité indéterminée, quasi erratique ("parfois"), du moment.'] Genette, 'Discours,' 154

16 'Reciprocal metaphor' designates a form of metaphorization involving two or more metaphors in which the given degree for the one is the constructed degree for the other. In the passages in question, an altar is described as a hedge in one, a hedge as an altar in the other; in the first the altar is the main, non-metaphorical context, in the second that semantic function is covered by the hedge. Most descriptions of Elstir's paintings, for example, are based on reciprocal metaphor: seascapes give the illusion of landscapes and vice versa.

17 'Avec ... analepses ... *répétitives*, ou " rappels," nous n'échapperons plus à la redondance, car le récit y revient ouvertement, parfois explicitement, sur ses propres traces. Bien entendu, ces analepses en rappel peuvent rarement atteindre des dimensions textuelles très vastes: ce sont plutôt des allusions du récit à son propre passé.' Genette, 'Discours,' 95; Lewin, 54

18 'C'est en effet la fonction la plus constante des rappels, dans la *Recherche*, que de venir modifier après coup la signification des événements passés, soit en rendant signifiant ce qui ne l'était pas, soit en réfutant une première interprétation et en la remplaçant par une nouvelle.' Ibid., 96; Lewin, 56

19 '... *scène*, le plus souvent "dialoguée," dont nous avons déjà vu qu'elle réalise conventionnellement l'égalité de temps entre récit et histoire.' Ibid., 129; Lewin, 94

20 '... jamais le récit proustien ne s'arrête sur un objet ou un spectacle sans que cette station corresponde à un arrêt contemplatif du héros lui-même ... et donc jamais le morceau descriptif ne s'évade de la temporalité de l'histoire. Ibid., 134; Lewin, 100.

'... En fait, la "description' proustienne est moins une description de l'objet contemplé qu'un récit et une analyse de l'activité perceptive du personnage contemplant, de ses impressions, découvertes progressives, changements de distance et de perspective, erreurs et corrections, enthousiasmes ou déceptions, etc. Contemplation fort active en vérité, et qui contient "toute une histoire." Ibid., 136; Lewin, 102

'Une conclusion s'impose donc: c'est que la description, chez Proust, se résorbe en narration, et que le second type cononique de mouve-

ment – celui de la pause descriptive – n'y existe pas, pour cette évidente raison que la description y est tout sauf une pause du récit.
'... Absence du récit sommaire, absence de la pause descriptive: il ne subsiste donc plus au tableau du récit proustien que deux des mouvements traditionnels: la scène et l'ellipse.' Ibid., 138–9; Lewin, 105–6
21 Genette, *Nouveau discours*, 24–5
22 '... la description au contraire, parce qu'elle s'attarde sur des objets et des êtres considérés dans leur simultanéité, et qu'elle envisage les procès eux-mêmes comme des spectacles, semble suspendre le cours du temps et contribue à étaler le récit dans l'espace.' Genette, 'Frontières,' 59
23 Yet another factor that greatly contributes to the impression of slowness in Proustian narrative is its dominant form of narration: the iterative. Iterative narration does not tell a single event that may be located, with greater or less precision, in diegetic time, but rather gives an account – in a single act of narration – of many events bearing a certain similarity among them and occurring in a more or less indefinite period of time. Unlike the singulative narrative of events in which there is a clear progression, both logical and chronological, from one event to the other, in iterative narrative the series of events thus narrated cannot be individually located in diegetic time; nor do they establish relations of progression or causality among them. This accounts for the impression of a static world, even though in fact the story advances: Marcel does grow up; singular, irreversible events do happen, like the quarrel with Uncle Adolphe or Leonie's death. Cf Genette's 'Fréquence,' in 'Discours,' and John P. Houston, 'Les structures temporelles.'
24 Genette, *Nouveau discours*, 25
25 'To visualize the passage of time as the flow of a river is one of the oldest stock metaphors of European literature, going back to [Heraclitus]. Yet Proust succeeds in revitalizing the cliché by elaborating it with a profusion of precise and highly concrete details.' Stephen Ullmann, *The Image in the Modern French Novel*, 146; also cf *Style in the French Novel*, 256.
26 This simultaneous interplay of isotopies due to the polysemic potential of a lexeme is very similar to the one analysed in Shelley's metaphor – 'stain'$_1$ and 'stain'$_2$ (cf chapter 1, 3).
27 Black, *Models*, 37
28 In fact, this metaphoric contamination becomes an actual diegetic event in the supra-temporal sequence made up of the many intermittent accounts of the Intermediary Subject's activities with which the first part of *Du côté de chez Swann* is punctuated (1, 3–9; 43–4; 186–7). If in the first narrative (1, 3–9) being awake all night is a metaphoric identification by extension, for which the sick-traveller sequence alone is responsible, in the other two reprisals insomnia has become a diegetic

188   Notes to pages 102–7

actuality: 'C'est ainsi que, pendant longtemps, quand, réveillé la nuit, je me ressouvenais de Combray' (I, 43); 'C'est ainsi que je restais souvent jusqu'au matin à songer au temps de Combray (I, 186) (cf 'il faudra rester toute la nuit à souffrir sans remède,' from the sick-traveller sequence).

29 Dorrit Cohn in *Transparent Minds* also remarks on the disproportionate duration of analogies like the one under examination. Psychoanalogies may be 'arresting in a literal sense: the similes draw attention to themselves and away from the temporal progression of the narrative. They digress from or impede the sequence of recounted events, slowing the pace by continually expanding the time of narration over the narrated time' (43). Cohn's description of the retarding effect of psychoanalogies applies to all forms of what I have been calling metaphoric narration, whether the narrative is of inner mental processes or external diegetic events, or the character's perceptions of the external world. Metaphoric narration always draws attention to itself as discourse, and although it constitutes its own metaphoric narrative sequence, it is also a spectacle that plays on the simultaneous, therefore *spatial*, character of the associated image. All these features 'impede the sequence of recounted events,' slowing down the pace by 'expanding the time of narration over the narrated time.'

30 A 'descriptive pause' might also be legitimately called a *narrative* pause because it occurs between discourse and diegetic times – both being narrative times – rather than a pause resulting from the interrupting, non-narrative gnomic discourse. A narrative pause would then be opposed to a digressive or reflexive pause.

31 For a more detailed discussion of gnomic discourse see Cohn, *Transparent Minds*, 28ff, 147–53, 190.

32 Cf chapter 5, nn 11, 13.

33 Genette, 'Discours,' 148ff

34 '... aucune oeuvre romanesque, apparemment, n'a jamais fait de l'itératif un usage comparable – par l'extension textuelle, par l'importance thématique, par le degré d'élaboration technique – à celui qu'en fait Proust dans la *Recheche du temps perdu*.' Ibid., 148–9; Lewin, 117

35 '... la figure centrale du traitement proustien de la temporalité narrative est sans doute ce que j'ai nommé *syllepse* ... [les syllepses] opèrent un regroupement thématique des événements au mépris de leur succession chronologique "réelle" ... Syllepses temporelles, donc, et la réminiscence, à sa manière, en est une, vécue. Mais la métaphore est (en ce sens) une syllepse par analogie, ce qui lui permet, comme on sait, de *figurer* la réminiscence. On pourrait donc avoir dans la syllepse ce que Spitzer aurait appelé *l'etymon* stylistique proustien.' Genette, *Nouveau discours*, 27

36 Genette, 'Discours,' 121

37 '... la syllepse itérative n'est pas seulement un fait de fréquence: elle

touche aussi à l'ordre (puisque en synthétisant des événements "semblables" elle abolit leur succession) et à la durée (puisqu'elle élimine en même temps leurs intervalles) ...' Ibid., 178, Lewin, 155
38 Houston, 'Les structures temporelles,' 95
39 'Dans l'analogie entre le jour, la saison et l'année, Proust a trouvé la forme narrative la plus condensée.' Ibid., 100
40 Genette, 'Discours,' 147
41 See Shattuck, *Proust's Binoculars*, especially the last chapters, in which he deals with this topic.
42 'Loin de se circonscrire à une locale fonction expressive, la métaphore accède de la sorte à un décisif rôle d'organisation.
    '... dans la mesure où son exercice revient à dissoudre, conjointement ou séparément, les catégories du temps ou de l'espace, la métaphore ordinale joue le rôle d'une parfaite machine à subvertir la représentation.' Ricardou, *Nouveau problèmes*, 93
43 Gilles Deleuze, *Proust and Signs*, 44

6 Narrative modulations

1 Genette, *Nouveau discours*, 29
2 '... *distance*, c'est-à-dire ... la modulation quantitative ("combien?") de l'information narrative – la *perspective* en commandant de son côté la modulation qualitative: "par quel canal?"' Ibid., 29
3 See Genette, 'Frontières,' 'Discours,' and *Nouveau discours*.
4 '... l'imitation parfaite n'est plus une imitation, c'est la chose même, et finalement la seule imitation, c'est l'imparfaite. *Mimesis*, c'est *diégésis*.' Genette, 'Frontières,' 56
5 '... la diégèse est l'univers spatio-temporel désigné par le récit.' Genette, 'Discours,' 280
6 Ibid., 186
7 'Un récit, comme tout acte verbal, ne peut qu'*informer*, c'est-à-dire transmettre des significations.' Genette, *Nouveau discours*, 29
8 Chatman, *Story and Discourse*, 102
9 These Proustian fictional *loci* have no extratextual reference whatsoever, in spite of the many facile identifications that readers, and particularly, biographers and critics have made between Combray and Illiers, or Balbec and Cobourg and Trouville.
10 Genette, 'Métonymie chez Proust,' 42–5
11 Cf Hamon, 'Un discours constraint,' 137.
12 Genette, 'Métonymie chez Proust,' 51
13 '... autour de Mme Swann, tous les contrastes s'effacent, toutes les opositions disparaissent, toutes les cloisons s'évanouissent dans l'euphorie d'un espace continu.' Ibid., 51
14 Poulet has also remarked that 'space is, in fact, nothing but a set of viewpoints, each of which can only be discovered by turns and by

making perspectives succeed one another. And yet, does its true significance not lie in the totality of perspectives, as in those cubist paintings in which the painter attempts a simultaneous presentation of all the aspects of an object, which we usually cannot discover unless we see it by turns from different angles?' ['L'espace ne serait donc réellement qu'un ensemble de points de vue dont chacun ne peut être découvert qu'à son tour et en faisant se succéder les perspectives. Et pourtant sa signification véritable ne consiste-t-elle pas dans la totalité des perspectives, comme dans ces tableaux cubistes où le peintre s'essaye à donner à la fois d'un même objet tous les aspects qu'on ne peut d'ordinaire lui découvrir qu'en se plaçant tour à tour selon des angles différents?'] Poulet, 'Proust,' 435

This dissolution is a perceptible effect not only at the level of diegetic objects and space, but also at the level of characterization. Léo Bersani, among others, has observed this peculiar psychological disintegration as the result of *seemingly* unifying metaphorical correspondences:

'It is true that the network of metaphoric correspondences seems, at first sight, to confer a tight unity to the work. Nonetheless, and in a more original manner, all those correspondences bring about a certain psychological disintegration. Their effect is that of distancing us from a fixed centre which we might have been tempted to consider as the source of all the different images of the self.' ['Il est vrai que ce réseau de correspondances métaphoriques semble à première vue donner à l'oeuvre une unité fermée. Cependant, d'une manière plus originale, toutes ces correspondances opèrent une certaine désintégration psychologique. Elles ont pour effet de nous éloigner d'un centre fixe que nous aurions pu être tentés de considérer comme l'origine des différentes images du moi.'] Bersani, 'Déguisements du moi et art fragmentaire,' in *Recheche de Proust*, 25–6. See also Genette, 'Discours,' 200–3.

15 Cf Ricardou, *Problèmes*, 31. For the French version of this text, see chapter 3, n 6.

16 See Cohn's treatment of *psychoanalogy* and its clear narratorial source in *Transparent Minds*, 37–46.

Genette observes 'that the very existence of metaphor or simile, like any other trope, in itself constitutes an extradiegetic intervention of "the author" ... ' ['... que le fait même de la métaphore, ou de la comparison, comme de toute figure, constitue en soi une intervention extradiégétique de "l'auteur" ...'] 'Métonymie chez Proust,' 48

Gerald Prince sees in comparisons and analogies more or less explicit signals to the narratee and therefore a strong discursive activity oriented towards the narrator and his communication with the narratee. 'Introduction à l'étude du narrataire,' 85. See also Genette's 'fonction idéologique' and 'fonction de communication' in 'Discours,' 262–3.

Michel Leguern also insists on the metalinguistic function of metaphor: 'The metalinguistic function, which makes discourse focus on the code, is that which makes metaphor possible without motivating it. The essential motivations of metaphor are therefore due to the emotive function focused on the sender, or to the conative function, oriented towards the addressee.' ['La fonction métalinguistique, qui centre le discours sur le code, est celle qui permet la métaphore, mais sans la motiver. Les motivations essentielles de la métaphore viennent donc de la fonction émotive, cntrée sur le destinateur, ou de la fonction conative, qui est l'orientation vers le destinataire.'] *Sémantique*, 76

17 'Extrême médiation, et en même temps comble de l'immédiateté' Genette, 'Discours,' 189. See also *Nouveau discours*, 30ff.
18 '... la perspective narrative ... procède du choix (ou non) d'un "point de vue" *restrictif.*' Genette, 'Discours,' 203; Lewin 185-6 (italics mine)
19 Ibid., 209
20 'Par focalisation, j'entends donc bien une restriction de "champ," c'est-à-dire en fait une sélection de l'information narrative.' Genette, *Nouveau discours*, 49
21 Ibid., 49
22 According to Mieke Bal, for example, whose theory of focalization extends to the fictional characters themselves, *external focalization* in Genette implies not 'a restriction but a reversal of functions.' The real difference between external focalization and the two other forms, she claims, is not 'a difference between sources of vision [*instances "voyantes"*], but between objects of vision.' 'Dans la première distinction, celle entre le "récit non focalisé" et le "récit à focalisation interne," le terme a un sens restrictif ... Le troisième type [i.e. external focalization] cependant, se distingue du deuxième par un principe de classement tout différent. Il ne s'agit plus maintenant d'une restriction, mais d'un renversement de fonctions ... Entre le premier et le deuxième type [i.e. nonfocalization and internal focalization], la différence réside dans l'instance "qui voit" ... Entre le deuxième et le troisième type [i.e. internal and external focalization], la distinction n'est pas du même ordre. Dans le deuxième type, le personnage focalisé *voit*; dans le troisième il ne voit pas, il *est vu*. Ce n'est pas cette fois une différence entre les instances "voyantes" mais entre les objets de la vision.' Mieke Bal, 'Narration et focalisation,' 113

In a *purely relational* theory, however, the only source of focalization can be the narrator alone – focalization being understood *in all cases* as a restriction. Therefore, the restriction peculiar to external focalization takes the form of the *inaccessibility* to fictional minds. Furthermore, focalization is not restricted to material vision; it is a question not only of who *sees* (Bal's 'instances "voyantes"'), but of who *knows* and *when*. Genette's theory of focalization transcends the purely visual referent of the concept to account for the various degrees of *cognitive*, *spatial*, and *temporal* limitations imposed on the narrative.

23 'En focalisation externe, le foyer se trouve situé en un point de l'univers diégétique choisi par le narrateur, *hors de tout personnage*, excluant par là toute possibilité d'information sur les pensées de quiconque.' Genette, *Nouveau discours*, 50
24 Cf Genette, 'Discours,' 214–24.
25 Cf Genette, *Nouveau discours*, 52.
26 In *Nouveau discours du récit*, Genette amends his position on what in 1972 he had called 'focalisation sur le narrateur': 'This evidently concerns the restriction of the narrative information to the exclusive "knowledge" of the narrator *as such*, that is to say, to the hero's information at the time of the story, *completed by his ulterior information* – the whole remaining available to the hero become narrator. Only the first grouping deserves, *stricto sensu*, the term of "focalization"; for the second, what we have is an extradiegetic information.' ['Il s'agit évidemment de la restriction de l'information narrative au seul "savoir" du narrateur *en tant que tel*, c'est-à-dire à l'information du héros au moment de l'histoire *complétée par ses informations ultérieures* – le tout restant à la disposition du héros devenu narrateur. Seul le premier ensemble mérite *stricto sensu* le terme de "focalisation"; pour le second, il s'agit d'une information extradiégétique.'] Ibid., 51
27 'Nous avons déjà observé le caractère fortement subjectif des descriptions proustiennes, toujours liées à une activité perceptive du héros. Les descriptions proustiennes sont rigoureusement focalisées: non seulement leur "durée" n'excède jamais celle de la contemplation réelle, mais leur contenu n'excède jamais ce qui est effectivement perçu par le contemplateur.' Genette, 'Discours,' 218; Lewin, 204
28 Ullmann, *The Image in the Modern French Novel*, 159
29 Genette, 'Métonymie chez Proust,' 50
30 Curiously the text 'forgets' this. In the description of Mme Swann's winter salon, certain qualifiers deny the chrysanthemum's appearance in the earlier passage from 'Un amour': 'Odette avait *maintenant*': while the analeptic reference insists that Swann had never seen such a variety of colours; in fact the very same colours qualify the flowers in both passages.
31 Jean Weisberg emphasizes the role of logic in the presentation of diegetic space. Spatial deictics like here/there, above/below, etc, and logic-linguistic spatial categories, such as form, movement, sets, and the like, constitute the frame of reference in relation to which narrative space is defined. *L'espace romanesque*, 18
32 Cf Leguern, *Sémantique*, 56–8.
33 Albert Henry, like Leguern, insists on the rational, therefore discontinuous character of the simile: 'Metaphor tends to unifying reduction, it gives the illusion of reducing to unity. By contrast, as soon as there is comparison, we have a confrontation of two notions, *a confrontation that holds and is imposed, as such, on everyone*. Two concepts or two series

of concepts are brought together, the distance between them is maintained; the character of each one remains whole and distinct.' ['La métaphore tend à réduire à l'unité, elle donne l'illusion de réduire à l'unité. Au contraire, dès qu'il y a comparaison, il y a affrontement de deux notions, *affrontement qui subsiste et s'impose à tous, tel quel*. Deux concepts ou deux séries de concepts sont rapprochés et maintenus à distance l'un de l'autre; la personnalité de chacun reste distincte et entière.'] *Métonymie et métaphore*, 59

But the *cumulative* effect of simile in a narrative text is strongly metaphorical and tends to be perceived as performing the same kind of unification by extension as the so-called 'strict' metaphor.

34 Cf I, 681; 806; 813; II, 282.
35 Cf Crossman, *Metaphoric Narration* and Jean-Pierre Richard, *Proust et le monde sensible*. The fact that neither Crossman nor Richard makes any distinction between metaphorization in the narrative and in the gnomic discourses also illustrates to what an extent different methodological grids draw different pictures on the same set of virtual points that a text constitutes.

7 Narrative voice

1 This time the term *function* has its most common meaning: 'assigned duty or activity,' 'specific occupation or role.' The notion of vocal functions, then, is not the same as the Barthean, structural, narrative functions.

For these three aspects of narrative voice, see Genette, 'Discours,' 225-67.
2 Cf Jakobson, 'Linguistics,' 356-7.
3 'Le second est le *texte* narratif, auquel le narrateur peut se référer dans un discours en quelque sorte métalalinguistique (métanarratif en l'occurrence) pour en marquer les articulations, les connexions, les inter-relations, bref l'organisation interne.' Genette, 'Discours,' 261-2; Lewin, 255
4 Genette, *Nouveau discours*, 90
5 '... je préfère le terme plus général (et plus neutre) de "fonction interprétative" pour désigner cette fonction du narrateur. Il s'agit en effet de n'importe quel commentaire interprétatif formulé par le narrateur à propos des personnages, du contexte ou des événements ...' Suleiman, *Le roman à thèse*, 197
6 Genette, *Nouveau discours*, 90
7 Prince, 'Introduction à l'étude du narrataire,' 185
8 Ricardou, *Nouveau problèmes*, 94
9 Genette, 'Discours,' 222-3
10 Ibid., 189
11 Ibid., 178-82

12 Ibid., 242-3
13 'Le troisième type ne comporte aucune relation explicite entre les deux niveaux d'histoire: c'est l'acte de narration lui-même qui remplit une fonction dans la diégèse, indépendamment du contenu métadiégétique: fonction de distraction, par exemple, et/ou d'obstruction.' Ibid., 243; Lewin, 233
14 Ibid., 87-8
15 Cf chapter 3, 2.1.4, p 53
16 René Girard, *Deceit, Desire and the Novel*, 34
The model that the disciple follows, as Don Quixote that of Amadis, for example is 'the *mediator* of desire.' 'The straight line is present in the desire of Don Quixote, but it is not essential. The mediator is there, above that line, radiating toward both the subject and the object. The spatial metaphor which expresses this triple relationship is obviously the triangle. The object changes with each adventure but the triangle remains ... The triangle is no *Gestalt*. The real structures are intersubjective. They cannot be localized anywhere; the triangle has no reality whatever; it is a systematic metaphor, systematically pursued.' Ibid., 2
17 'Cet amour entre femmes était quelque chose de trop inconnu, dont rien ne permettait d'imaginer avec certitude, avec justesse, les plaisirs, la qualité.' III, 385
18 'Mais ce qui me torturait à imaginer chez Albertine, c'était *mon propre désir* perpétuel de plaire à de nouvelles femmes ... Comme il n'est de connaissance, on peut presque dire *qu'il n'est de jalousie que de soi-même.* III, 386 (italics mine)
19 In *Proust's Binoculars*, 101, Shattuck has examined the important role of oblivion in the *Recherche*: 'Proust wrote at length in order to create within the frame of his novel an interval of *oubli*, the forgetting which would allow the reader a true experience of remembering and recognizing ... Proust creates his compound vision of the world in a metaphor so extended we forget the first term and then recall it.'
20 Muller, *Les voix narratives*, 19
21 Genette, 'Discours,' 247
22 Other examples of the same motif are to be found in III, 286, 889, 1030.
'Aimantation, agglutination ou blottissement dynamisent certes le rapport de voisinage, sans l'intégrer pourtant en une continuité, sans en faire une collusion. Sédimentées ou aimantées, les sensations réunies par la mémoire y restent encore, que ce soit en *file* ou en *tas*, les unes à côté des autres. La rêverie tente alors d'intérioriser ce côte à côte, d'en dépasser la contiguïté vers des thèmes de fusion, ou du moins d'interpénétration. C'est l'intention par exemple du motif du *tissage*, si important dans la *Recherche*.' Richard, *Proust et le monde sensible*, 150
23 The exceptions to which Genette refers are to be found in II, 419-22 and III, 158-62, 252-8.

24 'Jusqu'à ce moment en effet, ces deux discours s'étaient juxtaposés, entrelacés, mais, à deux ou trois exceptions près, jamais tout à fait confondus: la voix de l'erreur et de la tribulation ne pouvait s'identifier à celle de la connaissance et de la sagesse ... A partir, au contraire, de la *révélation dernière* ... les deux voix peuvent se fondre et se confondre, ou se relayer dans un même discours, puisque désormais le *je pensais* du héros peut s'écrire "je comprenais," "je remarquais" ... c'est-à-dire coïncider avec le *je sais* du narrateur.' Genette, 'Discours,' 260; Lewin, 253–4
25 Muller, *Les voix narratives*, 16
26 The relative 'silence' of the experiencing self, in contrast with the clear and 'audible' voice of the narrating self, is mostly due to the emphasis on the hero's *silent meditations* to the detriment of his *social voice*. Unlike so many other characters in the *Recherche* whose speech is masterfully represented in all its idiolectal and idiosyncratic peculiarities – even to the extent of existing only in and by their speech, like the hotel manager at Balbec – Marcel as the narrator's *experiencing self* is seldom given a chance to speak. The fact that the hero's spoken language is so rarely quoted accounts for the blurred image of Marcel as a character participating with others in Proust's vast social fresco.
27 See Dorrit Cohn's interesting theory of consonant and dissonant psychonarration in *Transparent Minds*, 21–57. In consonant psychonarration the narrator can hardly be 'grasped as a separate entity within the text' (30).

Unlike consonant psychonarration, in which there is a perfect merging of the narrator's and the character's 'voices,' in dissonant psychonarration, there is a tendency to 'abstract analytical vocabulary,' to 'ex-cathedra statements, unmistakably set apart by their gnomic present' (28).
28 Cf 'Quand chantent à leur tour de nouveaux moments de plaisir qui passeraient de même, aussi grêles et linéaire, elles viennent leur apporter le soubassement, la consistance d'une riche orchestration,' II, 396
29 Deleuze, *Proust and Signs*, 41, 43

Conclusion

1 Group μ, *Rhétorique générale* 107
2 Leguern, *Sémantique*, 22. For a more detailed discussion see chapter 1, 3 of this study.
3 '... [*iconisation*] la dernière étape de la figurativisation du discours où nous distinguons deux phases: la *figuration* proprement dite qui rend compte de la conversion des thèmes en figures, et l'*iconisation* qui, prenant en charge les figures déjà constituées, les dote d'investissements particularisants, susceptibles de produire l'illusion référentielle.' Greimas, *Sémiotique*, 'iconicité'

4 'Il se peut que la référence au réel quotidien doive être abolie pour que soit libérée une autre sorte de référence à d'autres dimensions de la réalité.' Ricoeur, *La métaphore vive*, 187
5 'Au sens métaphorique correspondrait une référence métaphorique, comme au sens littéral impossible correspond une référence littérale impossible.

   '... Comment cette proximité dans le sens ne serait-elle pas en même temps une proximité dans les choses mêmes? N'est-ce pas de cette proximité que jaillit une nouvelle manière de voir? Ce serait alors la méprise catégoriale qui frayerait la voie à la nouvelle vision.

   '... la classification antérieure, liée à l'usage antérieur des mots, résiste et crée une sorte de vision stéréoscopique où le nouvel état de choses n'est perçu que dans l'épaisseur de l'état de choses disloqué par la méprise catégoriale.

   'Tel est le schéma de la référence dédoublée. Il consiste pour l'essentiel à faire correspondre une métaphorisation de la référence à la métaphorisation du sens.' Ibid., 290

Appendix: The operational concepts

1 'Que ce soit sur le plan du signifiant (phonique ou graphique) ou sur le plan du signifié (sens), la chaîne manifestée peut être considérée comme un hiérarchie de plans, où s'"articulent" des unités discrètes ...

   'La décomposition se poursuit, sur chacun des deux plans, jusqu'à un niveau atomique ou insécable. Sur le plan du signifiant, on atteindra ainsi le niveau des traits distinctifs, sur le plan du signifié, on atteindra le niveau des sèmes. Il est remarquable que toujours le dernier état de décomposition atteint soit infralinguistique: ni les traits distinctifs, ni les sèmes n'ont dans le langage d'existence explicite et indépendante. Les unités de signification, telles qu'elles se manifestent dans le discours, commencent au niveau immédiatement supérieur.' Group μ, *Rhétorique générale*, 30
2 'Les sèmes sont définis par des relations entre sémèmes, aussi bien sur la dimension paradigmatique que sur la dimension syntagmatique.' François Rastier, *Sémantique interprétative*, 29
3 '... dans le texte même, le sémème continue d'entretenir des relations paradigmatiques, puisque ses sèmes inhérents sont définis relativement à une classe de sémèmes dont les autres membres ne sont pas ordinairement présents en contexte.' Ibid., 77
4 '... "permettant le rapprochement de deux sémèmes voisins, par référence à une classe plus générale," alors qu'un sème spécifique ... [permet] d'opposer deux sémèmes très voisins, par une caractéristique propre'. B. Pottier, *Linguistique générale* (Paris: Klincksieck 1974) 330–1. Quoted in Rastier, *Sémantique*, 49
5 '... "structure paradigmatique constituée par des unités lexicales ("lex-

èmes") se partageant une zone commune de signification et se trouvant en opposition immédiate les un avec les autres" ... ' E. Coseriu, 'L'étude fonctionnelle du vocabulaire. Précis de lexématique,' 18. Quoted in Rastier, *Sémantique*, 49
6 Unless the context has called for sharper distinctions, in my foregoing analyses I have continued to use the term 'semantic field' to simplify matters.
7 See Greimas, *Sémantique structurale*.
8 'L'isotopie élémentaire comprend donc deux unités de la manifestation linguistique ... Une isotopie peut être établie dans une séquence linguistique d'une dimension inférieure, égale ou supérieure à celle de la phrase. Elle peut apparaître à n'importe quel niveau d'un texte; on peut en donner des exemples très simples au niveau phonologique: assonance, allitération, rime; au niveau syntaxique: accord par redondance de marques; au niveau sémantique: équivalence définitionnelle, triplication narrative ... D'où la possibilité d'une stylistique des isotopies.' Rastier, 'Systématique des isotopies,' in *Essais de sémiotique poétique*, 82-3
9 Cf Group μ, *Rhétorique de la poésie*, 34ff.
10 ' ... l'isotopie d'un texte: c'est la permanence d'une base classématique hiérarchisée, qui permet, grâce à l'ouverture des paradigmes que sont les catégories classématiques, les variations des unités de manifestation, variations qui, au lieu de détruire l'isotopie, ne font, au contraire, que la confirmer.' Greimas, *Sémantique structurale*, 96
11 Such a conceptual expansion has allowed us to devise such narrative homologues as 'spatial,' 'diegetic,' or 'temporal isotopies.'
12 'The manifestation of distinct sememes may establish an isotopy, regardless of whether each of those sememes has only one seme or a semic grouping common to the nuclear figures of all the other sememes. The sememes considered may not necessarily be articulated among themselves by simple logical relations (as in the case of semic categories). But the common seme or semic grouping defines a semic field [i.e. a 'lexical' field in context; all the sememes in that context would be selected according to a certain lexical field] which is the basis for the inventory of sememes in a class.

'This kind of isotopy is coded by rhetorical forms such as ekphrasis. It paves the way for a scientific redefinition of what the current theory of literature calls the *subject* of a text or sequence.

'The description of such isotopies constitutes a way of reading a text. So, for example, reading l'Education sentimentale or the Gospel according to Mark as political texts initially amounts to making an inventory, in those texts, of the sememes that belong to the field identified ... from the retained sememic field, as that of politics.'

['La manifestation de sémèmes distincts peut établir une isotopie, pour peu que chacun de ces sémèmes comporte un sème ou un

198 Notes to pages 163–4

groupement sémique commun aux figures nucléaires de tous les autres sémèmes. Sans que les sémèmes considérés soient nécessairement articulés entre eux par des relations logiques simples (comme c'est le cas pour les catégories sémiques), ce sème ou groupement sémique commun définit un champ (sémémique) qui constitue l'inventaire des sémèmes en classe.

'Ce genre d'isotopie est codé par des formes rhétoriques comme l'ekphrasis; il permettrait de redéfinir scientifiquement ce que la théorie de la littérature représentative appelle le *sujet* d'un texte ou d'une séquence.

'Décrire de telles isotopies est une façon de lire un texte; ainsi, par exemple, lire l'Education sentimentale ou l'évangile de Marc comme des textes politiques revient tout d'abord à inventorier dans ces textes les sémèmes appartenant à un champ identifié ... comme celui de la politque d'après le champ sémémique retenu.'] Rastier, 'Systématique des isotopies,' 85

13 'Les sèmes inhérents relèvent du système fonctionnel de la langue; et les sèmes afférents, d'autre types de codifications: normes socialisées, voire idiolectales.' Rastier, *Sémantique*, 44

14 'Un sème inhérent est une relation entre sémèmes au sein d'un même taxème, alors qu'un sème afférent est une relation d'un sémème avec un autre sémème qui n'appartient pas à son ensemble strict de définition' ... Ibid., 46

Bibliography

Critical and theoretical texts

Adam, Jean-Michel. *Linguistique et discours littéraire*. Paris: Larousse 1976
Bal, Mieke. 'Narration et focalisation: Pour une théorie des instances du récit.' *Poétique* 29 (1977), 107–27
Barthes, Roland. 'Introduction à l'analyse structurale des récits.' In R. Barthes et al., *Poétique du récit*. Paris: Seuil 1977 [1966]
– 'L'effet de réel.' *Communications* 11 (1968), 84–9
– *S/Z*. Paris: Seuil 1970
Benveniste, Emile. 'Les relations de temps dans le verbe français.' *Problèmes de linguistique générale*. Vol. 1. Paris: Gallimard 1966
Bersani, Léo. 'Déguisements du moi et art fragmentaire.' In R. Barthes et al., *Recherche de Proust*. Paris: Seuil 1980
Black, Max. *Models and Metaphors: Studies in Language and Philosophy*. Ithaca: Cornell University Press 1962
Brée, Germaine. *Du temps perdu au temps retrouvé*. Paris: Société d'édition 'Les Belles Lettres' 1969
Brooke-Rose, Christine. *A Grammar of Metaphor*. London: Secker & Warburg 1965
Chatman, Seymour. *Story and Discourse: Narrative Structure in Fiction and Film*. Ithaca: Cornell University Press 1978
Cohen, Jean. *Structure du langage poétique*. Paris: Flammarion 1966
– 'Théorie de la figure.' *Communications* 16 (1970), 3–25
Cohn, Dorrit. *Transparent Minds: Narrative Modes for Presenting Consciousness in Fiction*. Princeton: Princeton University Press 1978

- 'The Encirclement of Narrative: On Franz Stanzel's *Theorie des Erzählens.*' *Poetics Today* 2 (1981), 157–82
Coseriu, E. 'L'étude fonctionnelle du vocabulaire: Précis de lexématique.' *Cahiers de lexicologie* 29 (1976), 5–23
Crossman, Inge K. *Metaphoric Narration: The Structure and Function of Metaphors in 'A la recherche du temps perdu.'* Chapel Hill: North Carolina Studies in the Romance Languages and Literatures 1978
Deleuze, Gilles. *Proust and Signs*, trans. Richard Howard. New York: George Braziller 1972 [1964]
van Dijk, Teun A. *Some Aspects of Text Grammars: A Study in Theoretical Linguistics and Poetics*. The Hague: Mouton 1972
- *Text and Context*. London: Longman 1977
Dubois, Philippe. 'La métaphore filée et le fonctionnement du texte.' *Le Français Moderne* 43 no. 3 (1975), 202–13
Eco, Umberto. *Lector in fabula: la cooperazione interpretativa nei testi narrativi*. Milano: Bompiani 1979
Eisenstein, Sergei. *Film Form: Essays in Film Theory*. New York and London: Harcourt, Brace & World 1949
Genette, Gérard. 'Frontières du récit.' *Figures II*. Paris: Seuil 1969 [1966]
- 'Proust et le langage indirect.' *Figures II*. Paris: Seuil 1969
- 'Discours du récit.' *Figures III*. Paris: Seuil 1972
- *Narrative Discourse: An Essay in Method*, trans. Jane E. Lewin. Ithaca: Cornell University Press 1978 [1972]
- 'Métonymie chez Proust.' *Figures III*. Paris: Seuil 1972
- 'La rhétorique restrainte.' *Figures III*. Paris: Seuil 1972
- *Nouveau discours du récit*. Paris: Seuil 1983
Girard, René. *Deceit, Desire and the Novel: Self and Other in Literary Structure*, trans. Y. Freccero. Baltimore and London: Johns Hopkins 1965 [1961]
Greimas, A.J. *Sémantique structurale*. Paris: Larousse 1966
Greimas, A.J. and J. Courtès. *Sémiotique: Dictionnaire raisonné de la théorie du langage*. Paris: Hachette 1979
Group μ. *Rhétorique générale*. Paris; Seuil 1982 [1970]
- *Rhétorique de la poésie*. Bruxelles: Editions Complexe 1977
Hamon, Philippe. 'Qu'est-ce qu'une description?' *Poétique* 2 (1972), 465–85
- 'Un discours constraint.' In R. Barthes et al., *Littérature et réalité*. Paris: Seuil 1982 [1973]
- *Introduction à l'analyse du descriptif*. Paris: Hachette 1981
Henry, Albert. *Métonymie et métaphore*. Paris: Klincksieck 1971
Houston, John Porter. 'Les structures temporelles dans *A la recherche du temps perdu*.' In R. Barthes et al., *Recherche de Proust*. Paris: Seuil 1980
Jakobson, Roman. 'Linguistics and Poetics.' In *Style in Language*, ed. T.A. Sebeok. Cambridge: M.I.T. Press 1960
- *Essais de linguistique générale*. Paris: Minuit 1963
- *Huit questions de poétique*. Paris: Seuil 1977
Leguern, Michel. *Sémantique de la métaphore et de la métonymie*. Paris: Larousse 1973

Lezama Lima, José. 'Las imágenes posibles.' *Obras completas*. Vol. 2. México: Aguilar 1977 [1948]
Metz, Christian. *Essais sur la signification au cinéma*. Paris: Klincksieck 1968
Muller, Marcel. *Les voix narratives dans 'A la recherche du temps perdu.'* Genève: Droz 1965
Pottier, Bernard. *Linguistique générale*. Paris: Klincksieck 1974
Poulet, Georges. 'Proust.' *Etudes sur le temps humain*. Vol. 1. Plon, Editions du Rocher 1952
- *L'espace proustien*. Paris: Gallimard 1963/82
Prince, Gerald. 'Introduction à l'étude du narrataire.' *Poétique* 14 (1973), 179–96
- *Narratology: The Form and Function of Narrative*. Berlin: Mouton 1982
Rastier, François. 'Systématique des isotopies.' In *Essais de sémiotique poétique*, ed. A.J. Greimas. Paris: Larousse 1972
- *Sémantique interprétative*. Paris: P.U.F. 1987
Ricardou, Jean. *Problèmes du Nouveau Roman*. Paris: Seuil 1967
- 'La métaphore d'un bout à l'autre.' *Nouveaux problèmes du roman*. Paris: Seuil 1978
Richard, Jean-Pierre. *Proust et le monde sensible*. Paris: Seuil 1974
Richards, I.A. *The Philosophy of Rhetoric*. London: Oxford University Press 1936
Ricoeur, Paul. *La métapore vive*. Paris: Seuil 1975
- *The Rule of Metaphor: Multi-disciplinary Studies of the Creation of Meaning in Language*, trans. Robert Czerny with Kathleen McLaughlin and John Costello, SJ. Toronto: University of Toronto Press 1977
- *Temps et récit I*. Paris: Seuil 1983
- *Temps et récit II: La configuration dans le récit de fiction*. Paris: Seuil 1984
- *Temps et récit III: Le temps raconté*. Paris: Seuil 1985
Riffaterre, Michael. 'La métaphore filée dans la poésie surréaliste.' *Langue Française* 3 (September 1969), 46–60
- 'Système d'un genre descriptif.' *Poétique* 9 (1972), 14–30
- 'L'illusion référentielle.' In R. Barthes et al., *Littérature et réalité*. Paris: Seuil 1982 [1978]
Rimmon, Shlomith. 'A Comprehensive Theory of Narrative: Genette's *Figures III* and the Structuralist Study of Fiction.' *Poetics and Theory of Literature* 1 (1976), 33–62
Shattuck, Roger. *Proust's Binoculars*. Princeton: Princeton University Press 1962/1983
Stanzel, Franz. *A Theory of Narrative*, trans. Charlotte Goedsche. Cambridge: Cambridge University Press 1986 [1979]
Suleiman, Susan R. *Le roman à thèse, ou l'autorité fictive*. Paris: P.U.F. 1983
Todorov, Tzvetan. *Qu'est-ce que le structuralisme? Poétique 2*. Paris: Seuil 1968
Ullmann, Stephen. *Style in the French Novel*. Cambridge: Cambridge University Press 1957
- *The Image in the Modern French Novel*. Cambridge: Cambridge University Press 1960

Weisberg, Jean. *L'espace romanesque*. Lausanne: L'Age d'Homme 1978

Narrative texts

Christie, Agatha. *The Hollow*. London: Collins 1946
Conrad, Joseph. *Heart of Darkness*. New York: Norton 1963 [1902]
Cortázar, Julio. 'La noche boca arriba.' *Final del juego*. Buenos Aires: Editorial Sudamericana 1978
García Márquez, Gabriel. *Cien años de soledad*. Buenos Aires: Editorial Sudamericana 1971
Joyce, James. *Ulysses*. Harmondsworth: Penguin 1968 [1919/1922]
Lezama Lima, José. *Paradiso*. México: Era, 1968
– *Paradiso*, trans. Gregory Rabassa. New York: Farrar, Straus & Giroux 1974
Maupassant, Guy (de). 'Boule de suif.' *Boule de suif. La Maison Tellier*. Paris: Gallimard (Folio) 1973 [1880]
Proust, Marcel. *A la recherche du temps perdu*. 3 vols, ed. Pierre Clarac and André Ferré. Paris: Gallimard 1954
Robbe-Grillet, Alain. *La jalousie*. Paris: Minuit 1957
– *Dans le labyrinthe*. Paris: Minuit 1959

Glossary

Afferent semes 20, 164
Attributed or *connotative* meanings. Aspects of meaning that do not depend on the functional system of language but are 'the product of other types of codification: socialized, even idiolectal norms' (Rastier). Whether a given aspect of meaning is afferent largely depends on the local context. See also *Inherent semes*.

Allotopic 12
Non-isotopic. Belonging to an incompatible semantic field. See also *Isotopy*.

Anachrony 84–5
Temporal rupture in the flow of the narrative, marking the point of non-coincidence between the sequence of events in the *story* (diegetic time) and their *textual* sequence (discourse time). There are two kinds of anachrony:

(a) *Analepsis*: the narrative in course is interrupted in order to account for a given segment of the story's having occurred earlier in diegetic time (but *earlier* only in relation to that segment of the narrative in which the rupture occurs).

(b) *Prolepsis*: the narrative in course is interrupted to announce a given segment of the story occurring later in story time.

Analepsis 84. See *Anachrony*.

Associated image 25
An iconic form of meaning, characteristic of metaphor, and coexisting with more abstract or conceptual meanings. The associated

image results from the presence of incompatible semes, or semes relating disjunctively, in a metaphoric utterance.

Autodiegetic narrative 137. See *Narrator (status)*.

Back-reading 31, 32, 44
Retrospective or 'vertical' reading. A given segment of a text establishes meaningful relations (opposition, parallelism, contrast, etc.) with a non-contiguous segment. The reader is then forced to 'reread' the previous portion of the text in the light of the present one, thus abolishing the intervening *textual distance* between the two.

Bi-isotopic (or pluri-isotopic) text 32
A text in which two or more isotopies are active in the production of meaning. This is typical of metaphor, as well as of many other tropes.

Catalysts (weak functions) 48, 60. See *Functions (narrative)*.

Classeme 12, 161–2
Recurring seme of a very general, abstract nature, and responsible for the inclusion of a term in a *class*. See also *Generic semes*.

Componential analysis 160. See *Semic analysis*.

Conjunctive relation 17–18
A relation of similarity and/or compatibility established among semes isolated from different terms

Connector of isotopies 28
A word, phrase, or narrative element with a great polysemic potential, 'a unit of the discursive level which induces one or several different readings' (Greimas)

Constructed degree 13, 159
A meaning that is not *given* in the actual terms of an utterance or text but is arrived at by means of a semantic manipulation of the terms involved; hence a *constructed* meaning. See also *Given degree* and *Semantic manipulation*.

Content-isotopy 163
The recurrence of generic semes in a content-isotopy is not to be observed at the level of the manifestation in language but at an infralinguistic, and therefore, constructed level. A content-isotopy is, in fact, what is described by Greimas's original definition: a recurrence of classemes in a given phrase underlying the variety of terms used in its actual composition. See also *Expression-isotopy*.

Contextual meaning 22
The meaning of a term, not as it appears in dictionaries, but determined by context. A *sememe* is the contextual meaning of a *lexeme*. See also *Sememe*.

Co-text 68
The immediate verbal context as distinguished from the circumstantial *context*

Decomposition 160. See *Semic analysis*.

Glossary

Decomposition in mode χ, or referential 15, 69
A given context may require the isolation and manipulation of semantic features that *particularize* the meaning of the terms involved. Usually decomposition in the referential mode takes into account the 'parts' out of which the designated object is composed or made up; hence *referential* decomposition.

Decomposition in mode Σ, or conceptual 15, 69
A given context may require the isolation and manipulation of more abstract semes; a conceptual meaning of the term is thus isolated.

Diegetic 48, 115
That which belongs to the story and to the spatio-temporal universe of fiction. Thus, the term *diegesis*, unless otherwise qualified, should not be understood in the classical sense of 'pure narration' as opposed to 'representation.'

Diegetic isotopy 53
The coherence of the story elements as proposed by the created fictional world. Any other potential stories or storylike aspects that do not belong to this world are received as ruptures in the diegetic coherence of the narrative.

Dimension 161–2
The class of highest generality to which macro-generic semes, such as /animate/ vs. /inanimate/, are affixed. See also *Domain* and *Taxeme*.

Disjunctive relation 17–18, 20
A relation of opposition or of incompatibility established among semes isolated from terms belonging to different semantic fields

Domain 161–2
A class of great generality, more general than the taxeme and less than the dimension, to which meso-generic semes, such as /alimentation/, belong. See also *Dimension* and *Taxeme*.

Expression-isotopy 163
The iteration of any linguistic unit at the level of the manifestation in language: for example, 'at the phonological level: assonance, alliteration, rhyme; at the syntactic level: agreement by mark redundancy; at the semantic level: definitional equivalence, narrative triplication' (Rastier). See also *Content-isotopy*.

Extradiegetic 103
A narrative level outside the created fictional world, or diegetic universe. Thus, gnomic discourse, for example, is by nature extradiegetic.

Extradiegetic narrator 137. See *Narrative level* and *Narrator (status)*.

Focalization 120–2
A qualitative filter in the selection and regulation of narrative information. Focalization arises 'from the choice (or not) of a restrictive "point of view"' (Genette). There are three basic codes of focalization:

(a) *Zero, or non-focalization*: the narrator imposes minimal restrictions upon himself: he goes in and out of his most diverse characters' minds *ad libitum*; his freedom to go in and out of places, from which characters are absent, is equally great. The focus ('foyer') of the narrative is constantly displaced from one fictional mind to the next, almost indiscriminately.

(b) *Internal focalization*: the 'foyer' of the narrative coincides with *one fictional mind*; that is to say, the narrator restricts his freedom in order to select only the narrative information that the cognitive and spatio-temporal limitations of a given character may allow. The narrative may be focalized on one character consistently (*fixed* internal focalization), on a restricted number of characters, with alternating displacements of the 'foyer' (*variable* internal focalization), or, alternately, the different perspectives from which the same series of events is narrated (*multiple* internal focalization).

(c) *External focalization*: here the restriction is not constituted by the limitations of fictional minds but by the very *inacessibility* of fictional minds. 'In external focalization the focus [*foyer*] is located at a given point of the diegetic universe, chosen by the narrator, *outside all characters*, thereby excluding all possibility of informations on the thoughts of no matter who' (Genette).

Frame 69, 174

A structured set of interrelated data and informations describing a given cultural situation. 'In that sense, *a frame is always a virtual text or a condensed story*' (Eco).

Functional isotopy 54, 176–7

A form of narrative coherence that may be abstracted into a logical pattern of 'functions'

Functions (narrative) 60, 176–7

Barthes defines 'functions' as *terms* in a correlation; as segments of story that are related to one another either logically or chronologically. It is important to notice that, since functions are relations established among the various actions and events of a narrative, it is the analyst who chooses abstract names to designate the corresponding functions, like 'getting up,' 'pulling out a gun,' 'shooting,' etc., terms that are, of course, absent from the verbal texture of the narrative as such, and are only analytical constructs.

Functions are divided into two great classes: *functions, stricto sensu*, and *indexes*. In turn functions are divided into *kernels* and *catalysts*; indexes are likewise divided into two groups: *indexes* and *informants*.

Strong functions or *kernels* are those 'actions' or 'events' that relate to one another causally, thus constituting the essential framework of a tale. Weak functions or *catalysts* are the ones that fill up the spaces between kernels, and are responsible for such well-known effects as suspense, delays, etc.

Indexes, in the strong sense of the word, are thematic collections of

Glossary

semes, disseminated all along the narrative, producing atmosphere effects, symbolic meanings, etc., while *informants* are local collections of semes projecting characters and settings.

Generic semes 161
Units of meaning of great generality that are responsible for the inclusion of a term in a class. Pottier and Rastier call them *generic semes*, Greimas *classemes*, and Katz and Fodor *semantic markers*. See also *Specific semes*.

Given degree 13, 159
The actual terms that make up an utterance, statement, or text. The observable 'words' at the level of the manifestation in language. See also *Constructed degree*.

Gnomic discourse 103, 188
A form of discourse marked by the presence of 'ex cathedra statements,' and 'a highly abstract analytical vocabulary' (Cohn). Gnomic discourse is the most appropriate vehicle for the expression of opinions, generalizations, and abstractions of all kinds. It is opposed to the strict *narrative* discourse. Formally, it is marked by the timeless or gnomic present and the tendency to use the generalizing first-person plural and/or whatever forms of neutral pronouns exist in a given language.

Heterodiegetic narrator 137. See *Narrator (status)*.
Homodiegetic narrator 137. See *Narrator (status)*.
Homonym 32, 42–3, 71
A word with two completely different meanings. A lexeme appearing as an identical formal cover for two distinct and unrelated semic figures

Hypotactic 68, 71
Hypotaxis is the dependent or subordinate construction or relationship of clauses with connectives. In general, any hierarchical relation linking two terms, such as principal and subordinate; determinant and determined (Greimas). See *Paratactic*.

Indexes 176–7. See *Functions (narrative)*.
Infralinguistic level 159, 164
A level, analytically constructed, below the observable linguistic manifestation

Inherent semes 20, 164
What may currently be understood as 'denotative' meaning. An inherent seme 'depends on the functional system of language ... and entails a relationship between sememes within the same taxeme, whereas an afferent seme draws a relation between two sememes, the second of which *does not* belong to the strict set of definitions of the first' (Rastier). See also *Afferent semes*.

Intercalated narration 136. See *Time of narration*
Intradiegetic 137. See *Narrative level* and *Narrator (status)*.

208 Glossary

Invariant 11, 14, 22, 169–70

According to Group μ, the invariant is that aspect of metaphoric meaning constituted by the recurring *identical* generic semes making up the semic intersection.

In a semic analysis, the invariant semes may also be referred to as the specific semes that *particularize* the meaning of a term, thus giving it its semantic individuality and identity.

In terms of the concept of presupposition, the invariant is the presupposed term (Greimas).

Isotopy 12, 163

The iteration of generic semes gives a semantic coherence to an utterance or text. This semantic coherence, or isotopy, reduces the polysemic potential of words by selecting only the meaning(s) that may be compatible with the context. The semantic isotopy is largely responsible for the establishment of such a context.

Isotopy may be fully defined as 'the property of limited sets of units of meaning entailing an identifiable recurrence of identical semes and an absence of mutually excluding semes in a syntactic position of determination' (Group μ).

Iterative narrative 73, 91–2, 106–8, 187. See *Narrative frequency*.

Kernels (strong) 60, 176–7. See *Functions (narrative)*.

Level of the manifestation in language 10, 35

The actual, observable terms that make up an utterance or text

Lexematic level 10, 159–60. See *Phrastic level*.

Lexeme 160–1, 169–70

The word as it appears in dictionaries. The lexeme is the synthesis of its many contextual meanings, or sememes. See also *Sememe*.

Lexical field 161. See *Semantic field*.

Lexicalized metaphor 21, 26

A metaphor that has been worn out by use (e.g. 'the ship ploughs the waves')

Literalization of the figure 55–6, 69

The literal meaning of the given degree of a trope. This usually leads to the fantastic (such as the reading of 'chasseur arborescent' as a man full of branches) or to the absurd.

Macro-generic semes 161–2

Semes of greatest generality and abstraction, such as /animate/, that make up a very abstract class called dimension. See also *Dimension*.

Meso-generic semes 161–2

Generic semes of less generality than the macro-generic, such as /alimentation/, that make up a class less abstract than the dimension called domain. See also *Domain*.

Metadiegetic narrative 51–2, 139–40
A narrative that is inserted in another narrative, constituting a completely different diegetic universe from the first
Metalanguage 9
A language so devised as to be able to 'speak about' language. In our study, a metalanguage designates a semantic model that may 'speak' about metaphor without inevitably using metaphors to do so.
Metaphor 10, 12–13, 19–21, 168, 171
A breach in the isotopic coherence of the text pointing towards a virtual semantic field, which is alien to the main context. So that a rationally satisfactory meaning may be produced, a semantic manipulation ensues, whereby similar attributes from both fields are rearranged and brought into conjunction in a semic intersection. Those semes that remain incompatible and relate disjunctively also participate in the production of metaphoric meaning by generating an associated image, which is the iconic dimension of metaphor.
Metaphoric articulation 35–6, 40–7
Two narrative sequences are linked, textually, by a simile structure or by mere juxtaposition (*actual mode* of articulation). Their interaction is based on simultaneous conjunctive and disjunctive relations, thereby triggering metaphorization. The two sequences may be separated by a considerable textual distance, but are linked by back-reading. Due to a series of semantic or diegetic elements programmed to be read in conjunction, the two sequences relate metaphorically to each other (*virtual mode* of articulation).
Metaphoric configuration of a narrative sequence 36, 55, 59
The pattern of a sequence may serve as the blueprint in the construction of another. This similarity in the particular arrangement of the constituents (a conjunctive relation) is the basis for other differences between the two sequences (a disjunctive relation). The interplay of the identical in the midst of the different activates the process of metaphorization.
Metaphoric narration 34–5
A paranarrative dimension characteristic of a narrative text in which the process of metaphorization is at work on either or both levels: that of the manifestation in language, and that of the work's organization as a text
Micro-generic semes 161–2
Generic semes of weak generality, the least abstract and the closest to the specific or particularizing semes, making up a taxeme, a class of low generality that is very similar to the concept of the semantic field. See also *Taxeme* and *Semantic field*.

Narrative frequency 106ff
The even or uneven relations of repetition that are drawn between the story and the narrative discourse. In *singulative narrative* (also 74), an event happens once in story time and is told once in discourse time. In *repetitive narrative* (also 91), an event happening only once is narrated

several times. In *iterative narrative* (also 73ff, 91–2, 187), various similar events are given account of in one single act of narration.

Narrative intersection 44

A concept homologous to that of *semic intersection*: a series of similar narrative elements, in two otherwise very different sequences, are rearranged so as to pave the way to metaphorization. Similar functions in two sequences, similar descriptive arrangements or events may be brought together in order to read both sequences in conjunction and find metaphorical meanings (i.e. to find the identical in the midst of differences).

Narrative level 51–2, 137

A distinction between the main narrative establishing a given fictional universe and a secondary or *metadiegetic* narrative, which designates a fictional universe generated within the frame of the main one. See also *Metadiegetic narrative*.

Narrativization of a lexicalized metaphor 36, 55–6

A worn-out metaphor may become the underlying narrative program for a given sequence (see 'the call of the blood' as a narrativized metaphor in *Cien años de soledad*).

Narrator (status) 136–7

The status of the narrator may be defined:

(a) In terms of his *relation to the diegetic universe*: If the narrator does not participate in the fictional world he is *heterodiegetic* (the traditionally called third-person narrative). If he does participate, he is a *homodiegetic* narrator (*autodiegetic* if he tells his own story; *testimonial* if he tells somebody else's).

(b) In terms of *narrative level*: If he is the first narrator of the main narrative his status is *extradiegetic*; if he already figures in the main narrative as a character and *then* assumes the act of narration in order to tell a different story he becomes an *intradiegetic* narrator (like Marlow in *Heart of Darkness*).

Nuclear semes 161, 170. See *Specific semes*.

Paranarrative x, 36, 39, 88, 158, 164

A narrative with a purely virtual existence, developing parallel or alongside the main narrative; hence *para*-narrative. Metaphoric narration is thus conceived as a paranarrative dimension due to the series of semantic transformations and relations, typical of the process of metaphorization, that are homologous to the transformations and sequential nature of a strict narrative.

Paratactic 68

The term *parataxis* is opposed to *hypotaxis* in that there is no relationship of dependence or subordination between the terms, but merely of contiguity, of juxtaposition, of coordination without the use of coordinating elements, such as conjunctions. It has often been said that prose has an essentially hypotactic organization, while the structure of poetry is mainly paratactic. See *Hypotactic*.

Glossary

Phrastic (or lexematic) level 10, 35
A level of analysis that is restricted to the limits of the sentence
Prolepsis 84. See *Anachrony*.

Redundancy 14, 177
Strict repetition of units of discourse or of diegetic situations. Redundancy may also refer to the recurrence or iteration of semantic features, whether generic or specific semes.
Repetitive narrative 91–3, 106, 108–9. See *Narrative frequency*.
Revaluation 12–14, 31
A selection and rearrangement of semes with the object of producing a constructed meaning. See also *Semantic manipulation*.

Semantic decomposition 15. See *Semic analysis*.
Semantic distinguishers 161. See *Specific semes*.
Semantic features 160. See *Semes*.
Semantic field 161
A concept akin to that of 'lexical field,' which Coseriu defines as 'a paradigmatic structure made up of lexical units ("lexemes") sharing a common zone of meaning and establishing an immediate opposition one to the other.'
  Semantic field, like lexical field, designates a structured *set of words* related by a common zone of *meaning*, well beyond simple synonymy or morphological kinship. A semantic field is, then, like a lexical field, a set of lexical units related to each other by meaning, sharing a thematic zone of different degrees of generality.
Semantic manipulation 12, 14
The result of a semic analysis in which certain semes have been isolated, in compatibility with the main context, and have then been rearranged in order to generate a satisfactory meaning. See also *Revaluation*.
Semantic markers 161. See *Generic semes*.
Sememe 21, 160–1
Contextual meaning of a word. The sememe is a structured set of semes appearing in context. The sememe actualizes only one meaning; its existence is always *syntagmatic* and, therefore, always in context. The lexeme, by contrast, appears as a *paradigmatic* set of meanings. See also *Lexeme* and *Semes*.
Sememic isotopies 163, 197
Contextual meanings sharing the same thematic zone in a given text. The concept of sememic isotopies is very close to Eco's notion of 'entry' in the reader's 'encyclopaedia' of the world, or 'frame': a structured set of interrelated data and information describing a given cultural situation.
Semes 21–2, 160
Also called semantic features. Infralinguistic units of meaning that make up the global meaning of a sememe

Semic analysis 15, 159–60
A decomposition of the meaning of a term whereby smaller units of meaning are isolated. These infralinguistic units that make up or *compose* (hence the possibility of a *componential* analysis) the complex meaning of a term *in a given context*, are called semes or semantic features.

Semic figure 12, 161, 170
The specific semes that particularize the meaning of a word. Also called nuclear semes. See also *Specific semes*.

Semic intersection 14–15, 18
In the rhetorical operation called metaphor, certain semes from the semantic fields in confrontation are found to bear some similarity and are read in conjunction in order to find a rationally satisfactory meaning. This activity of selecting similar semes leads to the intellectual operation of constructing a semic intersection; that is, a zone of shared meaning from which differences may be read as metaphorically significant.

Singulative narrative 74, 106–7. See *Narrative frequency*.

Spatial isotopy 54
The diegetic universe of a narrative proposes a certain number of places as its spatial coordinate, which traditional narrative usually respects. That spatial coherence I have called spatial isotopy (which may be broken for metaphoric effects of meaning).

Specific semes 161
Those semantic features that particularize the meaning of a term. A specific seme brings 'two closely related sememes into opposition by means of *an individual feature*' (Pottier). Pottier and Rastier use the term *specific semes*, Greimas *semic figure* or *nuclear semes*, and Katz and Fodor *semantic distinguishers*.

Suppression-addition of semes 14–15, 18
The manipulation and rearrangement of semes depends on the fundamental operation of addition and/or suppression of semes. In the construction of a semic intersection, made up of similar semantic features, some semes are highlighted, others suppressed, for the sake of compatibility. Since metaphor extends to the totality of the terms, meanings that are shared only by the semic intersection, semes are added to some terms, while others are attenuated. The addition and/or suppression of semes is always determined by the main context of the utterance or text.

Sustained metaphor 29. See *Threaded metaphor*.

Syllepsis 107
As a rhetorical figure syllepsis is defined as the bringing together of two different meanings of a term, simultaneously active in the same syntactic structure (e.g. Pope's Whether the nymph shall ... / Or stain her honour or her new brocade).

As a narrative homologue, temporal syllepsis (Genette) designates the arrangement of events occurring at different times but accounted for in one and the same act of narration (iterative narrative).

Glossary

Taxeme 161–2
The class of lowest generality, below the domain and the dimension, to which micro-generic semes, such as /cutlery/, may be affixed. There is a close affinity between the concept of taxeme and that of lexical field. See also *Semantic field*.

Testimonial 137. See *Narrator (status)*.

Threaded metaphor 29, 38
Alternation of metaphoric and non-metaphoric terms, i.e. an alternation between isotopic and allotopic lexemes

Time of narration 103, 136
By the ineluctable constriction to choose a grammatical tense, the narrator must fix his temporal position *vis-à-vis* the fictional world he narrates: the past tense if his position is *ulterior*, the future tense if it is *anterior* (predictive narration), or the present tense of contemporaneous action if his position is *simultaneous* or *intercalated* (i.e. an alternation of narration and action).

Transformation (narrative) 34, 38
The passage from one state of affairs to another is the basic narrative operation. Narrative discourse would then appear as a series of such transformations (Greimas).

Transphrastic or discursive level 10, 28, 32–3, 159
A level of analysis situated beyond the sentence, in order to examine the organization of discourse (its combinations, segmentations; its constituent parts and their relation to the whole, etc.)

Ulterior narration 136. See *Time of narration*.

Index of Authors Cited

Adam, Jean-Michel, 43, 176

Bal, Mieke: focalization, 191
Barthes, Roland: functions (kernels, catalysts, indexes, and informants) 48, 60, 176–7; thematic fields, 177
Bersani, Léo, 190
Black, Max, 19–20, 101, 168, 169
Brooke-Rose, Christine, 174

Chatman, Seymour, 116
Christie, Agatha: *The Hollow*, 4–6
Cohen, Jean: semantic impertinence, 168–9
Cohn, Dorrit: consonance and dissonance, 195; gnomic discourse, 103, 188; psychoanalogies, 188, 190
Conrad, Joseph: *Heart of Darkness*, 47–50
Cortázar, Julio: 'La noche boca arriba,' 59–67
Coseriu, E.: lexical field, 162, 197
Crossman, Inge K., 174, 193

Deleuze, Gilles: complication, 112; essence, 151
van Dijk, Teun A.: metaphor: relational character of, 23; simile as deep structure of, 23
Dubois, Philippe: bi-isotopic text, 32, 173; semantic dissemination in threaded metaphor, 30–3, 172

Eco, Umberto, 40, 69, 174–5

García Márquez, Gabriel: *Cien años de soledad*, 55–6, 177–8
Genette, Gérard
- 'Discours du récit'
- narrative frequency: iterative narrative, 73, 91–2, 106–7, 187; repetitive narrative, 106–7, 108
- narrative modulations ('mood'): distance, 114–15; focalization, 120–2
- narrative tempo, 96–9
- narrative voice: extradiegetic and intradiegetic levels, 137; func-

tions of the narrator, 137–9; homodiegetic and heterodiegetic narrators, 137; time of narration, 136
- temporal structures of narrative: order (analepsis and prolepsis), 83–5
- 'Frontières du récit': description vs narration, 99; mimesis vs diegesis, 114–15
- 'Métonymie chez Proust': aesthetic radiation, 124; continuous space, 119; diegetic metaphor, 117; tableaux monochromes, 118
- *Nouveau discours du récit*: digressive pause, 99; focalization as selection of information, 120–1; focalization on the narrator, 122, 192; functions of the narrator, 137–8; iterative syllepsis, 107; narrative information, 115; narrative modulations, 114; narrativization by focalization, 81, 98
- 'Proust et le langage indirect,' 91, 185

Girard, René, 142, 194
Greimas, A. J.: back-reading (rétrolecture), 31, 173; classemes, 161; connector of isotopies, 28–9, 65, 172; iconicity, 154, 195; isotopy, 12, 163, 167; lexeme, 169–70; metaphor, 24, 171; seme, 161; sememe, 160–1, 169–70; semiotic nature of tropes, 10, 167; theme, 177; transformation, 3, 166
Group μ: given and constructed degrees of metaphor, 13; invariant, 14, 169; isotopy, 12, 168; revaluation (manipulation of semes), 13, 15, 169; semantic decomposition (semic analysis and infralinguistic units of meaning), 14–15, 160, 196; semantic extension, 18, 88, 170; semic intersection, 15, 18

Hamon, Philippe, 118
Henry, Albert, 192
Houston, John Porter, 73, 107

Jakobson, Roman, 3, 6, 7, 34, 137, 165
Joyce, James: *Ulysses*, 44–7

Leguern, Michel
- conceptual metaphor vs referential metonymy, 16, 169
- metaphor: associated image in, 25, 153, 171; definition of, 12; metalinguistic function of, 190–1
- simile, 129
Lezama Lima, José: 'Las imágenes posibles,' 57, 178; 'Mitos y cansancio clásico,' viii; *Paradiso*, 5, 6–7, 41–3, 57–9

Muller, Marcel, 52, 86, 145, 148, 183–4

Pottier, Bernard: generic and specific semes, 161, 196
Poulet, Georges, 185, 189–90
Prince, Gerald, 138, 190
Proust, Marcel: *A la recherche du temps perdu: Du côté de chez Swann*, 75–6, 86–90, 91–3, 100–3, 104–5, 111–12, 117–19, 122, 126–8, 130, 140–1, 145–6; *A l'ombre des jeunes filles en fleurs*, 70–7, 131, 133, 134, 151; *Le côté de Guermantes*, 39, 133–4, 146–7; *La prisonnière*, 90, 112, 131–2, 138–9, 149–51; *Sodome et Gomorrhe*, 141–4; *Le temps retrouvé*, 111, 138, 143–4, 147, 151–2

Rastier, François
- conjunctive and disjunctive relations, 17–21
- isotopy, 163, 197–8
- semes: generic and specific, 161; inherent and afferent, 164, 198; macro-, meso-, and micro-generic, 161–2

- sememes and semes (inter-
  definition), 160, 196
Ricardou, Jean
- 'le fantastique de l'écriture,' 56
- metaphor: ordinal, 111, 189; vs
  commentary, 139
- reading, 39, 119–20, 174
- summary of theoretical model,
  175–6
Richard, Jean-Pierre, 193, 194
Richards, I.A.: delegated efficacy of
  words, 169–70; vehicle and tenor
  (*see also* Group μ: given and
  constructed degrees of metaphor),
  13

Ricoeur, Paul: associated image, 25,
  171; double reference, 40, 154,
  175, 196; metaphor as discursive
  phenomenon, 28, 172; semantic
  event, 27, 171–2
Riffaterre, Michael, 29, 80, 172, 180

Shattuck, Roger, 111, 144, 194
Suleiman, Susan R.: interpreting
  function, 137, 193; redundancy,
  177

Ullmann, Stephen, 100, 122, 187

Weisberg, Jean: space, 192

UNIVERSITY OF TORONTO ROMANCE SERIES

1 **Guido Cavalcanti's Theory of Love**
  J.E. Shaw
2 **Aspects of Racinian Tragedy**
  John C. Lapp
3 **The Idea of Decadence in French Literature 1830–1900**
  A.E. Carter
4 *Le Roman de Renart* **dans la littérature française et dans les littératures étrangères au moyen âge**
  John Flinn
5 **Henry Céard: Idéaliste détrompé**
  Ronald Frazee
6 **La Chronique de Robert de Clari: Etude de la langue et du style**
  P.F. Dembowski
7 **Zola before the Rougon-Macquart**
  John C. Lapp
8 **The Idea of Art as Propaganda in France, 1750–1759: A Study in the History of Ideas**
  J.A. Leith
9 **Marivaux**
  E.J.H. Greene
10 **Sondages, 1830–1848: Romanciers français secondaires**
  John S. Wood

11 **The Sixth Sense: Individualism in French Poetry, 1686–1760**
   Robert Finch
12 **The Long Journey: Literary Themes of French Canada**
   Jack Warwick
13 **The Narreme in the Medieval Romance Epic: An Introduction to Narrative Structures**
   Eugene Dorfman
14 **Verlaine: A Study in Parallels**
   A.E. Carter
15 **An Index of Proper Names in French Arthurian Verse Romances 1150–1300**
   G.D. West
16 **Emery Bigot: Seventeenth-Century French Humanist**
   Leonard E. Doucette
17 **Diderot the Satirist: An Analysis of *Le Neveu de Rameau* and Related Works**
   Donal O'Gorman
18 **'Naturalisme pas mort': Lettres inédites de Paul Alexis à Emile Zola 1871–1900**
   B.H. Bakker
19 **Crispin Ier: La Vie et l'oeuvre de Raymond Poisson, comédien-poète du XVIIe siècle**
   A. Ross Curtis
20 **Tuscan and Etruscan: The Problem of Linguistic Substratum Influence in Central Italy**
   Herbert J. Izzo
21 ***Fécondité* d'Emile Zola; Roman à thèse, évangile, mythe**
   David Baguley
22 **Charles Baudelaire. Edgar Allan Poe: Sa Vie et ses ouvrages**
   W.T. Bandy
23 **Paul Claudel's *Le Soulier de Satin*: A Stylistic, Structuralist, and Psychoanalytic Interpretation**
   Joan Freilich
24 **Balzac's Recurring Characters**
   Anthony R. Pugh
25 **Morality and Social Class in Eighteenth-Century French Literature and Painting**
   Warren Roberts
26 **The Imagination of Maurice Barrès**
   Philip Ouston
27 **La Cité idéale dans *Travail* d'Emile Zola**
   F.I. Case

28 Critical Approaches to Rubén Darío
   Keith Ellis
29 Universal Language Schemes in England and France 1600–1800
   James Knowlson
30 Science and the Human Comedy: Natural Philosophy in French Literature from Rabelais to Maupertuis
   Harcourt Brown
31 Molière: An Archetypal Approach
   Harold C. Knutson
32 Blaise Cendrars: Discovery and Re-creation
   Jay Bochner
33 Francesco Guicciardini: The Historian's Craft
   Mark Phillips
34 Les Débuts de la lexicographie française: Estienne, Nicot et le *Thresor de la langue françoyse* (1606)
   T.R. Wooldridge
35 An Index of Proper Names in French Arthurian Prose Romances
   G.D. West
36 The Legendary Sources of Flaubert's *Saint Julien*
   B.F. Bart and R.F. Cook
37 The Rule of Metaphor: Multi-disciplinary Studies of the Creation of Meaning in Language
   Paul Ricoeur
38 The Rhetoric of Valéry's Prose *Aubades*
   Ursula Franklin
39 Unwrapping Balzac: A Reading of *La Peau de chagrin*
   Samuel Weber
40 The French Fictional Journal: Fictional Narcissism/Narcissistic Fiction
   Valerie Raoul
41 Correspondance générale d'Helvétius: Volume I: 1737–1756; letters 1–249
   Edition critique préparée par Peter Allan, Alan Dainard, Jean Orsoni et David Smith
42 The Narcissistic Text: A Reading of Camus' Fiction
   Brian T. Fitch
43 The Poetry of Francisco de la Torre
   Gethin Hughes
44 Shadows in the Cave: A Phenomenological Approach to Literary Criticism Based on Hispanic Texts
   Mario J. Valdés
45 The Concept of Reason in French Classical Literature 1635–1690
   Jeanne Haight

46 **A Muse for Heroes: Nine Centuries of the Epic in France**
   William Calin
47 **Cuba's Nicolás Guillén: Poetry and Ideology**
   Keith Ellis
48 **Fictional Meals and Their Function in the French Novel 1789–1848**
   James W. Brown
49 **The Composition of Pascal's** *Apologia*
   Anthony R. Pugh
50 **Surrealism and Quebec Literature: History of a Cultural Revolution**
   André G. Bourassa
51 **Correspondance générale d'Helvétius, Volume II: 1757–1760; lettres 250–464**
   Edition critique préparée par Peter Allan, Alan Dainard, Jean Orsoni et David Smith
52 **Theatre in French Canada: Laying the Foundations 1606–1867**
   Leonard E. Doucette
53 **Galdós and His Critics**
   Anthony Percival
54 **Towards a History of Literary Composition in Medieval Spain**
   Colbert I. Nepaulsingh
55 **José Bergamin: A Critical Introduction 1920–1936**
   Nigel Dennis
56 **Phenomenological Hermeneutics and the Study of Literature**
   Mario J. Valdés
57 **Beckett and Babel: An Investigation into the Status of the Bilingual Work**
   Brian T. Fitch
58 **Victor Segalen's Literary Encounter with China: Chinese Moulds, Western Thoughts**
   Yvonne Y. Hsieh
59 **Narrative Perspective in Fiction: A Phenomenological Mediation of Reader, Text, and World**
   Daniel Frank Chamberlain
60 **Marcel Proust and the Text as Macrometaphor**
   Lois Marie Jaeck
61 **Metaphoric Narration: Paranarrative Dimensions in** *A la recherche du temps perdu*
   Luz Aurora Pimentel

www.ingramcontent.com/pod-product-compliance
Lightning Source LLC
Chambersburg PA
CBHW020406080526
44584CB00014B/1199